Classic American Films

Classic American Films

Conversations with the Screenwriters

William Baer

PRAEGER

Westport, Connecticut
London

Library of Congress Cataloging-in-Publication Data

Baer, William, 1948–
   Classic American films : conversations with the screenwriters / William Baer.
     p. cm.
   Includes bibliographical references and index.
   ISBN 978–0–313–34898–3 (alk. paper)
   1. Screenwriters—United States—Interviews. I. Title.
PN1998.2.B346   2008
808.2′3—dc22   2007038556

British Library Cataloguing in Publication Data is available.

Library of Congress Catalog Card Number: 2007038556
ISBN: 978–0–313–34898–3

First published in 2008

Praeger Publishers, 88 Post Road West, Westport, CT 06881
An imprint of Greenwood Publishing Group, Inc.
www.praeger.com

Printed in the United States of America

The paper used in this book complies with the
Permanent Paper Standard issued by the National
Information Standards Organization (Z39.48–1984).

10 9 8 7 6 5 4 3 2 1

For my family and friends
(especially Joey)

Contents

Acknowledgments

Some of the interviews in this book, often in shortened formats, were first published in the following journals:

Creative Screenwriting—

"*Psycho*: A Conversation with Joseph Stefano"
"*American Graffiti*: A Conversation with Gloria Katz and Willard Huyck"
"*North by Northwest*: A Conversation with Ernest Lehman"
"*Jaws*: A Conversation with Carl Gottlieb"
"*The Wild Bunch*: A Conversation with Walon Green"
"*Rocky*: A Conversation with Sylvester Stallone"
"*The Exorcist*: A Conversation with William Peter Blatty"

Michigan Quarterly Review—

"*Singin' in the Rain*: A Conversation with Betty Comden and Adolph Green"
"*Rebel Without a Cause*: A Conversation with Stewart Stern"
"*Hud*: A Conversation with Irving Ravetch and Harriet Frank, Jr."

The South Carolina Review—

"*Tender Mercies*: A Conversation with Horton Foote"
"*On the Waterfront*: A Conversation with Budd Schulberg"

Screentalk—

"*The Sting*: A Conversation with David S. Ward"
"*The Sound of Music*: A Conversation with Ernest Lehman"

Aside from the writers themselves, I'm most grateful to my longtime friend Joseph Urbanczyk, one of the industry's most respected camera operators, who helped me time and again to facilitate my travel and lodging in Los Angeles. Two others who helped me were David Berry, an attorney in Los Angeles, and Wyatt Prunty, Director of the Sewanee Writers' Conference, who helped me arrange the interview with Horton Foote. I also greatly appreciate the financial assistance provided by the University of Evansville for several of my trips to meet with the screenwriters.

I'd also like to thank Jeanine Kerridge, Alicia Harris, Joyce Harrington, and Elissa Shetler, who performed the difficult task of transcribing these interviews from the audio tapes. Also invaluable in the editing process was my friend Dr. Mike Carson.

Finally, I'm very grateful to the editors who first published these interviews, sometimes in shortened formats: Erik Bauer of *Creative Screenwriting*; Laurence Goldstein of *Michigan Quarterly Review*; Wayne Chapman of *The South Carolina Review;* and Eric Lillelør of *Screentalk*.

Introduction

*In my opinion, the writer should have
the first and last word in filmmaking.*

—Orson Welles

Critics like "themes" and "oeuvres" and "auteurs" and even things like
"semiotics" and "dialectic polarities," but audiences like films. In the end,
it is always the individual films that really matter. Bruce Kawin wisely writes
in the preface of his highly regarded *A Short History of the Movies*, "Just as
the history of the novel is, to some extent, a catalogue of important novels,
the history of film as an art centers on important films." In this book, some
of the most significant, influential, and popular American films of the second half of the twentieth century are discussed in depth by the individuals
who first conceived them: the screenwriters.

Films, of course, are a highly collaborative endeavor, especially in
America, and the role of producers, directors, performers, cinematographers, editors, and others are all obviously crucial to a film's creation.
However, none of these talented people would ever have a single task to
perform without the screenwriters. In truth, they would all be out of work.
Everyone involved in film is totally dependent on the script, and everyone
who is working on a film is actively engaged in interpreting the words, the
narrative, and the vision of the screenwriter.

The interviews in this book allow us to engage fourteen classic American
films though the lens of the screenwriters. We follow these films from their
very beginnings; we watch the writers struggle and exhilarate in the creation of their scripts; we listen as they examine the crucial roles of their
directors and stars; and we hear their honest appraisals of the finished film
and its subsequent reception by both audiences and critics. The story of

every one of these classic films is a seemingly impossible creative odyssey that somehow ended in triumph for these indefatigable writers.

Thus, in its essence, this book is a tribute to the screenwriter, a figure often ignored or maligned in Hollywood. Before looking at the individual films discussed in these pages, it would be useful to briefly remind ourselves about the uncertain status of the screenwriter in American film history.

SCREENWRITERS IN THE STUDIO ERA

In the days before sound, the writer was virtually invisible. It was the age of the genius director and the international star. The writer, if noticed at all, was generally referred to as a "gag writer," a "title card writer," a "continuity writer," or, at best, a "scenarist." Of course, some of the greatest directors like Griffith, Chaplin, and Keaton wrote their own "scenarios." In more recent times, scholars have discovered a number of very detailed screenplays used by major Hollywood directors (like DeMille and Von Stroheim) that were written by writers who have never been fully appreciated for their important contributions to the "silent" cinema.

Then came *The Jazz Singer* in 1927. Suddenly, films began to "talk," and writers were desperately needed to supply the talk. Soon, anyone with any discernible writing talent was flocking west to Hollywood led by the Broadway playwrights (Sidney Howard, Robert E. Sherwood, S. N. Behrman, Clifford Odets, Lillian Hellman, and others), the journalists (Ben Hecht, Charles MacArthur, Dudley Nichols, the Mankiewicz brothers, Nunnally Johnson, and others), and even the novelists (F. Scott Fitzgerald, William Faulkner, Aldous Huxley, and Nathanael West).

This would inaugurate "the era of the producers," since they were, without question, the most powerful figures in the studio system of the thirties, forties, and early fifties. It was the studio moguls and their producers who decided *what* was done, *when* it was done, and *by whom* it was done. The contract studio writers of the time generally made good money, but they were treated as a kind of necessary nuisance by the studios. They worked long hours, punched a time clock, and worked six days a week in small cubicles with daily page quotas hanging over their heads. Often, several writers or teams of writers would work on the same project at the same time, and screenplays were endlessly written, rewritten, rewritten by other writers, and then polished indefinitely. As a result, it was often difficult to discern proper screen credit.

In such an environment, the studio writers were often considered "hacks," and Jack Warner condescendingly referred to them as "schmucks with Underwoods." He could also boast with smug satisfaction, "I've got America's best writer for $300 a week," after he brought William Faulkner to the Warner Bros. studio. Even director Joseph L. Mankiewicz, himself a writer, claimed that "The screenwriter is the highest-paid secretary in the world," and the highly successful scriptwriter Ben Hecht admitted that studio writers were treated like "butlers" in Hollywood. Maybe the best Hollywood anecdote about the frustrations of the studio screenwriters involves Robert Riskin, the author of such Frank Capra classics as *It Happened One Night*, *Mr. Deeds Goes to Town*, and *Lost Horizon*. Supposedly, Riskin entered Capra's office one day, angrily tossed 120 blank pages across the director's desk, and said, "Here! Let's see you give *that* the Capra touch!"

Unfortunately, the problems of the screenwriters were further exacerbated in the thirties by an internal conflict over the attempt to unionize in 1933. The so-called "Screenwriters' War" was an ugly civil war within the ranks of the studio writers over the nascent Screen Writers Guild. Some of the studio writers were perfectly content and very grateful for their studio jobs and their high Depression salaries, while others were extremely concerned about Communist influence in the newly founded union. As a result, the union's legitimate contractual issues—credits, royalties, minimum salary, benefits, etc.—were eventually lost in the confrontation over politics; and those loyal to the moguls and/or concerned about Communist influence formed an alternate, short-lived guild, the Screen Playwrights, in 1936. In the end, the Screen Writers Guild won out, and they settled legally and contractually with the studios in 1941. However, the internal battle scars of this bitter confrontation would again rear its ugly head during the House Un-American Activities Committee (HUAC) hearings of 1947 and the subsequent blacklistings of many screenwriters.

Despite all these problems, and despite their virtual anonymity with the public, many of the studio writers during the "Golden Age of Cinema" were able to craft masterful scripts that reflected personal visions and styles. A few of the many distinguished screenwriters of that period were Ben Hecht, Preston Sturges, Samuel Raphelson, Nunnally Johnson, Robert Riskin, the Epstein brothers, and Herman Mankiewicz.

SCREENWRITERS IN THE POST-STUDIO ERA

All the films discussed in this book were written and produced in the second half of the twentieth century. *Singin' in the Rain*, the earliest film considered, was first released in 1952. By the early fifties, the Hollywood studio system had started to crumble for a number of significant reasons: the Supreme Court's 1948 antimonopoly decision against the studios, the rising threat of television, the damaging publicity surrounding the HUAC hearings, and the increasing power of the film stars. A number of Hollywood icons, like Cary Grant, realized that they were popular enough with the public that they could leave the studios, set up their own production companies, and make the films *they* wanted to make. Naturally, they needed screenplays, and this created more opportunities for the screenwriters, some of whom also left the studios and began to work independently. It seemed that this might be a new era for the screenwriter, one of increased recognition and prestige, and then something happened in France. It was called auteurism.

In 1948, Alexandre Astruc wrote an article in André Bazin's influential film journal, *Cahiers du Cinema*, claiming that the true "author" of the film was any director who was able to exert his own personal style and vision during the production of his films. Astruc's point of view was soon championed by a number of young French critics who wrote for *Cahiers*, like François Truffaut, and they began to carefully examine American films made during the previous few decades searching for directors whose body of work displayed a personal, "authorial" style. The obvious examples of Hitchcock and Welles were explored at length, and other notable Hollywood directors like John Ford and Howard Hawks began receiving the artistic recognition and attention they deserved. In the United States, the cause of auteurism was vigorously championed by Andrew Sarris in his important articles in *Film Comment* in 1962.

Once again, the screenwriter had been pushed into the background as the film directors of the past and the present were enthusiastically exalted as creative superstars. Of course, Astruc's original notion had much more validity in Europe where many of the finest directors—like Renoir, Fellini, and Bergman—were also the writers or coauthors of their scripts. However, the situation was very different in America, especially within the studio system, where the producer was king, and all his directors, stars, and writers were generally used as interchangeable parts to create the great films of the day.

Finally, in the mid-seventies, the proponents of the writers struck back, led by Richard Corliss's articles in *Film Comment* attacking the auteurism proposed by his mentor Sarris and challenging the auteuristic demeaning of the role of the screenwriter. Corliss's subsequent book, *Talking Pictures: Screenwriters in the American Cinema, 1927–1973*, examined one-hundred films by thirty-five screenwriters whose work was not only crucial to American film history but also revealed the writers' uniquely personal "auteurist" styles.

Two years later in *The New York Review of Books*, Gore Vidal took a similar though far more acerbic position in "Who Makes the Movies," which ridiculed the notion of auteurism, exalted the screenwriter, and denigrated the director, who was described, at best, as an "interpreter" of the writer's work and, at worst, a "technician-hustler" or "hustler-plagiarist" (because he's always "telling stories that are not his"). According to Vidal:

> In the Fifties when I came to MGM as a contract writer and took my place at the Writer's Table in the commissary, the Wise Hack used to tell us newcomers, "The director is the brother-in-law." Apparently the ambitious man became a producer (that's where the power was). The talented man became a writer (that's where the creation was). The pretty man became a star.

Yet, despite these vigorous challenges to auteurism, the principle of the dominance of the director is still generally accepted, and the writers of films, with few exceptions, are generally unknown by the public. Nevertheless, from the fifties on, the Hollywood screenwriter has seen his salary increased, his reputation within the industry enhanced, and, due to more creative contractual agreements, he is often better able to protect his work than he could in the past. Over the past few decades, various writers have also been able to secure "producer" status on their films, and many young screenwriters have been able to make the transition to film directors. Yet, as Pat McGilligan pointed out in *Backstory* (1986), "[S]creenwriting, for all its genuine 'progress,' remains an 'invisible' profession." Writers are still not cited in most film reviews, which chatter on incessantly about the director, the stars, and the special effects. Also, writers are often frustrated to discover that their work has been altered, rewritten, or poorly executed. As recently as the 2003 Academy Awards, the host Steve Martin could joke to his Hollywood audience:

> Finally, the studios are getting much more respectful of writers. I handed in a script last year, and the studio didn't change one word. The word they didn't change was on page 87.

THE FILMS

The films discussed in this book are all American classics from the second half of the twentieth century and cover a wide range of genres: dramas, musicals, horror films, thrillers, a sports film, and a Western:

Singin' in the Rain (1952): Written by musical legends Betty Comden and Adolph Green and directed by Gene Kelly and Stanley Donen, this clever, witty, and rousing film is generally considered to be the greatest musical of the Studio era. Begun as a "catalogue" picture (to incorporate the various songs of Arthur Freed and his musical collaborator Nacio Herb Brown), Comden and Green were able to craft an ingenious story line about the coming of the "talkies" and thus create one of the best film musicals ever made.

On the Waterfront (1954): Budd Schulberg's powerful script about a conscience-ridden longshoreman who stands up to the mob was brilliantly directed by Elia Kazan and powerfully performed by Marlon Brando in his most compelling role. The film, which won Best Picture at the 1954 Oscars, is generally considered one of the greatest of all American films, in a class with *Casablanca*, *Citizen Kane*, and the great Griffith masterpieces.

Rebel Without a Cause (1955): The quintessential film about the angst of American adolescence was written by the renowned screenwriter Stewart Stern. His screenplay, which confronted the fifties' social phenomenon of "juvenile delinquency," was directed by Nicholas Ray and memorably performed by James Dean.

North by Northwest (1959): Written by screenwriting legend Ernest Lehman, this original thriller began with a few of Alfred Hitchcock's disparate notions, which Lehman wove into a masterful, seamless narrative that stands with *The 39 Steps* as the greatest Hitchcock thriller and one of the best ever written for film.

Psycho (1960): When Alfred Hitchcock decided to enter into the popular horror genre of the late fifties, he hired a young writer, Joseph Stefano, to adapt a peculiar horror novel entitled *Psycho*, which was loosely based on the depravities of the real-life monster, Edward Gein. Stefano radically transformed the novel, and Hitchcock masterfully directed the script and the unforgettable performance of Anthony Perkins as Norman Bates. The result was the most acclaimed horror film in the history of cinema. This fact was reaffirmed at the beginning of the new millennium, when the American Film Institute polled "1,500 leaders of the American movie community" to determine the best one-hundred film thrillers of all time (the "most heart-pounding movies"), and *Psycho* was chosen number one. (*Jaws* was number two; *The Exorcist* was number three; and *North by Northwest* was number four.)

Hud (1963): Legendary screenwriters Irving Ravetch and Harriet Frank, Jr., took a minor character from Larry McMurtry's first novel *Horseman, Pass By*, and transformed him into one of the most eerily compelling characters in motion picture history. The Ravetches' uniquely close relation with the film's director Martin Ritt, and also with its leading actor, Paul Newman, led to a devastating cinematic character-study of evil and self-absorption.

The Sound of Music (1965): The bankrupt 20th Century Fox gambled everything on the talents of screenwriting genius Ernest Lehman to transform Rogers and Hammerstein's Broadway play into a successful film. Despite the endless predictions of doom in Hollywood, Lehman's masterful script, as directed by Robert Wise, broke all existing box office records, won Best Picture at the 1965 Oscars, saved the moribund studio, and became one of the most popular films ever made.

The Wild Bunch (1969): Although this film was originally seen as a "revisionist" Western because of its lyric violence and apparent cynicism, Walon Green, writing one of his first screenplays, imbued his strikingly original narrative with just enough idealism (his outlaws' fundamental sense of loyalty and courage) to make it one of the great Western classics, and, at least until now, one of the last.

American Graffiti (1973): This exuberant and irresistible paean to the youth culture of the early, still-innocent sixties was generally conceived by its director, George Lucas, and then written by his collegiate friend Willard Huyck of the University of Southern California (USC) and Willard's wife Gloria Katz of the University of California, Los Angeles (UCLA). The film's extraordinary success revolutionized Hollywood thinking about the nature of film audiences and about the potential talents of American film students.

The Sting (1973): This incredibly clever and meticulously written script by film school graduate David Ward turned into one of the most popular and entertaining films ever made. Directed by George Roy Hill and starring Paul Newman and Robert Redford, it won Best Picture of the Year at the 1973 Oscars.

The Exorcist (1973): In 1971, William Peter Blatty's psychological novel of demonic possession was first published, eventually selling 13 million copies. When Blatty, a well-known screenwriter in Hollywood, adapted his own novel, he was able to secure sole producer status and choose William Friedkin as his director. The resulting film became an immediate classic, and like all the other great "horror" films, it was much more than just a horror film.

Jaws (1975): The adaptation of Peter Benchley's novel to the screen was one of the most difficult cinematic projects ever undertaken. The film's awesome success was due to the incredible persistence of the film's young director, Steven Spielberg, and the amazing talents of its young screenwriter, Carl Gottlieb, who wrote much of the script on the set.

Rocky (1976): Sports movies were supposedly dead-on-arrival in Hollywood, especially boxing movies, when a young unknown actor and screenwriter wrote the screenplay for the most popular and successful sports film ever made. The story of Sylvester Stallone's determination not only to protect his script but also to perform as the film's leading character serves as an astonishing parallel to the noble triumph of his unforgettable character Rocky.

Tender Mercies (1983): One of America's greatest playwrights and screenwriters, Horton Foote, wrote this powerful, understated story of a man's extremely difficult and gradual regeneration. The script is an unforgettable testament to the power of love, and it was brilliantly directed by Bruce Beresford and featured Robert Duvall in an Oscar-winning performance.

CLASSIC AMERICAN FILMS

The idea for this book first occurred nearly two decades ago when I was a student in Max Lamb's class about screenwriters at USC. Max had worked for a long time in the industry, most notably for Robert Wise, and he would often bring many of his writer friends to class to meet with his eager students. One day, he showed up with the irrepressible Julius J. Epstein, who with his twin brother, Philip G. Epstein, had written most of *Casablanca* before Howard Koch and Casey Robinson made their own contributions to that classic script. Julius astonished us all by bluntly dismissing *Casablanca* as "nothing but cornpone" and claiming that he didn't even like the film. Almost all of his comments about the great film that he'd done so much to create were totally disparaging, and it was very clear that he was much more interested in talking about his numerous other films, especially *Reuben, Reuben*, a film I'd never cared for.

After class I talked more with Max and Julius, further convinced that Julius's responses to *Casablanca* were only partially authentic. I was convinced that he "doth protest too much," maybe because of all the endless questions about *which* of the script's writers had contributed *what* to the famous screenplay, or maybe because he felt that the film had dwarfed all his other accomplishments over a long lifetime of writing for the cinema. Regardless, I felt certain that if I could just get Julius alone for an hour or two, I could get him to open up about the film. So a few years later, when I was finally ready to initiate the interviews for this book, I called up Julius, and he immediately agreed to talk to me about *Casablanca*—and about nothing else. Now back in his early days, Julius and his twin brother Philip had grown up tough Jewish kids in New York City before they went off to Penn State so they could fight on the collegiate boxing team (bantamweights). As a result, Julius went to Penn State's homecoming football game every fall, so we planned our interview for a few days after he got back. Sadly, Julius, already 88 years old at the time, went to the football game and suffered a severe, incapacitating stroke which permanently precluded the possibility of our discussions about *Casablanca*.

The tragedy of Julius's sudden illness made me even more determined to press on with my planned series of single-film interviews. It seemed to me that there were just too many good stories that needed to be told and recorded. Of course, I was fully aware that there were already several good books containing screenwriter interviews, notably Pat McGilligan's *Backstory* (now a four-book series) but the conversations in both McGilligan's book and the other interview books covered the *entire* creative life of the screenwriters, thus leaving very little time to discuss their most significant achievements. So, I contacted Joseph Stefano, he agreed to meet with me, and we had a long conversation about his masterful script for Hitchcock's *Psycho*. That was the beginning.

Amazingly, every single interview I did for this book was a remarkable experience. The writers were honest, lively, informative, and fun. They were proud of their work but also humble and self-effacing. There was none of that terrible ego or self-promotion that one always associates with Hollywood, and it was a great pleasure to have the opportunity to meet with these talented writers and discuss their work. As cited earlier, Orson Welles once said that "the writer should have the first and last word in filmmaking." This book has allowed those who wrote the "words" which were eventually interpreted and adapted by directors, cinematographers, performers, editors, etc., into American film classics, to sit back, reconsider their distinguished work, and have the "last word."

CHAPTER 1

Singin' in the Rain (1952)

A CONVERSATION WITH BETTY COMDEN
AND ADOLPH GREEN

Betty Comden (1915–2006) and Adolph Green (1914–2002) were legends of the American musical who distinguished themselves as playwrights, screenwriters, and lyricists. Both born in New York City, they began their careers as cabaret performers in Greenwich Village and eventually created their own nightclub act, *The Revuers*, which included Judy Holliday. Their first Broadway musical, *On the Town*, with music by Leonard Bernstein, was a great success, and it led to a studio contract with Metro-Goldwyn-Mayer. Writing for the famous Arthur Freed musical unit at MGM, they wrote the scripts for various musical features including: *The Barkleys of Broadway* (1949) with Fred Astaire and Ginger Rogers; *On the Town* (1949) starring Gene Kelly and Frank Sinatra; *Singin' in the Rain* (1952) with Gene Kelly, Debbie Reynolds, and Donald O'Connor; Vincente Minnelli's *The Band Wagon* (1953) featuring Fred Astaire and Cyd Charisse, for which they were nominated for an Academy Award; *It's Always Fair Weather* (1955) with Gene Kelly and Cyd Charisse, for which they were again nominated for an Academy Award; and Vincente Minnelli's *Bells Are Ringing* (1960) with Judy Holliday. At the same time, they were also writing award-winning musicals for the Broadway stage including *Billion Dollar Baby* (1945), *Bells are Ringing* (1957), *Applause* (1970), and *On the Twentieth Century* (1978). Their sixty-year collaboration produced seven

Tony awards, and in 1991 they received Lifetime Achievement Awards in the Performing Arts at the Kennedy Center in Washington, D.C.

In 1946, after the great success of your Broadway musical, On the Town— *with its score by your friend Leonard Bernstein—you were offered a Hollywood contract to write musicals for the Arthur Freed unit at Metro-Goldwyn-Mayer. What was Arthur Freed like?*

COMDEN: He was actually a very complicated man. Before becoming a producer, he was a songwriter and a great lyricist. He was also a man who was used to working with highly talented people, and that's what made the Freed unit so unusual. More than anybody else in Hollywood, Arthur brought people out from New York who were not necessarily movie people and put them to work. People like Alan Jay Lerner; Vincente Minnelli; Oliver Smith, the designer; and anyone else he thought was exceptionally talented. That was one of his greatest gifts: the ability to bring people together and get them to work together.

GREEN: Arthur had a real "instinct" about things, and he also had a most invaluable assistant in Roger Edens, his second-in-command. Roger was extremely important at MGM; he was just like Arthur's co-producer—his partner, really—and he was involved in every aspect of the Freed productions.

COMDEN: The writing, the music, everything. And Roger was a very talented musician himself.

So you dealt more with Edens?

COMDEN: Yes, right from the very beginning.

GREEN: We only dealt with Arthur on and off. He was very friendly and nice and helpful, and he was *never* a tyrant or anything like that, but he was always so busy. So, Roger was the one we worked with every day.

COMDEN: As members of the Freed unit, we had a very unusual experience for writers in Hollywood. The unit had a reputation for being very respectful of all its various talents, particularly the writers, and it was true. No other writer was *ever* put on one of our pictures, and no one was ever brought in to rewrite anything. Never. Which was very unusual.

GREEN: And very pleasant. Although our office in the Administration Building was barely better than a prison cell! It was bleak and stark, and our window looked out on the Smith and Salisbury Mortuary. *That* was our daily view.

COMDEN: Arthur was right down the hall in the corner office ... in his suite of offices.

GREEN: So we'd come in early every day, and we'd work like mad in that little room.

COMDEN: When we first arrived in 1946, we were stunned to learn that our first assignment was *Good News*, a rather hokey campus football story from 1925! We were considered—I hate to use the word, but it was our reputation back then—rather sophisticated New Yorkers, and then we were handed *Good News*!

GREEN: We'd done *On the Town* and our second Broadway show *Billion Dollar Baby*, and our reputation was for sharp satire and sophisticated dialogue, and then we got *Good News* which was pretty much "old-hat" when it was first produced on the stage. But it was a tremendous hit in New York, and it had a wonderful score.

COMDEN: So we were trying to come up with new and clever ways to rewrite it, and Arthur said, "No, kids, just write *Good News*." So we did our best to keep to the original story line.

Then you wrote The Barkleys of Broadway *for Fred Astaire and Ginger Rogers, and then you adapted your own* On the Town; *both of which came out in 1949. I'm jumping ahead a bit to get to* Singin' in the Rain.

GREEN: Absolutely. "Skip all that!" as the Bellman said to the Baker in "The Hunting of the Snark" when the Baker started his sad story: "My father and mother were honest, though poor—." So the Baker did as requested, " 'I skip forty years,' said the Baker in tears."

Well, let's not skip that many years, but let's jump ahead to the summer of 1950, after the success of the film version of On the Town, *which starred Gene Kelly and Frank Sinatra. Arthur Freed called you back to Hollywood for what was known as a "catalogue" picture—a picture that's created around the songs of one songwriter or team of songwriters.*

COMDEN: Yes, we walked into Arthur's office, and he said, "Well, your next movie is . . ."

GREEN: "Kids!"

COMDEN: That's right, "kids,"—he always called us "kids"—"Well, kids, your next movie is going to be called *Singin' in the Rain*, and it's going to have all my songs in it." And that was that. That was the *whole* assignment. And it may not sound very difficult, but it was terribly hard to do, almost impossible.

Is that because you have to make all these unrelated songs somehow fit into the story you're creating?

COMDEN: That's right, you have to create a whole new story with characters and situations that fit the already existing songs. It's like working backwards.

And, of course, you're obligated to include the most popular songs.

COMDEN: Yes, but the very first thing you have to do is come up with an overall idea for the movie that'll be appropriate to the general feeling of the songs. And that was very hard to do, but we finally figured it out.

GREEN: Finally! It took us quite a long time before we realized that the songs would fit best in the time period for which they'd been written. Most of them, at least.

COMDEN: Which was the changeover period in Hollywood from the silents to the talkies, when Arthur Freed and his partner, Nacio Herb Brown, wrote many of their songs for the early film musicals.

GREEN: "Broadway Melody," for example—which was a very big hit when it came out in February of 1929.

COMDEN: And "Singin' in the Rain."

GREEN: "Singin' in the Rain" was first used in *The Hollywood Revue of 1929* directed by Charles Riesner.

How many Freed-Brown songs were there?

COMDEN: About a hundred or so. He gave us a huge stack of songs and said, "Go write a movie."

GREEN: But a movie about what? *That* was the problem. All we knew was, that at some point in the film, someone would be out in the rain and singing about it.

I've read that you were never crazy about the title. And both Kelly and Donen have also claimed that they never liked it.

COMDEN: It really didn't bother us. We liked the song; we liked lots of the Brown-Freed songs.

GREEN: The problem wasn't the title; it was that we had no picture to go with it!

When you arrived in May 1950 to write Singin' in the Rain, *you didn't realize that you'd be writing a catalogue picture. You assumed that you'd be writing* both *the story and the lyrics for your next film.*

COMDEN: We did. It was our own mistake because our previous agent had told us that it was in our contract that we'd *always* write our own lyrics, unless they were using songs by Irving Berlin, Cole Porter, and a few others.

GREEN: So we went on strike! We didn't work for about six weeks.

COMDEN: We stood firm, saying, "Look at our contract!" Then Irving Lazar, our new agent, came over one day and read the whole contract, and there was no such clause. So we were wrong.

It's a good thing. We might not have Singin' in the Rain.

COMDEN: That's true.

GREEN: So, Arthur said, "OK, kids, let's get to work." And we knew we had no choice, so we got to work.

The key to Singin' in the Rain, *as we've already discussed, was setting the film in the late twenties when the "silent" films gradually gave way to "talking" pictures. Back in your earlier days as performers in New York, you apparently did a satirical sketch in your show, "The Revuers," about the Hollywood transition period—and especially about the resultant problems with synchronization. What was the sketch about?*

COMDEN: Well, first, I should mention that Adolph is quite an expert on the movies. He knows everything about the history of film.

GREEN: And Betty knows a great deal too.

COMDEN: So even back when we were performing our nightclub act with Judy Holliday, which consisted of a variety of sketches and satirical songs, we had this one about the first time sound and image met on film—nearly!

GREEN: It was a sketch about a movie actor called Donald Ronald. And we first showed him in a silent film, and then we showed him in an early talkie. Sort of like Al Jolson. And I walked on and I said ... [mouthing the words out of sync].

COMDEN: [Saying the words for Adolph] "Hello, old man. Won't you come in? What's that you say? She's dead! No, no, no! I'll go for the doctor. Oh, Nellie, Nellie, my own!"

GREEN: So we used that directly in the movie.

COMDEN: The other bit, of course, was that some of the actors forgot to keep close to the hidden microphones, so the sound kept modulating up and down, and you could only hear part of a song.

GREEN: I sang a song called "Honeybunch." The lyrics went: "Honeybunch, you drive me frantic with your smile. Honeybunch, you're worthwhile." [Singing the lyrics with the sound drop outs] "Honeybun ... frantic with ... while." So we used that in the movie, too.

Apparently, the technicians working with the footage from Singin' in the Rain *were so confused by the "non-synchronization" scene that the answer print was actually delayed for a few weeks.*

COMDEN: Yes, they kept trying to make it match, and Gene and Stanley kept calling them up saying, "Where's the print? What's holding things up?" And they were very embarrassed, but they finally admitted, "We can't get this thing in sync." So Gene and Stanley had to explain to them that that was the point. It shouldn't be in sync!

Given that you're both great lovers of the silent pictures that you saw when you were younger, I wonder if either of you actually ever saw John Gilbert's His Glorious Night *(1929), which supposedly ruined his career? Especially when he repeated, "I love you, I love you, I love you...."*

GREEN: I saw it.

In a movie theater when it first came out?

GREEN: Yes.

What was the audience reaction? Was it really as shocking as we've been told?

GREEN: Well, it was quite a shock, and it ended his career, pretty much overnight. It was very sad. As a kid, I was crazy about John Gilbert, but when I heard him speak for the first time in *His Glorious Night*, it definitely didn't sound like him—or, at least, like what I expected him to sound like. And when he kept saying "I love you, I love you, I love you," the audience laughed out loud. It's true.

COMDEN: A lot of the silent stars had voices that didn't seem to fit their screen personalities.

GREEN: And, in some cases, the sound hadn't been properly adjusted to equalize their voices and make them sound okay.

Apparently, they delayed making a talkie with Garbo because they were afraid her accent wouldn't work. But the audiences loved it.

GREEN: Yes, in Garbo's case, her voice—accent and all—sounded exactly like what she looked like. It was a perfect match. But poor John Gilbert had no such luck. He was the biggest star in films back then, and the studio had to pay him enormous sums of money over the next seven years while his career just frittered away. It's a very sad story, but our picture was funny!

It's especially funny when Gene Kelly insists on saying the line.

GREEN: "I love you, I love you, I love you."

COMDEN: Yes, and he thinks it's a great idea!

GREEN: Yes, we liked that picture a lot. We've gradually gotten to like it.

Singin' in the Rain?

COMDEN: He's just kidding! You can't always tell with him.

GREEN: Yes, I'm sorry. As a matter of fact, we loved it from the very beginning, but we had no idea it would reach such epic proportions as it grew older. Initially, it was pretty much brushed off since it came out right after ...

COMDEN: *An American in Paris.*

GREEN: ... which got so much publicity and so many favorable notices.

COMDEN: And was considered "Art."

GREEN: So our picture didn't seem as important. Mainly because it was full of laughter—that sinful, superficial thing called laughter.

COMDEN: But *we* knew it was good from the start. Even before Gene decided to do the picture, we read the script to a number of people, and the response was always terrific.

In that excellent introduction you wrote for the published screenplay of Singin' in the Rain *in 1972, you mentioned that, at one point, you were considering a "singing cowboy" plot revolving around Howard Keel before you knew that Gene Kelly would be the lead.*

COMDEN: Yes, briefly. We were searching around for ideas at the time, and since we didn't have Gene yet, we had to consider other actors who might be available.

How did your good friend Gene Kelly get involved?

GREEN: Well, at first, he couldn't even consider the idea because he was in the middle of shooting *An American in Paris.*

COMDEN: We used to go down to the set where he was shooting, but we had to wait until he was finished with the picture. Finally, we did an "audition" for him, and we read him the script. At that time, Gene had his choice of anything that he wanted to do, but he fell in love with *Singin' in the Rain* right away.

I believe you first met Gene Kelly in the summer of 1939 at the Westport Country Playhouse?

COMDEN: Yes, the Westport Country Playhouse was a wonderful summer theater; it was a revue, and we were in it.

GREEN: Meaning our nightclub act, "The Revuers," with Judy Holliday, Alvin Hammer, and Joan Frank.

COMDEN: And there were a number of other people on the bill including Gene.

Was he was working as a choreographer? Or a master of ceremonies?

COMDEN: No, he was dancing.

GREEN: He had a dancing act. It's true that he was trying to get some work as a choreographer, which he did later, but, at the time, he was just a hoofer—and he had a very good act.

COMDEN: He was such an attractive guy—adorable, wonderful-looking—and very funny.

Going back to when you first began to write the script, you were apparently struggling with three possible openings for the film. What were they?

COMDEN: Well, one was the premiere of the new silent film in New York City; the second was a magazine interview where he's telling lies about his past; and the third was a sequence from the silent movie that was being premiered, *The Royal Rascal*.

GREEN: But they all felt too much like "openings." None of them made it seem like the plot was really starting. So we had these three unsatisfactory ideas, and we knew we'd have to use one of them, and we were in total despair. We were ready to give the money back.

Was it really that bad?

GREEN: It was. We were *always* in despair at the beginning of all our projects, but *Singin' in the Rain* was just impossible. We were ready to give up and go back to New York.

COMDEN: We thought we'd never solve it.

Then your husband came out for a visit.

COMDEN: That's right, my husband, Steve, came out to be with me, and we read him all three openings, and he said, "Why not use *all* the openings?" And we realized that he was right, and we worked it all out, and it solved the problem.

GREEN: All three ideas ended up in there—intertwined—and it worked. And Gene sure looked great in that white hat and the white coat at the premiere.

COMDEN: Yes, didn't he look terrific?

After he decided to do the picture, you began meeting with Kelly and his co-director Stanley Donen to discuss structure and go over the film shot-by-shot.

COMDEN: Yes, we worked at the studio during the day, but, in the evenings, we'd often go over to Gene's house. Then, we'd talk about the movie and discuss what we needed to do.

Did you act out the scenes?

GREEN: By that time, it wasn't necessary. Gene and Stanley knew the script well enough. So we'd read parts out loud or turn to certain pages and say, "Hey, I think we need to do this here." It was mostly patching things up, discussing costumes, sometimes deciding to rewrite two scenes into one—those kinds of things.

COMDEN: We had a great shorthand with both Gene and Stanley because we were all old friends, going back to our nightclub days. So we didn't have to explain things to them. Another director might have said, "What is this craziness? What do you think you're doing?" Or "How the hell are we going to do that?" But Gene and Stanley were used to the way our minds worked.

GREEN: Other directors might have panicked and thrown out the whole script. So we were very lucky. Gene and Stanley were always able to visualize the script. And as much as a film can ever resemble its script, *Singin' in the Rain* was extremely close to the screenplay. Wouldn't you say so, Betty?

COMDEN: It certainly was. Fortunately for us, Gene and Stanley were both so visually creative, and they had that masterful sense of pace. In so many movies, things are leaden and heavy . . .

GREEN: Belabored.

COMDEN: . . . usually because the director spends too much time on things. But in *Singin' in the Rain*, there isn't a wasted second. The important points are made in every scene, and then it moves right along to the next scene. It's brilliantly done.

There's no doubt about that. Now, I'd like to ask you a couple of questions about the casting of the picture. Debbie Reynolds was a very talented seventeen-year-old with limited film experience and only one year of dance training when she was unexpectedly given the lead in Singin' in the Rain. *Her "Aba Dabba Honeymoon" number with Carleton Carpenter from* Two Weeks with Love *(1950) had brought her some attention, but I wonder if you were concerned about the studio's choice?*

COMDEN: We weren't worried. We'd seen Debbie perform one evening. She got up and sang and danced, and she was very cute and talented. She wasn't really a dancer, but she worked very hard at it, and it paid off.

GREEN: Everyone considered Debbie "up and coming" at the time. She was very cute and funny, and we were both convinced when she performed for us that night.

COMDEN: It turned out to be a great call. So was the casting of Jean Hagen. She was wonderful too.

How about Donald O'Connor? He was borrowed from another studio for the role of Cosmo, but I've read that Arthur Freed really wanted Oscar Levant for Kelly's sidekick?

GREEN: Well, we actually started writing the script with Oscar in mind.

COMDEN: Oscar had been the sidekick in *American in Paris*, and it was more or less assumed that he'd do the same thing in *Singin' in the Rain*.

GREEN: It was very difficult for us because Oscar happened to be a very close personal friend.

Was it Kelly's decision?

COMDEN: Yes, Gene went to Arthur and said, "I don't want to work with Oscar again. This is a different kind of movie, and I need somebody who's more of an entertainer—somebody I can dance with."

GREEN: He didn't want any more of those scenes with Oscar sitting at the piano and Gene dancing on top of the piano. We felt terrible about it, but we knew that Gene was right, even though we loved Oscar.

COMDEN: So we went to Arthur and warned him, "Oscar's going to be very upset about this." But Arthur reassured us, "Don't worry, kids. Oscar's a good friend. I'll tell him myself." So we assumed that Oscar knew. Then one day, I was talking to Oscar on the phone, and I said, "We just feel terrible about the movie, Oscar," and he said, "What? What?" And that's how he found out about it. Arthur never told him.

GREEN: Arthur was like that sometimes. He didn't want to give the bad news, even though he'd told us it was no problem. So Oscar was furious at Betty.

COMDEN: It lasted about four months.

Why was he mad at you?

COMDEN: I was the messenger!

GREEN: He didn't blame me because I wasn't the one on the phone.

COMDEN: So I was the "guilty" one. It was terrible, but, gradually, we made up. And, of course, Gene was absolutely right. He needed someone to dance with, and Donald was his first choice.

GREEN: Early on, Gene brought Donald to the studio to see what he could do, and he had him do every single dance step that Donald knew—and every joke, and every pratfall. Later, of course, they were all used brilliantly in that crazy number, "Make 'Em Laugh."

Back when you were writing the role of Lina Lamont, were you thinking of Judy Holiday's Billie Dawn character in Born Yesterday?

COMDEN: Not really. We felt that a character like that—with that kind of voice and with that kind of a nasty personality—had nothing to do with Judy.

GREEN: But we did wonder if it might raise some questions. Which it did. Although, oddly enough, never from Judy herself.

COMDEN: Well, we tried very hard to avoid any possible resemblance. We made her a total heavy, not a little girl who was finding herself, like Billie Dawn.

Singin' in the Rain *is full of film references—to Clara Bow, Busby Berkeley, John Gilbert, George Raft, Louise Brooks, etc.—and a number of people believe that the character of R. F. Simpson was modeled on Arthur Freed himself. Is there any truth to that?*

COMDEN: I've never heard that before. It certainly wasn't intentional, and he sure didn't look like him!

People claim, for example, that Arthur Freed was known to be clumsy, and that he would often have difficulty making up his mind about things.

COMDEN: Well, it's certainly true that Arthur could have trouble making up his mind sometimes. It's also true that he occasionally took credit for certain things that he shouldn't have. Like in the movie, when Simpson claims that he warned everybody about the coming threat of the talkies.

GREEN: Yes, Arthur could have done that, but, I suppose, many other producers could have done it as well.

Is it true that the studio was worried about your satire of the powerful gossip columnist Louella Parsons?

COMDEN: I've never heard that either. Arthur never told us to "go easy" on that character, or anything like that. Did he, Adolph?

GREEN: No, but I guess she is a bit Louella-ish.

I've heard that she enjoyed it very much.

GREEN: She probably did. Dora Bailey wasn't a mean character in the film, and she wasn't even that dopey.

COMDEN: In real life, Louella Parsons could seem quite formidable and scary. And she had the ability to damage people's careers if she didn't like them. But we didn't create a character like that. Dora's a bit silly and gushing, but she's very likeable.

One important change from the earlier script to the film is the replacement of the "Wedding of the Painted Doll" number for "Make 'Em Laugh," which Arthur Freed wrote the night before rehearsals. Apparently, since he was held in such affection by the people who worked for him, no one pointed out—in public, at least—the song's marked similarity with Cole Porter's song "Be a Clown," which, ironically, was first sung by Gene Kelly and Judy Garland in The Pirate *(1948), which Arthur Freed produced. What was your reaction to all this?*

COMDEN: We just looked at each other, raised our eyebrows, and moved on.

GREEN: We shrugged our shoulders and said nothing. Everybody did.

COMDEN: Should I tell the story about Irving?

GREEN: Sure. Why not?

COMDEN: On the very day that they were shooting the song, Arthur brought Irving Berlin down to the studio. He was very proud of both the song and the number. So, Gene was in the process of shooting the number, and Irving walks onto the set, and we were all horrified. We were all thinking, "My God, Irving's going to hear the song and recognize the similarity! What's going to happen?" Then they put the song on the track, and it played for a little bit, while Arthur's sitting right there with Irving, feeling very proud of it.

So, obviously, he had no idea?

COMDEN: He had no idea. No clue. So Irving's listening, and he's listening, and then you could see his face changing. Then, he turned to Arthur and said, "Who wrote that song?" And Arthur, who had written it himself, suddenly got very flustered and said, "Oh, well, we … that is, the kids … we all got together and … come along, Irving!" Then Arthur pulled Irving away, and they left the set, and we all fell on the floor laughing.

So, he must have realized at that very moment?

GREEN: He must have.

COMDEN: But how he could have written it in the first place—and not realized—is still a mystery. We have no idea, and we never brought it up with Arthur, either before or after that day.

I don't know how Cole Porter took it, but it's a wonderful sequence in the movie—one of the best musical numbers in film history.

GREEN: It's great.

COMDEN: It's fabulous, but the song's exactly like "Be a Clown."

The only non-Freed song in the movie was the tongue-twister, "Moses Supposes," which Roger Eden set to your lyrics. Was the song finished before you left for the East Coast?

COMDEN: I think so. We incorporated it into the film while we were still out there, didn't we?

GREEN: I think we did.

As production actually got under way on Singin' in the Rain, *you went back to New York to prepare another play for Broadway. While you were gone, Kelly and Donen never altered a line of your script without your consent, and they occasionally called you up from Hollywood during the shooting of the film. Can you remember any of these long-distance discussions?*

COMDEN: One was about the tour of the studio lot with Gene and Debbie. Originally, it included three songs. Then we got a call from Gene that he wanted just one—a love song.

GREEN: Originally, they were taking a tour of various locales on the set—India, China, Germany, etc.—a world tour in five minutes around the studio. But Gene wanted the chance to sing a love song in a single location, and he was right. So we wrote the scene for the sound stage, and we sent it through the mail.

When did you finally see the completed film?

GREEN: It must have been when we went out there to get our next assignment, which was *The Band Wagon*. *Singin' in the Rain* hadn't been released yet, and we saw it in some grubby little equipment room—not even a screening room—and we carried in two chairs and sat down and watched it for the first time.

COMDEN: It was wonderful!

GREEN: We were thrilled!

Were you all alone?

GREEN: All alone.

COMDEN: All alone. And it just knocked us out!

Could you tell me about the party you attended with Charles Chaplin soon after the film was released?

COMDEN: Was it at Charlie's house?

GREEN: No, it was at the Contes'. Nick and Ruth Conte. And Charlie came in.

COMDEN: Yes, he came into the party, and he said, "I've just seen this marvelous picture!"

GREEN: He didn't know we had anything to do with it, and he started raving about the film and describing it to everyone.

COMDEN: And we said, "Oh, really?" And we listened for a while, and then we admitted, "That's our movie, Charlie!"

GREEN: It was so thrilling because we were always such great Chaplin fans.

Although you weren't actually on the set for most of the filming, you're both very familiar with how Kelly and Donen worked together as collaborative directors. Could you describe it?

COMDEN: They worked very closely and discussed everything. Stanley is a great cameraman, and he knows all about the angles and the set-ups. As a former dancer, he also knew which particular angles would be best suited to which steps and how to shoot them all. But it wasn't simply a matter that Gene did the dancing and Stanley did the camera; they really did everything together, collaboratively—the choreography, working with the other actors, and everything else.

One thing about Gene Kelly that's obvious from watching the film is his artistic generosity—his willingness to showcase such remarkable, show-stopping dancers as both Donald O'Connor and Cyd Charisse.

GREEN: That's the way he was. The picture always came first.

COMDEN: Gene was always smart enough to surround himself with wonderful exciting people. He didn't want to be the only star. *He* was the one who'd insisted on Donald O'Connor.

GREEN: Yes, he wanted him like mad! Gene knew that the more great entertainers the film had, the better it could be.

He not only gives whole dance numbers to other performers, but, in other scenes, he spotlights other characters rather than himself. Like when Cyd Charisse appears in the "Broadway Melody" number dressed in that dazzling green outfit.

COMDEN: Well, Gene couldn't wear that! Sorry!

GREEN: And, as you know, that was the first time that Cyd ever really "came across" in a film. She'd been in pictures for a number of years by then, but Gene and Stanley knew exactly how to highlight her talents.

COMDEN: And that's what Gene wanted. He never felt competitive with his co-stars.

GREEN: All he cared about was the film.

I'd like to ask your response to several of the musical numbers in the film starting with "Singin' in the Rain," which has become the most famous musical scene in motion picture history. Gene Kelly often said that it was the easiest dance he ever did, and that the real difficulty was the problems faced by the technical crew. But it's also well known that he had a 103-degree fever that day; that everyone was worried that he might catch pneumonia; and that, between takes, when he was drenched from all that water, he would leave the sound stage to stand in the hot California sun and try to warm himself up.

COMDEN: Yes, that's all true, and he did the scene rather quickly as well, didn't he?

Yes, I believe it was two days.

GREEN: It's an amazing scene! Marvelous!

The only real criticism that ever pops up about Singin' in the Rain *is "The Broadway Melody" sequence, which is, as Gene Kelly has always admitted, too long (over twelve minutes)—and which doesn't fit that well into the narrative of such a tightly structured and fast-paced film. How do you feel about it?*

COMDEN: Well, it was kind of a developing tradition back then. The theater in New York City started having all those second-act ballets after Agnes DeMille's *Oklahoma*. We had one in *On the Town*, and most of the shows were using them. Then, when the musicals were made into films, the ballets were included. *An American in Paris*, of course, had a very daring ballet, so Arthur Freed decided that he wanted a big ballet at the end of *Singin' in the Rain*—even though it didn't really fit in the film. But we had no control over it.

GREEN: But it turned out surprisingly well.

COMDEN: Yes, it did. But, if we'd had anything to say about it back then, we would have made it shorter and more appropriate to the film. It's not really our favorite part of the picture, except for looking at Cyd Charisse.

Is it true that, since Donald O'Connor had a television commitment to Colgate Comedy Hour, they brought in Cyd Charisse for "The Broadway Melody"?

COMDEN: I don't think we ever knew about that.

Did you originally include O'Connor in the number?

GREEN: No, we didn't, but we definitely didn't have Cyd in mind either.

How do you feel about the scarf dance—which Kelly claims was one of the most difficult things he ever did?

GREEN: We've grown to love it!

Which implies you weren't so sure in the beginning?

COMDEN: Well, at first, I think we were a little taken aback.

It goes on so long that it heightens your awareness of what they're actually doing with that huge scarf. And then you start wondering how the heck they're actually doing it.

COMDEN: And why? We don't really care. It's not at all like the rest of the movie.

GREEN: It's a symbolic umbilical cord of sorts!

COMDEN: I think she's a bit sexier than that.

GREEN: Well, yes, but it's umbilical, too. It *has* to be.

COMDEN: Oh, I don't think so. Our first disagreement!

GREEN: Yes! Or maybe not, now that I think of it!

COMDEN: But we love every foot of that film!

GREEN: Every foot! Even that tired New York number!

One of the two musical numbers that was cut from the film was Kelly's "All I Do is Dream of You," which he sang and danced in his bedroom on the night he first met Kathy Seldon. It was cut from the film because it slowed down the narrative, but Kelly has always said that it was one of the best dances he ever did in his whole career. I wonder if you ever saw it?

GREEN: Yes, I'd forgotten about that number, but we did see it once, and it was wonderful. But it would have slowed down the picture—just like Debbie singing "You Are My Lucky Star"—so they both had to go.

COMDEN: And "Lucky Star" was a very nice scene, too. Very charming.

Given the decline of the great studios, I wonder what you think about the future of Hollywood musicals?

COMDEN: There really haven't been any first-rate musical films since *Cabaret*, and that was over twenty-five years ago. It's very hard to make them now because the days of the big studios with all their various departments—performers, writers, arrangers, choreographers, costumers, and so on—are gone. Back then a producer could pick whatever he needed for a musical right off the lot.

GREEN: In those days, if they decided on a number they wanted, the set could be up the very next day and they could be shooting the scene.

COMDEN: But it's a different world now; it's much more difficult.

How do you feel about the training of younger people today? Can they dance as well, for example?

COMDEN: I think young people today are very well-trained, especially in the regional and local theaters and in the colleges.

GREEN: I have the feeling that there are even *more* people prepared for musical theater now than there were back then.

COMDEN: They're getting serious training in the colleges.

GREEN: It's not just, "Wow, I'd like to be in a play."

COMDEN: But nowadays, since everything costs so damn much, it would be very hard to finance a musical film.

It's a tragedy. If American film ever stood for anything, especially abroad, it was the musical and the western. And both have fallen into disrepair.

GREEN: They have. And, as for the musicals, even television, which used to have all kinds of Saturday night revues—with top entertainers and dancers—does nothing anymore.

COMDEN: Which is a terrible shame given all the talented young people out there. Last night, Adolph went to a show called *Swing*, and he said the cast was full of kids who could really sing and dance.

GREEN: The dancing was terrific.

COMDEN: But, of course, being a star is very different. There can only be one Astaire in a generation, maybe in every several generations. And one Gene Kelly. They don't come along very often, but maybe there'll be more in the future.

But if it wasn't for the Hollywood musicals, no one would have known who Fred Astaire was.

GREEN: That's true. There's no place to showcase such an extraordinary talent.

François Truffaut once claimed that he'd memorized every single shot of Singin' in the Rain—*and that it had inspired him to make his own film about filmmaking,* La Nuit Américaine (Day for Night, 1973).

COMDEN: Yes, we learned about that in Paris one time, at a party given by Gloria and James Jones. When we arrived, we were absolutely delighted to learn that Truffaut was also there. Then, suddenly, he rushed across the room rather breathlessly talking about *Chantons sous la pluie*. Through his interpreter we learned that *Singin' in the Rain* was his favorite film and that he knew every shot in the film. We were flattered to death.

GREEN: And he told us that Alain Resnais felt the same way. So, we were feeling very good at that party!

Singin' in the Rain *was one of over forty musicals that Arthur Freed produced for MGM and one of countless Hollywood musicals, yet it has been rated by the American Film Institute as one of the top ten American films, and rated by both* Sight and Sound *and* Entertainment Weekly *as one of the top ten films of all time. Why do you think it's so special?*

COMDEN: Because it's perfect! Perfect! Oh, no, just kidding. . . .

GREEN: But it *is* perfect!

COMDEN: OK, but trying to be a bit more objective, I think its uniqueness is the comedy.

GREEN: It's really funny!

COMDEN: And there aren't many like that. Most musicals aren't very funny at all. So, that's part of it. Then, there's the extraordinary talents of Gene Kelly and both directors and everyone else involved with the picture. Every department at the studio was in top form for *Singin' in the Rain*. Everything pulled together perfectly.

And what about that script? It's a very clever story.

COMDEN: That's true! We have to admit, we think it's a marvelous script!

GREEN: We're very proud of it.

You've even grown to love the scarf dance!

GREEN: Yes, we have!

COMDEN: Even the scarf dance!

CHAPTER 2

On the Waterfront (1954)

A CONVERSATION WITH BUDD SCHULBERG

Budd Schulberg was born in New York City and raised in Hollywood, where his father was a major film producer at Paramount, Columbia, and Selznick International. After graduating from Dartmouth in 1936, Schulberg spent a summer in the Soviet Union, and he joined the Communist Party the following year. The second of his four prewar screenplays, *Winter Carnival* (1939), was cowritten with F. Scott Fitzgerald, and his first novel, *What Makes Sammy Run?* (1941), was a very successful and controversial exposé of the Hollywood film industry. Disillusioned with the attempts of CPUSA (Communist Party of the United States of America) to edit his novel, Schulberg left the Party in 1940. In 1943, he joined the U.S. Navy, became a lieutenant in the Office of Strategic Services, and was awarded an Army Commendation Ribbon for gathering photographic evidence of war crimes for the Nuremberg Trials of 1945–46. After his Navy service, Schulberg returned to novel writing, publishing *The Harder They Fall* in 1947 and *The Disenchanted* in 1950. The following year, he testified at the HUAC hearings and, in 1953, he published a collection of short stories entitled *Some Faces in the Crowd*. In 1954, Columbia Pictures released *On the Waterfront*, written by Schulberg, directed by Elia Kazan, and starring Marlon Brando and Eva Marie Saint. The film won eight Academy Awards, including Best Picture, Best Director, and Best Screenplay. His subsequent films include: *The Harder They Fall* (1956) with Humphrey Bogart; Elia Kazan's *A Face in the Crowd* (1957); and Nick Ray's *Wind*

Across the Everglades (1958). Since that time, Schulberg has written numerous books including *Moving Pictures: Memories of a Hollywood Prince* (1981) and *Sparring with Hemingway: And Other Legends of the Fight Game* (1995). In 2003, he was inducted into the International Boxing Hall of Fame.

In 1948, Malcolm Johnson wrote a series of articles for the New York Sun *about corruption on the New York/New Jersey waterfront, particularly within the International Longshoremen's Association (ILA). Johnson eventually won a Pulitzer prize for his exposé, and, as pressure mounted for a government investigation, Joe Curtis, the nephew of Columbia Picture's Harry Cohn, bought the film rights from Johnson and hired you to write the script. Is that correct?*

SCHULBERG: Yes, that's right. And Robert Siodmak—a very good director, by the way—was supposed to direct it.

Did you complete the script?
SCHULBERG: Yes, I did. It had Terry Malloy in it, and I remember that the police were more involved in the story than in the later versions.

Did you discuss the project with Malcolm Johnson?
SCHULBERG: I did talk to Mac Johnson about it, and I did some other research, but I didn't get very deep into the bowels of the story—as I did later.

At the time of the original exposé, was it just a "New York story," or was it syndicated across the country?
SCHULBERG: Just New York, I think. I don't believe it was very well known in the rest of the country, although more so after Mac won the Pulitzer prize.

So who killed the project?
SCHULBERG: Harry Cohn.

Even though his nephew had purchased the rights?
SCHULBERG: Yes, and then everything fell apart. But, oddly enough, in my contract with Columbia, everything relating to the story—my screenplay, the rights, the whole thing—reverted back to me after twelve months.

Now around the same time, Arthur Miller, encouraged by Elia Kazan, was also researching the waterfront story, and he eventually completed a screenplay entitled The Hook *which Kazan tried, without success, to get funded in Hollywood. Did you ever read* The Hook?
SCHULBERG: No, I've never seen it, but I'd like to. I'm naturally very curious about it. Another coincidence is that, totally independent of each other, we were both greatly influenced by the murder of Peter Panto. Panto was a young longshoreman who became the model for my Joey

Doyle in *Waterfront*. The Panto murder was an extremely notorious murder case in New York City at the time—the brutal killing of a young reformer on the docks—and I understand that it triggered Miller's interest in the waterfront story—as it did mine.

Were you aware that both you and Arthur Miller—who greatly admired your 1947 boxing novel, The Harder They Fall—*were simultaneously working on screenplays about the same general subject?*

SCHULBERG: No, I didn't. And I don't know if he knew about me.

Have you ever discussed the coincidence with Miller?

SCHULBERG: Oddly enough, no. But I'd like to. And I'd like to read his script.

Now when both projects seemed dead, you were unexpectedly contacted by Elia Kazan. When did you first meet?

SCHULBERG: I think it was early '52. I can't remember the exact date when he came out to the farm to visit me. He wanted to ask me if I'd be interested in writing a film with an "eastern" background. He wanted to get away from Hollywood and shoot his next film out of New York City.

And you'd never met him before?

SCHULBERG: Never, but I'd seen him on the stage, of course.

Now, at the time Kazan contacted you, you'd already left Hollywood behind and were living on a farm in Bucks County, Pennsylvania. You'd written three successful novels, including What Makes Sammy Run? *and you seemed uninterested in getting reinvolved with Hollywood.*

SCHULBERG: That's right. I thought I'd left it forever, and that's exactly what I told Kazan when he came to visit me. I didn't like the way they treated writers in Hollywood, and I was fed up. I was perfectly content writing novels on the farm.

So why did you decide to work with Kazan?

SCHULBERG: Because he said that he would treat me the same way that he'd always treated his playwrights—in the same way that he'd treated Arthur Miller and Tennessee Williams and Bill Inge. He said, "I'll treat it exactly like a play. I'll make suggestions, but you'll have the final word." Naturally, this greatly impressed me, and I decided to plunge in.

Apparently the first film idea that you and Kazan discussed related to "The Trenton Six."

SCHULBERG: Yes, and when Kazan left at the end of that first meeting, I told him I'd explore "The Trenton Six" situation, which I did. I went over to Trenton a number of times and sounded out the idea of doing a screenplay on "The Trenton Six" case. Then, when we got back together,

Kazan asked me what I thought, and I told him it was a very interesting case—especially the social themes and all that—but I admitted that I was very frustrated by the fact that I'd done this waterfront script which was just sitting in my desk collecting dust. So, we ended up talking more and more about the waterfront story, and he decided to do it.

At that point, you pretty much decided to start over—beginning with a whole year of research down on the docks.

SCHULBERG: Yes. I started hanging around the waterfront, and I became completely absorbed in my research. It really began to take over my life. The longer I hung out down there, the more involved with the men and their problems I became. I sat in on their meetings, I drank with them in their bars, and I slept with them and their families in their flats. In time, I even won over Father John Corridan, the tough Roman Catholic priest at St. Xavier's in Hell's Kitchen, who, at first, was very cynical about my "Hollywood" project. He definitely didn't want his men exploited to make some Hollywood movie, but, eventually, he decided that it was an untold story that needed telling. "We're not getting through to the press," he finally admitted. "The *Times* isn't telling the story, and maybe you can be our—whatever you want to call it—our spokesman."

So you were on a kind of probation with Father Corridan. He had to learn to trust you.

SCHULBERG: Yes, he was continually testing me, and I finally won him over. Then, I went to the *Times* and convinced them to let me write a piece on the waterfront problem.

And you also wrote pieces in the Saturday Evening Post *and* Commonweal.

SCHULBERG: I did, and I was glad to do it.

Could you discuss Father Corridan, who helped you with your research and had such a profound impact on the script and the film?

SCHULBERG: He was absolutely amazing to me. I had never been around the Catholic Church before, and the figure of "Father John," as they call him on the docks, was unlike anything I could have ever imagined. He was very smart, very tough, and very radical. If he didn't have a cassock on, he would've passed for any of the Irish longshoremen on the docks. He looked just like them, and he talked their language. I remember the first time I introduced him to Gadg [Kazan], who was incredulous. "Are you sure he's a priest?" Gadg asked me later. He even wondered if Father Corridan wasn't really some kind of waterfront rebel in disguise, but I assured him that he was the real thing. What I came to realize, as I continued my research on the docks, was that Father Corridan was really filling the vacuum that had been left by the racketeer control of the unions, like the ILA. There was no other leadership for the men, who were being exploited by the very labor leaders who should have been helping them. In those days, there was $8 billion worth of cargo passing through the New York/New Jersey docks, and the mob was taking 10% off the top, and still ripping off the 25,000 longshoremen who had to pay bribes—kickbacks—to the hiring bosses in the shape-ups. So, what Father Corridan was trying to do was teach the men honest unionism: how to stand up for their rights. So, he was conducting much more than just a seminar down there; he was leading a kind of silent rebellion and encouraging the men to stand up for themselves. Underneath all his toughness, Father Corridan had studied economics at the University of St. Louis, and he was very, very smart on the economic issues, but it was extremely dangerous trying to get those sons of bitches off the workers' backs. I've already mentioned Peter Panto, and "Cockeye" Dunn alone—just in the Chelsea area—killed no less than thirty-three people.

He did it himself, or he had them killed?

SCHULBERG: Both. Many he killed himself. Eventually, he was convicted and went to the chair. And Father Corridan played a role in his conviction.

When you were hanging around the docks, did you ever see "Cockeye" Dunn or Eddie McGurn, his partner on the Lower West Side?

SCHULBERG: I never saw Dunn, but I did see Eddie. He was a very, very slick character. Very gentlemanly.

Was he a model for Charley "the Gent" Malloy?

SCHULBERG: Yes, he was. He was a lot like Charley. Very well tailored. Eddie, oddly enough—especially considering that Cockeye got the chair and was electrocuted—ended up down in Key Biscayne with a lot of money. He was in one of the big country clubs down there, living like a wealthy retiree. I wonder if he's still there?

How about Anthony de Vincenzo, the dock boss who was sympathetic to the rebels in Hoboken? Many people have assumed that he served as a model for Terry Malloy. Is there any truth to that?

SCHULBERG: Not really. I don't want to hurt Tony's feelings because he's a very heroic person, but the truth is, I didn't meet "Tony Mike" de Vincenzo until after I'd written Terry Malloy. But he was a disciple of Father Corridan, and he had been an ex-boxer, and his nickname "Tony Mike" had the initials TM, so people naturally assumed that he was the model for Terry. But it was all coincidence. During the first year of my research, I hung out, almost exclusively, in the Chelsea area of the Lower West Side—on this side of the river. And I didn't even meet Tony Mike until we began scouting locations over in Hoboken. Later, thinking he was the model for Terry, Tony sued—or threatened to sue—the studio, and they gave him $5,000. And I didn't mind. Even though he didn't really inspire the character, he was a heroic guy and deserving, in my opinion, of the five thousand bucks.

You once mentioned that in the early stages of your collaboration with Kazan, his wife Molly often participated in the discussions. What was her contribution at that stage of the script's development?

SCHULBERG: Yes, Molly was very active in the early discussions. She'd worked with a lot of playwrights, and she was very good at analysis. She had an excellent story mind. She was also a professional film critic for *The New Leader*. So Molly was both politically and professionally engaged, and long before the "Spiegel period" of advising about structure, she was very involved.

When the script was finally done, you and Kazan took the Super Chief to Los Angeles to meet Darryl Zanuck at 20th Century Fox. Kazan owed Zanuck a picture, and he was extremely confident that Zanuck would produce the picture, but things didn't go as he expected.

SCHULBERG: That's right. As we rode west on the Super Chief, Kazan was overflowing with enthusiasm and confidence. He kept saying that the *Waterfront* script was a great piece of work—in a class with *Salesman* and *Streetcar*. "I've been so lucky that I've had these three scripts: *Salesman*, *Streetcar*, and *Waterfront*! Darryl will love it!" He was exuberant, but I was worried, and I told him so. "Look, Gadg, I'm not so sure they're going to like it." I knew that Hollywood made very few films about the working class, about laborers and their work—you could count them on one hand. But Gadg was astonished by the idea, and he totally dismissed it, "How could they *not* like it? It's terrific!" Then, we arrived in Los Angeles.

And there's no limousine.

SCHULBERG: No limousine.

I know that you've discussed some of this in that excellent article you wrote for the New York Times Magazine *back in 1989 [January 6], but could you recollect what happened when you got to Los Angeles?*

SCHULBERG: Well, there was no studio limo waiting at the train station. So Kazan, always very down-to-earth, acted like it was nothing, saying, "Oh, who wants a limo anyway? Let's take a cab." Then we got to the Beverly Hills Hotel, and we asked for our messages, and there weren't any—and, most important, there was no message from Zanuck inviting us down to Palm Springs to play croquet over the weekend. Then we went up to our suite, and I looked around the room, and I saw no flowers, and I said to Gadg, "I don't see any flowers." But he was getting quite irritated at me, and he said, "What are you, spoiled or something? What the hell are you talking about limos and croquet and flowers for? Who the hell wants flowers? I hate flowers!" But I knew better. I said, "Gadg, I think we're in big trouble. I was raised in this town, and I know how it works, and we're in big trouble." But he refused to believe me. Then Monday came, and we waited all morning, and we never heard anything about an appointment with Zanuck. I knew we were in very serious trouble. Finally, in the afternoon, we were given an appointment, but we were left waiting in Zanuck's outer office. I remember that the actress Bella Darvi, Zanuck's latest European import, was sitting there with us, and she was called in first. She was in there quite a long time, and Gadg was seething. Finally, we were called into Darryl's huge inner office—as big as Mussolini's—and Darryl was all excited about CinemaScope. He gave us this exuberant little speech about the progress of the motion picture business: how it started with flickers, got natural movement, then sound, then color, and now CinemaScope. He was exhilarated. He started raving about *Prince Valiant*, and how glorious it would be in CinemaScope, "It's so exciting!" He told us that he was so excited about it that he couldn't get to sleep at night thinking about CinemaScope—knowing full well that Gadg had told him that *Waterfront* should be shot in a flat black and white. Finally, after about a ten-minute oration, Kazan says, "How about our picture, Darryl?" There was a long pause, and then Zanuck finally said, "I'm sorry, boys, but I don't like a single thing about it." Stunned, we moved forward, almost like two enforcers, and Darryl took a step backwards behind his desk, and Kazan pressed him, "Not a single thing?" And Zanuck said—which stabbed me right in the heart—"What have you got here, boys? All you've got is a lot of sweaty longshoremen. I think what you've written is exactly what the American people don't want to see." I was crushed, and so was Gadg. We left Zanuck, we went over to our own studio office, and we trashed the place. I saw Kazan just a few nights ago, and we were talking about it again. We just went crazy. We turned over the desk, we flung papers all around in the room, and we threw the chairs at the wall. It was like a spontaneous combustion. We didn't plan it, and we didn't talk about it. It just happened. We'd been treated very badly, and we were both furious and frustrated.

Then you went back to the hotel.

SCHULBERG: Yes. We took a typewriter and returned to the Beverly Hills Hotel. Kazan began wondering if we could do the story as a play, and I started thinking about a novel, but then Kazan's indomitable determination came back, and he said, "No, we're going to do it. I'm going to stick with this thing if I have to get a 16-millimeter camera and shoot it myself!"

Then he tried the other studios.

SCHULBERG: Yes, he tried them all, and they all turned it down: Warner Bros., Paramount, MGM, Columbia, all of them. Eventually, I scheduled a flight to go back home to Pennsylvania. We were so depressed that we didn't leave the hotel, and we hung around the suite in our bathrobes. But, strangely enough, we began working on the script again. Kazan would say something about one of the scenes, and we'd discuss it, and then one of us would sit down and type for a while. When I think back on it now, our behavior seems very odd. Then, suddenly, when the project seemed totally dead, we had a completely unexpected and amazing stroke of good fortune from the cinematic gods.

Sam Spiegel.

SCHULBERG: Yes. Sam Spiegel. If Sam hadn't wandered across the hall at the Beverly Hills Hotel, I doubt that *On the Waterfront* would have ever been made. It was the night before my flight back home, and Spiegel was planning a big party across the hall in his suite, and he came over and knocked on our door, dressed in an elegant midnight blue suit and smelling of crushed lilacs. He looked us over—still unshaven and looking quite disreputable—and he said, "Why don't you boys get dressed up and come on over? I'm having a beautiful party tonight." Then he named all the people—the movie stars and the socialites—who'd be there. It was a typical Spiegel production, especially considering the fact that he'd just done a movie called *Melba* that he couldn't give away. No one was interested in the picture, and I'm not sure if it ever came out. That's the way Sam was. Whenever he was in big trouble—which he was many times in his life— he'd hole up in the Beverly Hills Hotel, run up his bills, give champagne parties, and live the high life without a cent in his pocket—always assuming that he'd somehow figure a way out of his troubles. He was a pirate. When things were good—like when he did *The African Queen*—he'd celebrate hard, and when things were bad—as with *Melba*—he'd celebrate even harder. So he invited us over, but we said, no, that we really didn't feel like going to a party. We especially weren't in the mood for facing all the Hollywood people who'd know about our failure with *Waterfront* and who'd be asking us all night, "So, what happened?" But Spiegel hadn't heard yet, and he looked us over and said, "Are you boys in trouble?" And we told him the whole story, with Gadg taking the lead. When we finished, Spiegel grew pensive for a moment and then said, "Why not come over tomorrow morning and tell me the waterfront story?" And I said, "But Sam, I'm leaving for the airport at eight sharp." "Then," Spiegel decided, "I'll see you at seven. I'll leave the door unlocked, so I won't have to get up." So early the next morning, I crossed the hallway, waded through the post-party litter, and found Sam Spiegel still lying in bed. He was inert, barely awake, and said nothing more than "Hmmm" when I spoke to him. So with my time running out, I began pacing around his huge bed and passionately describing the story of Terry Malloy and his problems on the waterfront. When I was done, Spiegel was absolutely motionless in the bed, there was a long silence, and I wondered if he was still awake. Then his sleepy head rose up a bit, and he looked at me and said, "I'll do it. We'll make the picture." And we did.

Originally, you'd thought of John Garfield for the role of Terry Malloy, and you'd even discussed it with him before he died in 1952. Was he interested in the film?

SCHULBERG: Yes, he was. Ironically, Brando seemed to be Garfield's nemesis. When they first did *A Streetcar Named Desire* on Broadway, Irene Mayer, who was the producer, wanted John Garfield, the "movie star," for the role of Stanley. And I believe he would've been excellent in the play, just right for the role. But Kazan had other ideas, and he had a knockdown fight with Irene about it. Kazan said, "Look, Irene, I love Julie [Garfield]. I've been in *Golden Boy* and many other Group Theatre plays with Julie. He's a terrific actor, but there's just that little extra magical mysterious something in Brando." Which, of course, there was. Garfield was a marvelous actor, but Brando's got that crazy mystery about him. And now, for *On the Waterfront*, Kazan felt the same way about Brando, but Brando turned it down. But I was certain that he hadn't read it because I'd inserted tiny bits of paper into the script—a sneaky trick I'd learned in my O.S.S. counterintelligence days—and when it came back, they hadn't moved a bit.

Is that when Sinatra got involved?

SCHULBERG: Yes. Then we talked to Frankie about it—thinking, hell, he comes from Hoboken, he was terrific in *From Here to Eternity*, and he could definitely do it.

How did you feel about that? Were you comfortable with Sinatra as Terry Malloy?

SCHULBERG: Yes. I think he could've done it, and I think he could've done it very well. I think either Sinatra or Garfield could have played the role.

Earlier, when you were writing the script, did you have Garfield in mind?

SCHULBERG: Not really. I knew, sort of in passing, that he might be a possibility, but I didn't write it for Garfield. But I do remember him calling me at my apartment, and just begging me to read the script, convinced that he was just perfect for the role. And he was.

So how did Kazan and Spiegel convince Brando to take the part?

SCHULBERG: It was mostly Spiegel. He's the great seducer. He wined and dined Brando, and fawned over him, and reminded him how much he owed to Kazan. After all, there really wouldn't have been a Brando without Kazan in the first place. As I mentioned before, Kazan and Irene Mayer almost broke up over their fight on *Streetcar*. She didn't know anything about "Marlon Brando"—he was just some kid in the Actors Studio. She thought Kazan was nuts.

How about the role of Edie? Is it true that Grace Kelly turned down the role for Hitchcock's Rear Window?

SCHULBERG: I don't remember that, and I'm not sure it's true. I remember that Kazan and I went through the entire Screen Actors book—the Players' Guide—picture after picture, trying to find the right Edie, and we couldn't find her. We were looking for an unknown for Edie, and we talked to lots and lots of promising young actresses, and Kazan read quite a few people for the role. But we had no success. Then I happened to see Eva Marie Saint in a play on Broadway. I can't remember the name of the play, and she only had a small role in it, but I was very impressed. So, I mentioned her to Kazan—who was always very thorough about every-thing—and he went to the play and, afterwards, invited Eva to come and talk with him about *Waterfront*. And Kazan, as he often did, decided on the basis of that discussion. I can still remember seeing her in that play—one scene, in particular—where she was really, really lovely. We couldn't find anybody else who looked like that: truly virginal, not just in a sexual sense, but innocent in a true and complete sense.

The script went through many rewrites—with a great deal of input from both Kazan and Spiegel. Did either of them have markedly different ideas from your own?

SCHULBERG: It was more a matter of a different point of view. Spiegel was obsessed with structure, and he was very good at it. Both Kazan and I were very impressed, although Sam could drive you to distraction. At the same time, Kazan and I were more focused on telling the union story, the social story—which worried Spiegel who wanted more entertainment and more of the love story.

That makes sense. He was the producer.

SCHULBERG: That's right, and it worked out very well in the end.

Yes, because the film accomplishes both objectives.

SCHULBERG: It does, but some things were lost in my opinion. I saw it again recently in Paris, and I guess the fact that it was cut down to an almost ninety-minute movie does give it a thrust that it wouldn't have had if it had maintained some of the richness—some of the texture—of the earlier drafts. I always wanted to include more of the waterfront in its true social context. For example, there's that one odd scene remaining in the movie where you see the back of "Mr. Big" in his living room. But, I'm afraid, the message is lost on the audience—the point that the problem isn't just Johnny Friendly because there's somebody even further upstairs.

But I think you're underestimating the film. That point does come through in that scene, and it's reinforced by the thug's earlier reference to "Mr. Upstairs" at the wedding reception, and the photo that Terry shatters in the bar, and even Cobb's "I'll be back" at the end of the film. Even though the priest and Edie smile like they've succeeded, Cobb's still there yelling that he'll "be back," and I think the audience knows that he will.

SCHULBERG: Well, that's another interesting thing, that "I'll be back." When we later did *Waterfront* as a play, we ended with that line, and it worked very well, despite people's natural expectations from having seen the movie. Those "I'll be back" lines are a very good example of how film editing can manipulate a motion picture. For instance, at the end of the picture, if instead of that medium shot on Lee Cobb, the camera moved right up to him—and Kazan did shots like that—right up on his face saying, "I'll be back, I'll be back, and I'll remember every one of you!," and the film ended that way, then you'd have a very different movie. That's what the audience would leave with. But if it ends "I'll be back, I'll be back, I'll remember every one of you!" And then the camera swings past Cobb to Edie and Father Barry, and then cuts to Brando, and the music comes up, then it's a whole different ending—and a whole different movie.

Spiegel may have had his way, ending the film with a certain amount of comfort for the audience, but it's still very significant that Johnny's there at the end—as with the Mr. Upstairs shot—reminding the audience that the waterfront corruption is very deep and broad, and reaches much higher than Johnny Friendly.

SCHULBERG: They always say that the most famous of all Hollywood clichés—maybe it was Zanuck, I don't know—is that "If you want to send a message, call Western Union." But I always believed in sending messages, and that brief Mr. Upstairs shot was a concession to me, although I'm glad to say Kazan was on my side.

There's also the scene where Terry throws the gun at the framed photograph of Johnny Friendly standing with someone we assume is "higher up."

SCHULBERG: When I was watching the picture in Paris recently, I wondered if that comes through. I must admit I had my doubts.

It does come through.

SCHULBERG: I'm very glad to hear it. I hope so.

In an earlier draft of the script, Terry takes Edie to a seedy boxing arena where she watches him lose an inconsequential lightheavy bout for forty dollars. Why was the scene cut?

SCHULBERG: For the same reason that Father Barry going to the wake for Joey Doyle was cut out: to keep the film moving forward, without digression or distraction. It was something that wasn't absolutely necessary, something that could be taken out. But that reasoning can be fatal sometimes in film. I lost some important chunks of *The Harder They Fall* in exactly the same way. Somebody says, "Look, what if we try this? Let's take it out, and try it without it, and see if it works? And if it doesn't work, we'll put it back in." But they never put it back in. *Never.*

But with the boxing scene, isn't it better to cut it for another reason: because it once again shows Terry as a complete "loser," and we've already had so much of that in the picture.

SCHULBERG: That's true, and it's much cleaner without it. That was Spiegel. He made a real contribution in terms of producing a tighter story and a more effective film.

Similarly, the relationship of Terry and Charley is much more interesting and subtle in the final script. In earlier drafts, Charley was extremely conde-scending to his younger brother and even tried to seduce Edie away from Terry at one point. Do you remember how the Charley character metamorphosed into someone the audience cares about?

SCHULBERG: I'd forgotten about that. But I still remember that Kazan, as he did in the theater, was always talking about working on the relationships—improving the relationships. And making them more personal.

And more intimate. The closer relationship between the brothers powerfully enhances Terry's motivation at the end of the film when he goes off with the gun looking for Johnny Friendly.

SCHULBERG: That's right. The closer relationship is the trigger for the third act.

Another excellent revision in the developing script was to combine the "Palookaville" dialogue on the roof with the "contender" speech in the back of the taxicab. The scene in the back of the cab has become one of the most famous in the history of cinema. Did you have any idea of its power when you wrote it?

SCHULBERG: No, not at all. At that point, I was very much into Terry's mind, and the dialogue came out very naturally. Last week, they showed the scene at the Garden before the Knicks game, ending it with the line, "Take me to the Garden." Spike Lee called me afterwards, and he said, "Budd, you had a big moment at the Garden tonight. The crowd went crazy." But I had no idea when I wrote it that it would become a classic scene.

Do you know what happened during the shooting of that scene that created such a rift between Rod Steiger and Marlon Brando?

SCHULBERG: Yes, I was there. Whenever you shoot a scene like that, you first shoot the whole thing with the two of them in a sort of medium-close shot, and then you shoot each one individually, with the other actor behind the camera feeding the lines to the one on camera. So Brando went first, Steiger fed him his lines, and everything went fine. But when it came time for Marlon to read his lines behind the camera to Steiger, he said, "No, I'm sorry, I have to go back to the city," and he didn't do it. So

Kazan read Brando's lines, and Steiger, with some justification, was steaming, although Brando had been allowed, on other days, to leave the set early to meet with his psychiatrist. So I think Brando might have had Kazan's permission to leave early that day, but Rod was naturally outraged by Marlon's lack of professional courtesy. He was also, I believe, a bit jealous of Brando, but, regardless, he was terribly effective in that scene—just wonderful.

Why was the film shot in Hoboken?

SCHULBERG: There were a number of reasons. One was the loud traffic noise in New York. Kazan felt he could control the exterior noises better in New Jersey. Another factor was Spiegel's arrangement with the Hoboken police.

Let's talk about that. Given the film's portrayal of mob corruption in the union, Joseph P. Ryan, the president of the longshoremen's union, threatened a boycott of the picture. There were also death threats on Elia Kazan and others involved with the production. What was it like making the film in Hoboken under police protection?

SCHULBERG: Very uneasy. We'd arranged with the Hoboken Chief of Police, Arthur Marotta, for his brother, Lieutenant Marotta, and a group of plainclothesmen and some uniformed police to serve as a sort of protective group on the set. But, nevertheless, there was the very real fear that we might be attacked. I never got any specific death threats myself, but I did get some scary phone calls. People calling up at midnight and hanging up, things like that.

Weren't there some incidents?

SCHULBERG: There was a lot of yelling from the nearby piers trying to sabotage the picture. And, sometimes, the mob goons would stand at the back of the set and watch—sort of in fascination—and then one day, just after lunch break, some goons actually grabbed Kazan and shoved him up against the wall. But, fortunately, the Marines arrived in time, Lieutenant Marotta and the cops, and they rescued Kazan. That was the only time that there was actual physical intimidation.

It's amazing that you got through shooting as cleanly as you did.

SCHULBERG: It is. At the time we were there, things were very tense on the docks. Very tense. The rebels were gaining in strength and making big inroads around the harbor, and a union election was coming up, and it was an open question whether the old racket-ridden ILA or the new reform group would take over the union. So things were extremely tense and dangerous. It was my hope—and the hope of Father Corridan—that we could get the film out in time to affect the election. But, I felt that Spiegel wanted exactly the opposite. He didn't want the film involved in the day-to-day struggles of the men, and I felt that he postponed it intentionally.

Yet the shooting schedule was very tight, and Kazan shot it quickly.

SCHULBERG: Yes. In thirty-five days.

And with a fairly low budget.

SCHULBERG: Just eight-hundred thousand dollars.

Did the mob have a very significant influence in Hollywood back then? I've been told stories by a number of people—including the screenwriter of a well-known gangster film—that anyone who was writing such a film would be visited by anonymous representatives of the mob.

SCHULBERG: There was a good deal of mob influence in Hollywood. The powerful IATSE [International Alliance of Theatrical Stage Employees] union was mob-controlled, and we had many workers on the set who were answering to mob-controlled union bosses. There were also a number of important Hollywood people, like Harry Cohn, who had mob "connections." Or, should I say "friends"? They weren't really part of the mob, but they were very friendly with mob figures. And then there were many other Hollywood executives who had no involvement with the mob at all, but who were greatly intimidated by it—very afraid.

Were you ever contacted about Waterfront?

SCHULBERG: No, I was never contacted directly. No visits or anything like that. But there were a lot of threats down at Xavier's. Father Corridan was quite concerned, and he warned me to be careful and to tell him if I got any direct threats, but I didn't. But I was often threatened indirectly, through other people who told me what some of the mob guys were saying.

It couldn't have hurt to have all the old heavyweight contenders on the set. Where did they come from? And was it your idea to cast them in the picture?

SCHULBERG: Yes, it was. At one point, I said to Kazan, "I'm sick of all these Hollywood heavies. I've seen the real mob goons down on the docks, and I know what they look like, and I think we should bring in real fighters." And I must say, Kazan was marvelously open to the idea. Instead of saying, as most directors would have, "I'll cast them myself," he said, "Great, bring them in." So, I brought them all to Kazan—Tony Galento, Abe Simon, Tami Mauriello, and Lee Oma—and he decided to use them. But, you know, the poor screenwriter never gets credit for anything! About two years ago, when they did a new print of *On the Waterfront*, they had a big screening at the Museum of Modern Art, and Marty Scorsese made a very generous presentation that day about the film, and, in praising Kazan's devotion to realism, he talked about Gadg's bold idea to cast the boxers as the thugs.

How do you think they did in the film, especially Tony Galento—whom I knew as a kid in Orange, New Jersey, and who was also in one of your later films, Wind Across the Everglades?

SCHULBERG: Yes, I think Tony's entire acting career was in "Schulberg" films! He was a natural actor, and I think he was terrific, except that he couldn't remember his lines.

Well, in Waterfront, *he mostly said "Definitely" a lot.*

SCHULBERG: Yes, and he said it very well.

He did. And now, I'd like to get back to some of the thematic aspects of the film. On the Waterfront, *very honestly, depicts the religious failings and triumphs of the waterfront dockworkers, and it never falls into the contemporary compunction to ridicule religion and faith. Not only are Edie and Father Barry serious Roman Catholics, but the film is full of religious symbolism: Dugan rising on the pallet after his martyrdom, or Terry's calvary at the end of the film. How conscious were you of the religious underpinnings of the script?*

SCHULBERG: I felt it was very important. I was very moved by my experiences on the docks—being part of the Xavier movement—and I came to understand why Christianity has its unique power and how its ideas have spread so powerfully around the world over the last two thousand years. I had a lifelong interest and concern about the underdog, and I came to a better understanding of the teachings of Christ and the fact that what he was saying was, basically, that if you do it to the least of mine, you do it to me—and that I am my brother's keeper. Before that, I'd always thought of Catholicism as the top brass, with the gold and the showiness and the didacticism. But my experiences on the docks made me realize that it's much more than that. It's the story of concern for the underdog, and so was *Waterfront*, and when Father Barry says to the men in the hold of the ship, if you do it to Dugan—or whoever you do it to—it's a crucifixion. That it's a crucifixion that's happening right here, right now. And I believe that myself. I related to it then, and I still do. When I pick up a newspaper and read that some young, innocent girl who's been trying to help poor kids in the inner city gets stabbed or something, it immediately jumps out at me that she's been crucified. So it wasn't difficult for me, even without being a Roman Catholic, to feel the power of Christ on the docks—the power to teach and to help the men organize.

You've said that you based Karl Malden's powerful "Christ on the Waterfront" speech on an actual sermon by Father Corridan.

SCHULBERG: That's right. It was an impassioned speech that he gave at a communion breakfast for the longshoremen. It was very stirring and moving, and the men talked about it all the time, and, later, I got to talk to Father Corridan about it. It was amazing. It said everything that needed to be said. I can't praise him enough for what he did back then.

Maybe it's time for the inevitable HUAC question. It's become common-place "wisdom" about On the Waterfront *that you and Elia Kazan, having both testified before HUAC, were consciously trying to justify your decision by making Terry Malloy—a "testifier"—the sympathetic hero of the film. Is that characterization true?*

SCHULBERG: No, it's not, and I've always felt that the "supposed" connection with the Hollywood hearings was an unfortunate and mislead-ing aspect of a number of critical responses to the film. On the other hand, I realize that some of those people, aware of what happened during the hearings, would *never* believe that *Waterfront* is anything but what they *want* it to be. But the sad thing is, it trivializes the film—and all the old longshoremen feel the same way I do about it because it trivializes the incredible pressure that the longshoremen were facing during the Water-front Crime Commission hearings. I was down there every day—every sin-gle day, for forty days—at the Crime Commission hearings, and I was down in the basement of Xavier's when Father Corridan was saying to the men, "Boys, this is your chance to tell it like it is! This is it. You can break the hold of the mob if you've got the nerve." And the guys were scared to death, understandably, because he was urging them to testify against the mob. And all of my experiences, and my research, and my writing fed back to Kazan. And, at the time, we were still searching for the right ending for the film, still working out the final development of Terry's story, and it was attending those Waterfront Crime hearings, watching those brave men testify against the mob—with the mob sitting right there facing them, all dangerous, dangerous killers—that made me say to Kazan, "I feel like real life is writing our script. It's writing the end of our film." Because Terry's story *had* to climax with the Waterfront hearings, and nothing else would have made any sense. But some people, who know nothing about how the script was written, have invented the story that Kazan came to me and said, "Budd, I want you to write a script that justifies my testimony," but it's not true, and I wouldn't have been interested. That's something you do in a memoir, not in a film.

But it's reasonable that people have wondered about it, especially with Miller writing The Crucible *and talking so openly about its relationship to HUAC. So when people saw* On the Waterfront, *they could ask, quite logi-cally, is Arthur Miller's old pal Kazan now making a movie to justify his own position about HUAC?*

SCHULBERG: That's quite true, and I understand that people might wonder about it, but it was never my intention. Never.

But did you ever worry about it? I mean, once you saw where the script was going, did either you or Kazan worry about the fact that it might be misleading to people?—that it might lead them back to HUAC?

SCHULBERG: No. I swear to God, when I was writing the script and we were making the film, I never thought about it at all. Maybe that sounds dumb now, in retrospect, with hindsight, but at the time we were writing and making *Waterfront*, I was only thinking about the men, the workers. I was very involved in the reality of their lives and their stories. Men were being killed, families were being destroyed, and some of the workers left town—one guy from Hoboken shipped out on a freighter to Australia. That was the reality, and that was my only concern at the time. I never stopped to think, "Oh, my god, what if people take this the wrong way?" It never entered my mind, and though I can't speak for Kazan, I never had the sense that he thought about it either.

And you never discussed it?

SCHULBERG: No, we didn't. Never.

That's amazing, especially with the hindsight. And no matter what you say, history's going to be written the way they want it to be written.

SCHULBERG: I know. Exactly. They've already been writing the history the way they want it to be written. Awhile back, they showed the film at UCLA in a little series about "sell-outs" or something like that, and I read over the professorial notes about how everything was related to HUAC, and it all sounds very knowledgeable, and professional, and convincing, and so on, but it's absolutely incorrect. The idea that Kazan said to me, "Look, Budd, instead of Hollywood boys we'll make them longshoremen, and then we'll tell it our way," is ludicrous. We never discussed it. *On the Waterfront* came out of the real life stories of the men on the docks, and my experiences and research down on the waterfront.

Which was a story that you were involved with long before HUAC, due to Malcolm Johnson and Joe Curtis.

SCHULBERG: That's right.

Regarding the realism of the film, I know that you admire the American social novelists—like Twain, Norris, and Steinbeck—but the script for On the Waterfront *also has many characteristics in common with the Italian Neo-realist movement: working class protagonists, social oppression, social consciousness, etc. Do you think that any of those Italian films influenced your vision of the film?*

SCHULBERG: I love those films, but I never set out to imitate them in any way. But since I'd always enjoyed them so much, maybe they affected me subconsciously. I don't really know.

In the end, On the Waterfront *defied Zanuck and all the naysayers. It won eight Oscars and was a huge critical and box office success. When you look at the film now, is there anything you're unsatisfied with?*

SCHULBERG: Very little. There's that shot at the end, which we discussed earlier, of Edie and Father Barry smiling. In my opinion, that was the only phony touch in the picture, the only "Hollywood" touch—the only "let's give it a happy ending" touch. If you were really down on the docks that morning, you wouldn't be smiling, right? For one thing, Terry might be dying; he could be bleeding to death; and Edie would have been terrified, wondering whether he was going to make it or not. That shot's always bothered me, and every time I see it, I wince.

Anything else? How about Leonard Bernstein's highly dramatic score?

SCHULBERG: It's a fantastic score, and Lenny Bernstein was a genius. I've heard the score played at the Hollywood Bowl, and it's a marvelous piece of music. But from the poor old writer's point of view, I thought it was too loud at times in the film. I also thought it was too obtrusive at times, and that it led the audience reaction too much—telling them how to feel, rather than letting them react to the story. But overall, I think it's marvelous. I especially like the way it sets the tone right at the beginning of the picture with the percussion, the drums.

In 1955, you published Waterfront, *a novel based on the Terry Malloy story. As you pointed out in the book's introduction, the novel "required retelling his story from another point of view, and with a different end in mind." The different point of view is that of Father Barry, who really becomes the main character in the novel, and the "different end" is a much more realistic one. Edie (called Katie in the novel) goes back to Marygrove. Terry Malloy is murdered by the mob—with ice picks—and his body is dumped in the Jersey swamps. Johnny Friendly, convicted of perjury, gets a year's sentence and is expected back on the docks in seven or eight months. And Father Barry, given a reprieve from a threatened transfer to a "safer" parish, is determined to press on despite the odds against him. Given these changes at the conclusion of the novel, are you still comfortable with the ending of the film?*

SCHULBERG: Yes, except for the things I've already mentioned. I still feel that the film version of the story is right for film, even though I made a number of changes for the novel.

It's now fifty years since Malcolm Johnson's award-winning exposé in the New York Sun. *How much progress has been made on the New York/New Jersey docks? And within the longshoremen's union?*

SCHULBERG: There's been a lot of good changes, and at least one was due to the film. Once people saw what a shape-up was really like, things had to change in New York, and they did.

They never shape anymore?

SCHULBERG: No, that's been knocked off for years, and many other changes were made as well. Father Corridan always felt that the creation of the Bi-State Waterfront Commission—which was an idea of his—was greatly helped by the success of the movie. The Bi-State Commission has, to some extent, cleaned up operations on the docks. There are no longer dock bosses recruited right out of Sing-Sing—actual murderers—like in the old days. They now check prison records and stuff like that. On the other hand, it's no secret that the Jersey docks are still being exploited, if not controlled, by the mob, and that the docks in Brooklyn are still manipulated by hand-me-downs from the Anastasias, from Tony Anastasia and Albert A. So the mob influence is still very strong, even though good progress has been made. You can't really stamp it out entirely. There's too much money down there, although the Brooklyn docks are dying compared to the Jersey docks. But whenever there's so much money moving around, there's going to be mob involvement and exploitation. Everybody knows the mob is still around. It's just much more subtle now; it's more sophisticated.

But the situation for the ordinary worker has improved?

SCHULBERG: Very much so. Things are much, much better.

Last year, the American Film Institute listed On the Waterfront *as the eighth best film in American cinema history—and, personally, I think that's not high enough. Looking back, after nearly fifty years, what are your fondest memories of the long and difficult process to get the film completed?*

SCHULBERG: Working with Kazan. Working with Gadg was a real joy, and it definitely spoiled me. Our relationship was so close during the making of that film that I have a unique feeling of involvement with every single frame of that picture. There's nothing in it, with a few tiny exceptions, that I'm not comfortable with. How many writers can say that? In our very first meeting in Pennsylvania, Kazan had promised that he wouldn't "change a single word of the script" without my permission, and he was always true to his promise. And as the script was slowly forming and progressing, we got along marvelously. We were so creatively in sync that it seemed as if we were almost married in our minds—in our ways of thinking. Gadg would say, "What if we tried this?" And I'd say, "That's a damn good idea, let's try it," and vice versa. We got into a sort of shorthand communication that was like we were in each other's minds. It used to almost scare me sometimes. Years later, especially after working with Nick Ray on *Everglades*, I realized what a charmed existence I'd had working with Kazan. It was an amazing experience.

I doubt there are many films—and certainly not many great ones—where the writer and the director worked so closely from the very beginning to the very end, and for such a long period of time.

SCHULBERG: That's right. And I can't imagine any other director allowing a writer to become an almost alter ego like I became on *Waterfront*. It's an extraordinary testimony to Kazan's talent and confidence. He was a great genius as a director, and maybe part of that genius was that he really and truly appreciated his writers, whether it was me, or Steinbeck, or Williams, or Bill Inge, or Paul Osborn. With Gadg, writers were writers— and it made no difference to him whether they were playwrights or screenwriters. Kazan was keenly aware that too many film directors forget that in the beginning is the word. But he knew it, and he always respected it, and I'm very grateful that he did.

That's a good place to end. Thanks very much.
SCHULBERG: Thank you.

CHAPTER 3

Rebel Without a Cause (1955)

A CONVERSATION WITH STEWART STERN

Stewart Stern was raised in New York City, and after graduating Phi Beta Kappa from the University of Iowa, he served in the U.S. Army during World War II. After a brief stint on Broadway and some work in Hollywood, he returned to New York City to write for live television before resuming his screenwriting career. The first of his Hollywood screenplays was Fred Zinnemann's *Teresa* (1951) for which he was nominated for an Academy Award, and his next feature was Nicholas Ray's *Rebel Without a Cause* (1955) starring James Dean and Natalie Wood. His subsequent films, all marked by his characteristic emotional and psychological intensity, include *The Rack* (1956) starring Paul Newman; *The James Dean Story* (1957), a documentary codirected by Robert Altman; *The Ugly American* (1963) starring Marlon Brando; and Paul Newman's *Rachel, Rachel* (1968) starring Joanne Woodward, which also received an Academy Award nomination for screenwriting. He also wrote the Oscar-winning short *Benjy* (1951) directed by Fred Zinnemann, and the Emmy Award-winning teleplay *Sybil* (1976) starring Sally Field. No longer writing for film, Stewart Stern has lived, since 1986, in Seattle, Washington, with his wife, artist Marilee Stiles Stern.

You always felt that it was a party at Gene Kelly's house in 1954 that helped you get the writing assignment for Rebel Without a Cause.

STERN: That's right. At the time, I was living in New York, and I'd come out to Los Angeles for Christmas vacation and was taken to Gene's party by my cousin Arthur Loew, Jr. Marilyn Monroe was there, and Nick Ray, Stanley Donen, Adolph [Green] and Betty [Comden], and others. The usual Gene Kelly crowd. At one point that night, as they were planning to play charades, Nick Ray, whom I'd never met before, came over and said that he'd seen my first film, Fred Zinnemann's *Teresa*, and that he liked it very much. Then he said, "Maybe you'd like to come out to the studio and talk some time?" Or something like that. What I didn't know was that Lenny Rosenman, who'd done the score for *East of Eden*, and who was a friend and roommate of Jimmy Dean's in New York, had talked to Nick about me because Nick was having script problems with *Rebel*— which Irving Shulman was writing at the time. I also didn't know that Jimmy, whom I'd only met a few days before the Kelly party, had similarly talked to Nick about me. So Nick got interested, screened *Teresa*, and decided to approach me at the party. Eventually, I went to Warner Bros., talked things over with Nick, and was given the job.

Rebel had a long studio history before you came on the project. The title came from an actual case study of a disturbed young man written by Dr. Robert Lindner in 1944. Three years later, Warner Bros. bought the screen rights, and Marlon Brando was contracted to play the lead. The studio, however, never followed through. But, after the box office success of The Wild One, *Warners approved a completely different project about "juvenile delinquency" that was suggested by Nick Ray and given the title of Lindner's book. When the novelist Leon Uris wrote an unsatisfactory screenplay, Irving Shulman, the author of* The Amboy Dukes, *was hired to do a second version. But Ray was still dissatisfied, and he made up his mind to "get a young, beginning writer," and you were hired to do a brand new script. Apparently, you never read the Uris script. Was the Shulman version very useful?*

STERN: It wasn't useful until it was clear that I didn't *have* to use it; then I used some of his best ideas, even though Irving and I had very different sensibilities. At the time, I was in my eighth year of therapy, and I was "hot" with it. *Everything* seemed psychologically motivated to me, and there was very little of that kind of psychological approach in Irving's script. I also couldn't identify with the kids in his script; they seemed awfully macho to me, and I was always afraid of the macho guys in high school. So I had a very different perspective, and I wanted to go in a different direction. For one thing, I couldn't wait to blame the parents. I also wanted to start from scratch and do my own research. Nevertheless, there were a number of things that Irving used—like the setting of the planetarium—which I liked very much, especially when I saw it for the first time. It was like a Greek temple, like the Theater Dionysus, and the way the steps came down from its great doors reminded me of the skene that used to stand in front of the back wall of the ancient Greek theaters—where they did the sacrifices. The king always came from there, and often died there, and the gods came down on the roof of it. So it seemed like an amazing place to round out the story of *Rebel*. I felt that the story should begin there and that some crucial, concluding event should take place there as well—maybe a sacrifice of some kind. So that was one thing I was grateful to Irving for. Another aspect of his script that I liked was something that Nick conceived in his original pitch to Warner Bros. called "Blind Run." The blind run was a head-on confrontation—with two cars coming at each other in the Sepulveda Tunnel—and whichever driver swerved out of the way first was called "chicken." But since I'm terrified of heights, I agreed with Irving that an even worse possibility would be driving toward the edge of cliff, as fast as you can, and then rolling out of the car before it went over the precipice. So that's why Millertown Bluff appears in the picture; although, in Irving's original version of the chickie run, Buzz survived and Jim was just an observer. I also kept the character names that Irving had created—Jim, Judy, and Plato—and I used a scene of his that took place in a drive-in theater, but it never made it into the picture.

So, with those few ideas, you began your research?

STERN: Yes. I asked Nick if he would facilitate my going to juvenile hall, and he did. Nick loved the way that the reception part of the juvenile office was laid out—with the booths and glass windows—so you could see the other people through the windows, and he wanted me to exploit that setting to develop the relationships of the characters. So I went down to juvenile hall, and the first kid I interviewed was a famous actor's son, who'd just gotten out of jail. He'd been in a lot of trouble, and he'd had a really heartbreaking experience with his father when he left the facility. I learned a great deal talking with him. So, every night, from around five o'clock into the early morning, I was at juvenile hall, and they gave me a clipboard, and I talked to an awful lot of troubled young kids. After about three days, I was even given access to some selected files: the psychiatric testing, the inkblots, and all the stuff they did in processing those kids.

Did you talk to the kids privately?

STERN: Yes. They were brought in from their holding areas, and we'd have a private conference.

Did they know you were a screenwriter?

STERN: No. They assumed I was a social worker or something. Someone they could talk to. Someone who would listen.

Did any of the kids' specific experiences impact the script?

STERN: There was one young boy who'd been brought in for killing some ducklings—which I changed to puppies for the film. In talking to that kid, I discovered a great deal about Plato. And there was one very large girl who was having a terrible time with her father, but she was too young to understand any of the sexual connotations. She only knew that he was constantly rejecting her. She wasn't allowed to wear lipstick—or do anything to make herself look more feminine—even though her father allowed her younger sister to do it. And that became a kind of signal for the relationship between Judy and her father in the picture. It was very, very important for me to talk to those kids before I wrote the script.

You were thirty-two at the time, and you'd been hired as a "young" writer. Was your relative youth an asset in comprehending the teenage angst and loneliness that James Dean—now a cultural icon in his famous red wind-breaker—so powerfully portrayed in the film?

STERN: I think it did. At thirty-two, I certainly wasn't a kid anymore, but I'd never been able to shake my own high school experiences. They were still very fresh in my mind. I clearly remembered my youthful, romantic idealization of certain high school kids who were older than I was—or who were more athletic than I was. I understood the longing to be accepted by them and to be "chosen" as a friend by one of them: to be taught, to be protected, and to be taken out of my creative shell. When I was in high school, I wanted to be a painter, and I never participated in athletics. My dad wasn't that kind of father, and he rarely played sports himself. When my parents sent me off to summer camp, I always felt terribly isolated and even hid myself when the whistle blew for after-supper baseball. I was terrified of having to get up to bat, or having to catch a ball. So, I was always searching for someone who'd take care of me and show me how to do things. At the same time, I knew the problem from the other side as well, because in my high school days a number of other kids came to me for support. So, I knew what it felt like to befriend somebody who wasn't popular at a time when I had such a strong desire to be popular myself. I was forced to make difficult decisions. Should I be seen in the school hallway with someone who wasn't "in" with the girls who set all the social patterns? Decisions like that had been incredibly painful for me, and I was still trying to work them out when I was in the army. By the time of *Rebel*, I was in therapy with Dr. Frederick Hacker and dealing directly with those issues. I still am. I think I'm the oldest patient in the world, celebrating my fiftieth year in therapy. I can't tell you how many therapists have been cured just dealing with me!

I wanted to ask you about your war experience. In 1945, you were an infantryman in the Battle of the Bulge, and you were, for a time, listed as "missing in action."

STERN: That's right, but *I* didn't know I was missing. I knew where I was.

Were you with other soldiers?

STERN: Yes, but our division had been smashed to smithereens, and we had no overall organization. We were really just self-contained little groups fighting rearguard actions with raggedy elements of other divisions.

So, eventually, they discovered that your small group had survived?
STERN: That's right.

You once said that you felt your war experiences helped you understand your audience better.
STERN: Definitely. Because I was forced to deal with all kinds of different people that I'd never encountered before—and I found out that I didn't have to live in an "ivory tower" as I'd done in high school. For the first time, I realized that even rough, tough people could really like me if I was just myself—even if I wrote poetry and liked art. I also discovered, as I listened to other people's problems, that I sometimes had the answers they wanted, just as they sometimes had the answers I needed. I discovered an ability to communicate with a lot of very different people without being afraid, without having to hide who I was. It was like a miracle, and I really bonded with the infantry and with my group in particular. Before we went overseas, at Camp Atterbury in Indiana, I became very close friends with a big, powerful kid from the toughest part of Chicago named Jim Sramek. He was a very devout Catholic who'd snuck into the army at sixteen, and I was a sheltered Jewish doctor's boy who longed to be in the Navy, but we liked each other very much—even though he often kidded me about writing poetry—and when they made me staff sergeant, squad leader, I chose Sramek as my assistant. Then one night, when I was working in the office, there was a terrible ruckus in the barracks—a terrible fight. It took me quite a while to learn the truth, but apparently some guy had called me a kike, and Sramek had taken him apart. Naturally, it made a great impact on me, and we're still close friends today. He even named one of his ten children "Stewart." So I learned back then that I could be friends with all kinds of people, even ones very different from myself, and that we really could help each other. I remember during the German attack on the first morning of the Bulge, there was a kid in my squad named Rogers, and he was just shaking himself to pieces with fear, as I was too. He didn't know what to do; he didn't know whether to cuss or cry. So I diverted him. I knew that he liked to draw horses and cowboys, and I pulled out my notebook, and we stood in that trench full of freezing water with everything coming at us, and I showed him how to draw a horse in a rodeo scene. I'd learned in the army that I didn't have to abandon who I was—an artist—because I'd learned that it had weight with other people. It stunned me at the time, and I guess it still does. But I discovered that everyone, no matter how much tough armor he's created around himself, is, fundamentally, a sensitive, responsive person who needs just as much reassurance as the rest of us. And that gave me a great deal of strength and insight, and it also informed my writing of *Rebel*—especially this whole question of the masks we feel we need to wear in front of others—and what *exactly* defines a "man." I wanted to say something about that in the script, and I thought

that the Jim Stark/Plato relationship was striving for that. Here's one kid who's moved from town to town with a desperate need to be popular, and here's this other needy kid who hangs onto him—which Jim needs like a hole in the head. If I were rewriting it today, I would dramatize that even more—Jim's initial reluctance to let Plato hang around him.

In the film, he's very accepting of this nerdy, young kid.

STERN: Yes, right away.

And even though we admire Jim for that, it seems much more likely that he would have held him at arm's length for a while.

STERN: Yes, and then allowed him to get closer more gradually. But that's hindsight now. I do think the film offers an excellent counterpoint from Jim's point of view because Buzz offers him what he's offering to Plato, and there's that one special moment between them that's my favorite in the film.

Right before the race?

STERN: Yes, when they look over the cliff and talk. "I like you, you know that?" "Then why do we do this?" "We gotta do *something*, don't we?"

It's one of the best moments in the film, and it works because of the context of the danger. Given the circumstances, we can believe that such a powerful bond has developed so quickly between Jim and Buzz.

STERN: I think it still works.

Now after you'd been given the job by Nick Ray and approved by Warner Bros., you apparently couldn't get started on the script. Then you saw Kazan's On the Waterfront, *and it really got you going. Was that because the films had things in common, or was it just a matter of being inspired by a great movie and a great script?*

STERN: It was both. Writing has always been torture for me, and I'm terrified the whole time. A lot of writers are. And I just couldn't start the script. In more recent times, I would have been grateful for a short writer's block like I had on *Rebel* because it only lasted a few days, not months or years. But back then, I just couldn't shake loose on *Rebel*, and I'd heard that *On the Waterfront* was a very powerful film and that it also dealt with the problems of some young people—although from a very different social class. I also thought that Brando and Dean, as performers, had a lot in common, having seen Jimmy's performance in *East of Eden*. Jimmy's sensitivities and choices of behavior were very similar to Brando, so I hoped that seeing *Waterfront* would be illuminating for me in some way. And it was. When I saw the film, it opened up everything for me—even more than I realized at the time. Last year, in a class I taught at the University of Washington, I had some of my students track various significant objects in *On the* Waterfront. We watched the film five times together, and I was amazed by the jacket of Terry Malloy!

I was planning to ask you about that—if Dean's windbreaker was a little homage to Terry's jacket in On the Waterfront?

STERN: I guess it was, but I didn't realize it until a year ago.

That's amazing because it's so significant. It's not just about keeping "warm," it's—

STERN: It's a talisman. In both films, it's a talisman of protection, and it's also something that I'd used in my first film, *Teresa*, with the sergeant's scarf. So the impulse came from *Teresa*, but the specifics came right out of *On the Waterfront*, without my being aware of it. Thank you, Budd Schulberg!

So now you were under way—writing a script that David Dalton later described as "lean, provocative, psychologically charged and appropriately cosmic." You clearly wrote Rebel *with great confidence, with very few corrections and few rewrites. Were you writing with the actual cast in mind? Warner Bros. had apparently considered Tab Hunter and Robert Wagner for the Dean role, and Margaret O'Brien and others for the Natalie Wood role.*

STERN: I knew Jimmy was doing it, and that was it. I knew that other girls were coming in to test for the Judy role, even Jayne Mansfield. All kinds of people.

Was the Jayne Mansfield test serious?

STERN: From her point of view, I guess it was. I don't know whether Nick ever had any intention of using her.

You're well-known to be a very slow writer, but you wrote Rebel, *your second feature film, very fast. Was it really five weeks?*

STERN: It was more than that. I think that's a legend. When did they begin shooting?

The last script was dated March 25, and the shooting began on the thirtieth.

STERN: So I finished on March 25, and I'd begun writing on the first or second of January. I'm sure of that because I got stung on the eye by a bee at the time. So it took all of January, all of February, and most of March—eleven or twelve weeks to do the whole thing.

That's still pretty fast.

STERN: Yes, especially for me, and that was the *whole* thing because it included the research.

Nick Ray clearly felt that the fifties' phenomenon designated "juvenile delinquency" was the result of emotional deprivation and not material

deprivation—thus, a sad repercussion of middle-class malaise. Were you com-
pletely comfortable with that assessment?

STERN: I was. And I'd come across related material when I was doing research on the whole question of battle fatigue for *Teresa*. John Huston, of course, had done that wonderful documentary *Let There Be Light* about the treatment of shell-shocked soldiers with sodium amytol. The doctors couldn't find a way to treat the stammering, paralysis, and other phenomena that happened as a result of battle trauma until the "truth serum" let the patients relive the precipitating event, let it all surface. So my research made me realize that combat was merely an arena that could "trigger" feelings and behaviors which had their causes in precombat situations, and that such problems could have been triggered *without* a war. The initial damage could have happened in a kitchen somewhere with the dooming predictions of the parents. I'm convinced that many kids collapsed because of what their parents told them they were—or would be.

Living up to the parents' worst fears?

STERN: Yes, and often through subtle messages. For example, parents will often say, "Whatever you want to be is fine with us, we don't care, just be the best." But underneath that statement is a very important, understood caution *not* to be the very best because dad was the "best." And if you got to be "better" than dad, then dad was in some way going to be demeaned—or even killed. So the cautionary limit that a child often put on himself so that he could maintain the love and interest of his parents—and not be abandoned for having gone too far—was to set impossible standards and then, consequently, to fail to fulfill them despite trying very hard. So, I brought all of this with me in my thinking about the young people in *Rebel* and the problems they were going through. In the past, poverty had always been blamed for "juvenile delinquency," but the war made us realize that there were other, psychological causes—and that fact exacerbated the issue and made it more dramatic.

Sometimes when you're speaking about these issues, you seem to be talking from Plato's point of view, and at other times from Jim's point of view. How much did you identify with these two male characters?

STERN: I'm both of them. Of course, with some aspects of Jim, he's really the person I wish I'd been, while Plato is the me I always tried to leave behind but never could.

In an attempt to portray the psychological complexity of the Jim character, Nick Ray apparently envisioned a split-screen sequence in which Jim, while talking to his parents, has this odd reverie about entering a carnival shooting gallery and shooting a balloon that has his father's face on it. Is that true?

STERN: Yes, it is.

Did you actually write it, or did you just talk him out of it?

STERN: I wrote it. I wrote a couple of split-screen sequences, including one for Plato. Nick came up with the idea because he didn't know how to fill up the CinemaScope screen. He was very afraid of "big heads" taking over the screen, so he thought he could show, simultaneously, what these kids were doing and what they were fantasizing in their heads. He never did decide what would happen to the people in the foreground when the fantasy started. Do these other people shut up? Do they continue to move? Do they move in dumb show? Do they freeze? What happens? But even though Nick was undecided, he told me to write that scene, which I did. I sometimes read it aloud to people because it's hilarious. It's a terribly funny scene. So back then, I showed it to David Weisbart, the producer, and he said, "Well, what do you think?" And I said, "I think it's terrible. I hate it." And when David admitted that he felt the same way, I said, "He *can't* be allowed to do it, David," and he agreed, "I'll talk him out of it." So David laid down the law with Nick, and that was the end of it.

When the script was done in March, Ray sent you to his mentor, Elia Kazan, so Kazan could read the screenplay. You've said that it was a very unpleasant experience. What happened?

STERN: It was very uncomfortable, but not because of Kazan. Nick had instructed me to take Kazan the script, so I went to his home on the East Side somewhere, just down the block from Steinbeck's. Kazan was very gracious, and he gave me a sandwich, and I sat in the living room while he took the script inside—because Nick insisted that I wait there while Kazan read it. When Kazan was done, he handed me back the script, and I said goodbye.

He didn't say anything?

STERN: Not that I can remember.

Did he say anything to Ray?

STERN: I guess so, but I don't know what.

It sounds very strange.

STERN: It was. I remember standing in Kazan's house, watching a man I assumed was Steinbeck out the back window. He was about two gardens away, sitting in his backyard typing.

Now, just before shooting was about to start, James Dean vanished, and the bewildered studio was threatening to replace him. Then he called you up one night and asked your advice. What was he so worried about?

STERN: Nick. Nick in comparison to Kazan. By that time, there was a lot of talk about Kazan's *East of Eden* and how superb it was, and Jimmy said, "I really want this picture to be as good as *Eden*, but I'm worried that Nick might not be able to do what Kazan did." Then he said, "I just don't trust him the same way I trusted Kazan. What do you think?" And I said I didn't know. I also told him that I didn't plan to be on the set of *Rebel*. I said, "You and I have a different relationship than you have with Nick, and I don't want him seeing me in your dressing room and wondering what we're talking about. The most important thing to Nick, and to any director, is his relationship with his actors, and he already has a sense of ownership about you." Which he did. So Jimmy said, "Well, do *you* want me to do it?" And I said, "You're asking me if I want the most talked-about young actor in Hollywood to do my picture! But I'm not going to tell you to do it, because I'm not going to take that responsibility. We're friends, and I want it to stay that way."

So you didn't encourage him at all?

STERN: No. And, at the time, I really didn't know if *Rebel* would turn out to be good or bad. No one did, except David Weisbart, who later said that Nick made "a very good film out of marvelous script"—for which I've always been grateful.

So where were you when the shooting began? Was that when you were adapting Rod Serling's teleplay The Rack *for Paul Newman?*

STERN: No, not yet. I went back to my apartment in New York, where I lived when I was doing live television, and I used the opportunity of *Rebel's* shooting to pick up my furniture and drive it back across the country. I didn't start *The Rack* until I got to California.

So you moved furniture in order to avoid the set?

STERN: That's right.

Because of your friendship with James Dean?

STERN: Yes. But I did have an agreement with Nick that I would check in by phone every night to see if he needed any new lines for the next day's shooting. We had a deal: I'd write any new lines he wanted, but in my own words, and he agreed not to write anything himself.

Did you talk every night?

STERN: Just about. Maybe I missed a few.

When did you first see the finished film?

STERN: At a sneak preview, and I hated it. I was horrified! I thought it was endless and self-indulgent, and I was shocked by the raucousness of the color—which I later got to like. I remember meeting Jack Warner and David Weisbart in the lobby of that Encino theater, and I lost my composure and told them what I thought.

Did they do anything?

STERN: They cut parts of it out and reedited other parts. Quite a bit, in fact.

Now let's start with some of the larger issues. You've often criticized the film as well as your own script for being unfair to the parents, calling them, on one occasion, "cartoons." And while there's no doubt that all the adults in the script clearly risk stereotyping, it's also true that the script contains more development of the parents than the final film. Judy's father, for example, is much more sympathetic in the script, but the film eliminates a number of key lines and thus creates a one-sided villain.

STERN: Yes, and it hurts the film quite a bit.

Why do you think Ray simplified the parents?

STERN: Nick can be accused of a lot of things, but never subtlety. Just as all the colors had to be primary, so did the situations and the motives. Nick hated himself as a father because he felt he hadn't done right by his son. So, he took what was already a highly charged theme in the movie, and he overdid it. The changes in Jim's father, for example, were also oversimplified; they didn't have enough steps in the finished film.

It happened too fast and too easy.

STERN: That's right. Last year, at the Seattle Film Festival, I heard, for the first time, the original script performed in a rehearsed reading. In their version, which was cast locally, the relationship between Jim and his father was much more complex and affecting. It was clear that the kid who was playing Jim truly loved—and had reason to love—his father. He just wanted his father to be more of a man, and he was clearly on his father's side in the war against the mother. That Seattle script-reading, a tape of which was shown at the Sundance Screenwriter's Lab, had much more dimension and shading in certain scenes than the film, and I was very grateful for the experience. It was a revelation.

I'd like to turn now to the beginning of the film. After a week of filming Rebel *in black and white, Warner Bros. realized that the CinemaScope lens was only supposed to be used for color, so they told Nick Ray to start again and redo the movie's opening sequence in color. In doing so, he shortened it quite a bit. Christmas was changed to Easter, and the gang's terrorizing of the man with the Christmas packages—including the toy monkey—was cut out entirely. How do you feel about the opening now—which is basically James Dean lying in the street with the toy monkey?*

STERN: Well, Jimmy does it so well that I've always suspended my wish for the original beginning, but when I heard them perform that sequence in Seattle last year, and I remembered that the kids who terrorize the innocent man with the Christmas packages are the very same kids whom Jim meets at school—Buzz and his friends—I thought it was a terrible loss. Nevertheless, I'm glad they cut it out of the film because, in the footage they originally shot, the whole gang was dressed in suits!

Which doesn't make any sense at all. Now, let's jump to the end of the script, which ends with Plato shot down from the planetarium dome, and a definite reconciliation between the parents and the teenagers—especially Jim and his father. But in the film, not only is Jim reconciled with his dad, but his parents look at each other and smile, as if all their problems have been resolved, which is the most unbelievable thing in the whole film. So I guess my question is this: why did Nick Ray take the "happy" part of an already risky ending and extend it even further?

STERN: I can't answer that. I don't know.

And what about Jim and Plato? Originally, you had both of them dying at the end of the picture.

STERN: That's right.

Who changed it?

STERN: Nick said, "We can't do it." And I think David did, too. They felt we couldn't do it to the audience, but I still believe that after Plato is shot, Jimmy should also be shot when he drags himself over to zip up Plato's jacket.

Even more like a Greek play?

STERN: Yes.

So how do you feel about it now?

STERN: Oh, I'd love to see it that way. I still prefer it.

Then, possibly as a private joke, Rebel Without a Cause *ends with a man, who's carrying a briefcase, walking through the crime scene to the planetarium. The man is actually Nick Ray himself, and some critics have made the illogical assumption that he's supposed to be the professor arriving at the planetarium for the next day's work—despite the fact that, even from a distance, Ray looks nothing like the professor seen earlier in the film. What do you make of this?*

STERN: Maybe Nick wanted to be Alfred Hitchcock. He told me he was going to do it before shooting started. We were out at the planetarium one day discussing the ending when he gave me the news that he was going to make an entrance at the end of the film. I insisted that the film should end with Jimmy saying, "He was always cold," and leaving it right there. But Nick said, "Well, we have to have a reconciliation of some kind with the parents, and Jim has to introduce Judy—'This is my friend' or something like that"—and I said, "You're ruining the movie." And that was that.

So he did his cameo.

STERN: Yes, he was determined to do it. You can see it in his very determined walk!

Two of the most awkward moments in both the script and the film are Jim's mooing at the planetarium and Judy's kissing her father on the mouth. Both create a very palpable embarrassment in the audience: seeing the hero making a fool of himself in public and watching the pathetic and peculiar impulses of the heroine. Were you pleased with how Ray captured these difficult moments on film?

STERN: I was, and the more I see the movie, the more wondrous I think certain moments are. For example, I think the way Nick orchestrated the whole chicken run sequence is brilliant, and I feel the same way about the knife fight and most of the action at the mansion. I'm very grateful for much of the film. It's the finest work Nick ever did.

Rebel has wonderful moments all the way through, but I do think the knife fight is better in the script.

STERN: You do?

Yes, because in the script, Jim flat-out refuses to do it, and it isn't until Plato is drawn into it, that he takes action—which seems more reasonable. Then, once Jim's into the knife fight, he's more dominating than he is in the film. He knows exactly what he's doing. He seems more like someone to be reckoned with—someone who's done it before and who's had to move from town to town to escape his past.

STERN: That's true.

I think both of those factors tie in more appropriately with Jim Stark's character.

STERN: Yes, he really wanted to be good. He didn't want trouble, but he was "good" at trouble.

But having said all that, I still like the scene in the movie, even though the script seems more effective. Now, I'd like to ask you about a few of the performances, starting with James Dean's legendary characterization of Jim Stark. What was your reaction?

STERN: When I first saw it?

Yes. You'd created the character, and now your friend had portrayed him on film.

STERN: My recollection is that I loved what Jimmy did from the start. I thought that he was wonderful, but I had many reservations about Jimmy Backus when I first saw the film.

That was clearly the oddest casting choice, given that Jim Backus was a well-known comedian—a fact that has no relevance to contemporary audiences. So, what did you conclude about Backus's portrayal of Jim's father?

STERN: Seeing it again—and many times again!—I do think that he gave a very good performance. Not the one I would have preferred, but very good. The one I always hated was the autocratic grandmother. And I must admit, I was very put off by the performance of Jimmy's mother because I wanted her to be more like my own mother. I don't know why, but I expected her to look like my mother and sound like her, too. But I'm over that now, and I think she was very good.

I've noticed that young, contemporary audiences, who are always knocked out by Dean, sometimes find Natalie Wood's performance a bit off-putting, a mixture of believable anxiety with over-the-top acting.

STERN: When I wrote the script, I didn't think of Judy as having the hard edge that Natalie gave her in the film—a brittle edge. I thought of her as much softer and more confused and helpless. More like a lonesome child dressed up as a woman. So I wasn't prepared for Natalie's edgy, anxious performance, but I liked it.

After the success of the film, and possibly inspired by the French auteurists, Nick Ray made many unfounded and unfortunate claims as the "author" of the film. He even claims to have laid out the story essentials in a twenty-page outline called "The Blind Run," although I can find no evidence that anybody ever saw it.

STERN: I never did.

Even though Ray admitted that you wrote the screenplay, he insisted on a solo story credit for the Oscar nominations, and, later, a French novelization of the screenplay appeared in Paris which listed him as the sole author and made no mention of you. This must have been very difficult?

STERN: It was terrible.

Did you talk to him about it?

STERN: I wrote him an angry letter.

Did he respond?

STERN: We had a meeting. I was shocked that he wanted sole story credit. In those days, there were two separate Oscars, one for story and another for screenplay, and Nick wanted credit as the exclusive source. I was astonished. I'd never even seen "Blind Run," but I knew *exactly* what he'd contributed to my creation of the story for the screenplay. So, we had a meeting, and he made all kinds of false claims which I disputed, but he remained firm. Then all at once, he said, "If you want me to give you co-credit on the story, then I want co-credit on the script." And I said, "But you didn't write a word of it, Nick. There was *no* story until I wrote the screenplay, so I won't give you co-credit." But he wouldn't relent, and finally I got fed up and said, "If you insist on taking story credit, then I insist that you give Irving Shulman adaptation credit, because it will at least recognize, in some way, that there was another contribution I used beside the one you're claiming, and which I never even saw." So he agreed, and that was that.

Did Shulman really deserve credit for adaptation?

STERN: Not really, but I think all three of us should have shared the "story" credit.

So, in the end, the film reads, "Screen Play by Stewart Stern," "Adaptation by Irving Shulman," "From a story by Nicholas Ray." And since the Academy nominated the story and not the screenplay, the only one nominated for a writing award was Nick Ray.

STERN: That's right. It was exactly what I was afraid of, and it was outrageous. Terrible for me, and terrible for Irving.

It certainly was. What about the Writers Guild? Nowadays, the Guild has arbitration. Did you pursue anything along those lines?

STERN: No. It was only my second movie, and I'd just become a member of the Guild, and I didn't realize that the Guild would help me. I remember Nick saying, "I don't give a damn if you go to the Guild; it won't make any difference. I've got an agreement with Warner Bros. I sold them this thing, and they'll guarantee that I get sole credit." So I gave up, and I never went to either Warners or the Guild.

Tell me about La fureur de vivre.

STERN: Ironically, I was on my way to visit Nick in Paris when I first saw the book, a French novelization of *Rebel* "written by Nicholas Ray"! Nick was sick at the time, and I discovered the book when I'd stopped on the way to the hospital to buy him a gift. I was stunned and hurt. My screenplay shanghaied by Nick Ray! When I asked him about it, he denied any blame, "I had nothing to do with it, nothing to do with it at all. I had no control over it."

Unfortunately, the problem persists because some of Ray's enthusiasts have continued to perpetuate the myth of Nick Ray as the "author" of Rebel. *John Francis Kreidl, in his book on Ray, even claims that the director gave James Dean "carte blanche" to improvise on the set.*

STERN: Jimmy didn't improvise. Where did he improvise? He improvised, "See the monkey." That's it.

But that's the claim. Kreidl says that there was a "constant process of rescripting" on the set. Yet when one reads your final, preproduction script, dated March 25, 1955, it's perfectly clear that, except for the opening, the director and performers stayed very close to the script—with only the natural cuttings and adjustments that happen on every film. All the great scenes are in your script, and all the famous lines: "You're tearing me apart!" "If I had one day when I didn't have to be all confused and ashamed of everything—or I felt I belonged some place." "I got the bullets!" "You did everything a man could," and so on. So, what's the matter with these people?

STERN: I don't know. It's all lies, and it was all encouraged by Nick Ray. He couldn't be satisfied with being the director of a successful picture; he had to pretend that he wrote it as well. It's very unfortunate.

Now I'd like to shift back to your relationship with James Dean. Unfortunately, he never saw the completed film, dying as he did in a highway accident on the way to participate in a car race at a Salinas Speedway. How did you learn about the death of your close friend?

STERN: I was staying at my cousin Arthur Loew's house, and the phone rang. It was the producer Henry Ginsberg, and he asked for Arthur. When I told him Arthur was out at a restaurant having dinner, Henry said, "Well, I have some bad news. The kid's dead." So I said, "What kid?" and he said, "Jimmy. Jimmy was just killed in an accident." In a state of shock, I went out to the car and began driving to the restaurant to tell Arthur. On the way, I turned on the radio to see if anything was on the news since I really couldn't believe it. Eventually, I got to the restaurant, told Arthur, and then I drove around Hollywood by myself. I remember driving by Googie's where Jimmy used to hang out. I went to see if there was any reaction on the faces of the people there, but there wasn't. Finally, at some point that night, there was an announcement on the radio, and I saw people pulling off to the side of the road. It was as if there'd been an earthquake, and the people were afraid their cars would fall through the sidewalk. Many people pulled over and parked, and they began to get out of their cars. They were stunned. I'll never forget it.

It's truly amazing since he'd only had, up to that point, one released film, East of Eden.

STERN: Yes. But Jimmy'd made a huge impact. At Warners, they flew the flag at half-mast, and they even wondered whether they should release the picture. They said, "It'll look like we're riding on the coattails of his death, and we certainly don't want that." They got very virtuous for a while. Then Henry Ginsberg and I flew out to the funeral.

In Fairmont, Indiana?

STERN: Yes. We stayed with his family, the Winslows. We stayed on their farm, and then went to the funeral with them—Marcus, Ortense, and Markie.

Not long after his death, you reluctantly agreed to write the script for The James Dean Story, *a peculiar documentary codirected by Robert Altman.*

STERN: Yes, but I never wanted to do it because of misgivings about some of the effects *Rebel* had had—and about what Jimmy had come to represent. At first, I wasn't aware of what was happening, but not long after *Rebel* came out, I was on a cross-country flight. I was thumbing through my *Rebel* script for some reason, and the guy next to me said, "Oh, is that what a screenplay looks like?" And when I said yes, he asked what film it was, and I said, "It's a picture called *Rebel Without a Cause*." Then he told me that he hated the picture, and I asked him why. But first, I explained that I was the author of the script, and I asked him to be honest with me, and he was. He told me that he was a scout leader, and that many of the kids who'd fallen for Jimmy Dean were out of control. He said there'd been knife fights all over the schools since the movie came out, and I was shocked. That was exactly the opposite of what my purpose had been—and Jimmy's purpose too—we wanted to show that violence and leather boots and all that stuff *didn't* make a man. And that people needed to find each other's essential goodness and to reach out to each other and form families that really worked. Needless to say, I was extremely upset by what this honest man told me. So when Abby Greshler contacted me about making a documentary about Jimmy, I said no. I explained that I didn't want to add to the legend of violence, because it wasn't true, and Greshler abandoned his project. Then George W. George, a partner of Robert Altman, called me about their project and said, "Stewart, you've got to do this documentary because we're going to make it anyway, and I think you should be a part of it." So, I met with Altman, looked over the photos and stock footage of Jimmy, and studied the interviews they'd already filmed. Finally, I decided to do it if I could present Jimmy as I knew he would have wanted to be presented—as a man of peace, as a man who understood loneliness, and the difficult things that can happen to people. I felt that his beautiful letter to Markie explained his feelings best.

His young cousin?

STERN: Yes. Markie had sent him some drawings of soldiers and tanks and bombers, and Jimmy, very tactfully, told him that those things were easy to draw. He said that animals, and plants, and the earth itself were even harder to draw because they're harder to grow, and he asked Markie to draw those things. And that's what I wanted in the film.

So what went wrong?

STERN: Two things. One was my overripe writing—I got carried away with the poetic aspect of the script—and this was compounded by the second problem: Martin Gabel's narration. I pleaded with George to get Dennis Hopper to do the narration. Dennis had played one of the gang members in *Rebel*, he knew Jimmy pretty well, and he had the voice of youth. But they got Martin Gabel, who sounded like Rabbi Magnim. Everything was a pronouncement. He'd been beautifully trained in the old school, and he had this incredible voice, but it was too much—way too dramatic. So the images weren't allowed to just "be there," and neither were the interviews, and it was all underscored by Martin Gabel's incantation of my already purple script.

In the end, the documentary comes off as quite depressing.

STERN: It *is* depressing. And I didn't want that. I wanted it to be a tribute to Jimmy's talents and aspirations. I wanted it to challenge what was happening out there—this bizarre legend—with all these people pouring into Fairmont and chipping away at his headstone, and creating crazy myths about Jimmy still being alive and mutilated. I saw these things as a desire to hang onto the violence in some way, and that's what I wanted to crush.

Another of your close friends, Marlon Brando, apparently felt very uneasy around Dean and supposedly avoided him, believing that he was a deeply disturbed young man who desperately needed psychiatric help. Is that appraisal excessive?

STERN: Marlon may have felt that way about Jimmy, but it wouldn't have kept him away. Marlon doesn't stay away from people who need help—because Marlon knows what it's like to need help. He's one of the most emotionally naked people I've ever met, and the most willing to reach out to help other people. As for Jimmy, he was in therapy, which he'd begun not very long before he died. In fact, Nick had gotten him a therapist, and Jimmy was very happy about it. He felt that he was beginning to make strides, and that things were improving.

So you weren't overly concerned about him back then?

STERN: Not really. We mostly had a wonderful time together—lots of laughs. He was terribly funny, and terribly mischievous, and childlike, and magical. Off the set, you couldn't depend on him for two seconds, but the connections we had were always joyous.

That's missing in the documentary.

STERN: Yes, it is.

During your long and distinguished career, you had the opportunity to work with three of the most talented performers of the last fifty years—James Dean, Marlon Brando, and Paul Newman—and you also became good friends with all three men. Having written films for each of them, how would you characterize the uniqueness of their individual talents?

STERN: Well, Jimmy was extraordinarily intuitive and inventive, and he had an immediate connection with his whole emotional being. He was extremely quick to absorb things, and he was always hungry for information. He could also practicalize things which stayed impractical for other performers, things about the Method, for example, which he was able to simplify for himself. He understood the concept that "acting is doing," and he never worried about excessive emotional preparation. He might, for example, prepare by doing multiplication tables. By sixteens, say. How much is 16 times 16? How much is 16 times 17? Something that would force him to be intensely focused on a specific problem which might have absolutely nothing to do with his character's problems but which would give him the results he wanted without straining for the result.

The Dean "intensity."

STERN: Yes. He was always doing imaginative things that would get him where he wanted to be. He wasn't orthodox, and he never believed that things had to be done only one way. He did whatever worked. So did Marlon. But Marlon, of course, spent much more time studying with the best teachers, whereas Jimmy was in and out of the Actors Studio in maybe five sessions. I think he only did one scene there. So, he picked up things here and there, and he read a lot of stuff, although he didn't read very deeply. One of the things he picked up from Marlon was how to invest inanimate objects with meaning, and how to reveal character by the way you physically pick up something. Jimmy was a wildly gifted actor—a work still in progress.

Marlon Brando?

STERN: Marlon is prodigious. He's Mount Rushmore on a skateboard! There's no more monumental talent than Marlon's, or a more brilliant mind. It's a mind that comes out of watchfulness. He's the most mistrustful man I've ever met, and the most watchful. He can "read" anything. He comprehends the subtext of everything, whether it's an animal, a book, or a human being. He has a kind of insight that would paralyze me if I had it. It would *hurt* me to have it. He's hypersensitive, closely in touch with his emotional being. I won't talk about all the failings of Marlon, and all the flaws, which are gigantic. They're epic, epic. And deeply wounded. He's Job, authentically Job.

Are you talking personally or professionally?

STERN: Personally. He's a tyrant, a lover, and the most sensitive friend— the most helpful person in the world—and one of the funniest men I've ever encountered.

And Paul Newman?

STERN: Paul is the most complex of them all, and the most endearing and moving. He used to say that he was "too cerebral" as an actor, and he called himself an "emotional Republican." He felt that the other two guys—Brando and Dean—could do it without working for it. They could easily find their emotions, and he couldn't—the only way he could cry, he claimed, was to stare at a light bulb without blinking. So, he bashed himself for not being what they were, or what he thought they were. But then he'd say, "The old fox has something they don't have: tenacity. I'm the tortoise, and they're the hares. I can keep going." And he was right. He also has a wonderful mind. A legal mind, very analytical. He was never readily swept into any kind of hyperbolic emotional state. He was careful and watchful, and he had to be, because he was a very tiny child. I think he was 5'3" when he went into the Navy, and he did most of his growing while he was overseas. So, he was patient. He always accused himself of being too objective and linear, and he always accused me of being too baroque, and he concluded that these differences were the reason we worked so well together. Another thing about Paul is that he always abhorred celebrity—right from the beginning—and he was repulsed by theatrical behavior. He has, of course, a natural vanity and ego, but he has less of it than anybody in that position that I've ever come across except for Joanne [Woodward]. Even when he was younger, the world was always more important to Paul Newman than Paul Newman himself—as shown by his involvement with the civil rights movement, and the work he's silently done for a thousand other causes over the years, and often in the most personal ways. He's one of the most elegant human beings that I've ever come across. They both are. Paul and Joanne, as people and artists. I trust them absolutely—in a way that it's hard to trust anyone. As actors, directors, professionals, and people, they're a different breed, from a much, much different time.

In your career as a screenwriter, you were nominated for Academy Awards for Teresa *and* Rachel, Rachel; *you wrote an Oscar-winning documentary,* Benjy; *and you wrote such renowned works as* Rebel Without a Cause, The Ugly American, Sybil, *and others. But, eventually, you found yourself burned-out as a writer. What happened?*

STERN: A number of things. The fear of writing became overwhelming—especially the fear of not being able to write as well as I had in the past. This happened each time I started a new project, and there were long periods when I couldn't write. As time went by, the acclaim made it even harder. Every time a film was successfully finished, when everybody else was celebrating, I'd be worried if I could do it again. I'd find myself back at the beginning, helpless and terrified. It felt as if there'd been no achievement at all, and it wore me down.

Because you were back to square one?

STERN: Yes. Regardless of what everyone said, despite all their encouragement: "Well, this should be a breeze for you. Look what you've just finished."

That's what most people would expect. But you always put tremendous pressure on yourself.

STERN: Yes, it's killing. Another problem was that almost all my work has been very autobiographical and dealt with questions that I had about my own personal life at the time. My main character, my protagonist, would go out as a scout into the minefield and survive somehow, whereas, in real life, I could never really do things that way. Then, through therapy and life and living, I found myself with a changed life, and my earlier themes, whatever those themes might have been, were absorbed and integrated, and I couldn't go back to them. I couldn't write *Rebel* now, for example. I couldn't remember what I'd need to know. Also, somewhere along the line, I became acutely aware of the brevity of life, the fact that you have a limited amount of time left. In the past, I'd always try to find a metaphor for my screenplays that had some social application. So, whether it was *The Ugly American*, or *Sybil*, or *Rebel*, or *The Outsider*, or whatever it was, there was always some kind of social issue that related to my own private quest as an individual. I had the belief that if enough people saw *The Ugly American*, then we wouldn't make the same kind of political mistakes that we're still making. Or, that if enough people saw *Sybil* and understood that the abuse which children suffer can cause them to disintegrate into different aspects of themselves in order to stay sane, then public awareness would be raised and something good would come from it. But in almost every case, the limitations of the power of film to influence people came home to me—very strongly. Its power is limited. You really can't change the world with film. You can change a few things, but not much. So, I began to reconsider where I should focus my remaining energies. As you know, I'm very involved in the efforts to save the dwindling lowland gorillas still surviving in what remains of the rainforest in the Congo and Cameroon. There's an estimated 50,000 lowland gorillas left in the world. So what do you do about that? Do you make a movie about it? Or do you get involved with the people who are really doing something more immediate? *Gorillas in the Mist* let people know that gorillas are accessible beings, so everything helps in some way, I suppose, but eventually you get impatient with it all. You're not willing to go through three years writing a script which may or may not be made as a movie, and which, even if it's made, probably won't make the slightest difference. So I prefer to give my time to movements like Poachers-Into-Protectors. It's a race against time, and even though I don't think it's going to be won, I think you have to go down swinging. That doesn't mean that I would *never* write about it, and maybe all of this is a cop-out, but I grew sick to death of talking about nothing but movies and being part of a community where film was more important than anything else in life— and where the movies became more and more about other movies and less and less about real life. The happiest times in my life have been the periods when I wasn't living that way. I was happier in the army than I was in Hollywood, and I'm happier here in Seattle because I'm involved in real things, like my work at the zoo helping the gorillas. Does that answer your question?

Yes, but I also thought that you lost your confidence as a writer because so many people were forcing you to see things from their points of view that you started to feel as if you were writing what they *wanted you to write, rather than what* you *wanted to write?*

STERN: That's true. I began to lose confidence in my own ability to make choices. It was a kind of attrition. People were so eager to make contributions before you were ready for them that you began to automatically assume that they were right about things and that you were not. But I don't blame Hollywood. I had the best ride of any writer I know. Not necessarily financially, but I was always welcome on the set of every picture that I chose to be on, and, in many cases, I was there from the first casting interviews to the final cut. Only a few people in Hollywood had such opportunities, and I'm very grateful. But I did burn out in the end. There's no doubt about that.

And despite all of your Hollywood difficulties, you've always avoided falling into bitterness, and have always considered yourself very fortunate, even privileged. When you look back now, especially at your work on Rebel Without a Cause, *what stands out among your most pleasurable recollections?*

STERN: Being with Jimmy at Arthur's, night after night. Horsing around. Breaking his glasses the night before he shot his first scene. Jimmy picking me up to go to the studio on his motorcycle. Sweet young Natalie. Young Dennis. Memories like that. Things I'll never forget.

Thanks, Stewart. And thanks for Rebel.

STERN: Thank you.

CHAPTER 4

North by Northwest (1959)

A CONVERSATION WITH ERNEST LEHMAN

Ernest Lehman (1915–2005), one of the most acclaimed screenwriters in Hollywood history, was born in New York City. After graduating from City College of New York, he worked for a publicity agency that specialized in a Broadway/Hollywood clientele. His early short stories, often related to theater and film, began to appear in prestigious journals like *Collier's* and *Esquire*, and his short novel *Sweet Smell of Success* was first serialized in *Cosmopolitan*. After moving to Hollywood in 1953, his first screenplay was *Executive Suite* (1954), directed by Robert Wise and starring William Holden. His subsequent films include: Billy Wilder's *Sabrina* (1954), starring Humphrey Bogart and Audrey Hepburn; *The King and I* (1956), with Yul Brynner and Deborah Kerr; *Somebody Up There Likes Me* (1956) and *From the Terrace* (1960), both starring Paul Newman; Alfred Hitchcock's *North by Northwest* (1959), with Cary Grant and Eva Marie Saint; *West Side Story* (1961), starring Natalie Wood, which received the Academy Award for Best Picture; Robert Wise's *The Sound of Music* (1965) with Julie Andrews, which also received the Academy Award for Best Picture; Mike Nichols's *Who's Afraid of Virginia Woolf?* (1966), which was produced by Ernest Lehman, starring Elizabeth Taylor and Richard Burton; Gene Kelly's *Hello, Dolly!* (1969), with Barbra Streisand; *Portnoy's Complaint* (1972), which was produced and directed by Ernest Lehman; and Hitchcock's final film, *Family Plot* (1976). In 1995, his co-written screenplay for *Sabrina* was adapted for a remake, directed by Sydney Pollack and starring Harrison

Ford and Julia Ormond. Ernest Lehman was also the author of a number of successful novels, including *The French Atlantic Affair,* which was a national best seller in 1977. His various screenplays received five Writers Guild Awards and were nominated four times for Academy Awards. In 2001, he became the first writer in film history to receive a Lifetime Achievement Award from the Academy of Motion Picture Arts and Sciences.

In 1957, you were one of the most sought-after screenwriters in Hollywood, and Alfred Hitchcock decided that he'd like you to write his next picture.

LEHMAN: That's right. MGM had bought a novel called *The Wreck of the Mary Deare*, and they told me that Hitch wanted me to write it.

Had you met him before?

LEHMAN: Just once. We were introduced by Bernard Herrmann, and we had lunch together. Benny thought we'd get along well, and we did.

So why did you turn down The Wreck of the Mary Deare*?*

LEHMAN: When I read the novel, I just didn't see the movie in it. It was mostly a naval inquiry into something that had happened in the past, and I felt it would be too static.

But the book began with a very intriguing scene.

LEHMAN: Yes, the ship was found in a channel with nobody on board. But that was the only good scene in the whole novel. All the rest of it was the inquiry.

But Hitchcock still wanted you for the picture.

LEHMAN: My agent, who was also Hitchcock's agent, let me know that Hitch was very upset that I'd turned him down. I guess he wasn't used to that. So a couple of weeks later, my agent asked me if I'd be willing to have lunch with Hitchcock at the Polo Lounge. So I said, "Why not? I'm sure we'll have a good time together." And we did have a good time, and I came away thinking, "Maybe Hitch knows how to do the picture." So even though I still had my doubts, I decided to do it.

Did you talk much about the picture at that meeting?

LEHMAN: Not at all.

Then how did things go when you started working on the script?

LEHMAN: Well, I went to his house every day for about three weeks, and I realized that every time I brought up the subject of *Mary Deare*, he would change the subject. So, I began to suspect that he didn't know any more about how to do the picture than I did. Finally, I went to his house one morning and said, "I've got bad news for you, Hitch. You'll have to get another writer. I don't know how to write this picture." And he said, "Don't be silly, Ernie. We'll do something else." And I said, "But what'll we tell MGM?" And he said, "We won't tell them a thing." And that's how it evolved.

How did you break the news to MGM?

LEHMAN: That was later on, when we were working on *North by Northwest*, and Hitch said, "Don't you think it's time we told MGM that we're not doing *Mary Deare*?" Everybody at the studio thought we were moving along just fine with the picture. People used to salute me in the hallways and say, "Hello, Skipper, how's it going?" But Hitch wanted *me* to tell them, and I said, "I'm not going to tell them. *You're* going to have to do it." So, he did it. He went to a meeting and told them that it was taking too long to write *Mary Deare*, and that we were planning to do another script instead. The studio people, who apparently assumed that Hitch was now planning to do two pictures for the studio, were delighted. Then he glanced down at his wristwatch, said he had to go—because we didn't really have a story at that point—and left. And that was that.

After you'd decided to do an original script, I believe Hitchcock suggested a film on the life of Jack Sheperd, an eighteenth-century English escape artist?

LEHMAN: Yes. After the decision to drop *Mary Deare* was made, we spent a couple of months just talking about ideas and possibilities. And Hitch brought up a lot of subjects that I wasn't interested in, and, I guess, I brought up a few that he wasn't interested in. And one of his suggestions was a picture about an escape artist, which didn't interest me at all.

You once discussed the fact that, in those days, doing an original script was looked down on in Hollywood circles.

LEHMAN: That's right. It wasn't as highly regarded as it is now. If you were at a party back then, and somebody said, "What are you doing these days?" and if you answered, "I'm doing an original script," it suggested that you really weren't doing anything at all—since almost all of the pictures back then were adaptations of plays or novels.

And those scripts would have the prestige of the book or the play behind them.

LEHMAN: Exactly.

Was it different with this project, given that you were working with Hitchcock?

LEHMAN: Well, for me personally, none of this mattered anyway. I never went to a party where anyone said, "Oh, you're doing an original? Too bad." That never happened.

Once you were finally under way on the script, you decided to do "the Hitchcock picture to end all Hitchcock pictures." What did you mean by that?

LEHMAN: I meant something that was witty and entertaining, with lots of suspense, and all kinds of colorful locales—things like that. Everything that I'd enjoyed in Hitchcock pictures from the past.

The one I think of the most is The 39 Steps, *where you have someone who—from out of nowhere—falls into a complicated spy web, and the action of the film moves around quite a bit, up to Scotland and then back to London.*

LEHMAN: Was there humor in it?

Yes, especially between the leads. Remember when they were handcuffed together?

LEHMAN: Yes, I do. I think that was Robert Donat and Madeline Carroll.

It was. Now, in the process of writing the film, it seems that you began with a list of disparate ideas that Hitchcock mentioned as possible scenes for the movie. Could you discuss them?

LEHMAN: Yes. They were all wonderful, and I took them all down, and I never used most of them. For some reason, Hitch wanted to do the longest dolly shot in cinema history. The idea was that the shot would begin with an assembly line, and then you'd gradually see the parts of the car added and assembled, and, all the while, the camera's dollying for miles along with the assembly line, and then eventually there's a completed car, all built, and it's driven off the assembly line, and there's a dead body in the backseat.

Did you try to work that one into the script?

LEHMAN: Not really. It was intriguing, but it had no place in the picture. Then Hitch told me another one: there's a speech being made at the General Assembly of the United Nations, and the speaker suddenly stops. He's irritated, and he says he's not going to continue until the delegate from Brazil wakes up. So a UN page goes over to the man, taps him on the shoulder, and the delegate falls over dead. But he'd been doodling—and that's the only clue to the murder—and his doodling is a sketch of the antlers of moose. So I said, "Well, that's intriguing—now we've got the United Nations, and Detroit, and what might seem like a reference to northern Canada." And Hitch said that he'd always wanted to do a scene at Lake Louise where a family is having a reunion—a get-together—and a twelve-year-old girl takes a gun out of a baby carriage and shoots someone. I realize that all these ideas sound very peculiar and unrelated, but I took them all down and thought about them.

Wasn't there something in Alaska?

LEHMAN: Yes. There's a hole in the ice, and an Eskimo is fishing, and a hand suddenly comes up out of the water. As you can see, all these ideas seemed to be moving in a northwesterly direction, starting in New York. Hitch also mentioned something about wanting to do a shot where people take off in a little plane that has skis on the ice instead of wheels, and that reinforced the idea of heading northwest. So, I started calling the project *In a Northwesterly Direction.*

Where did Mount Rushmore come in?

LEHMAN: That also came up in those discussions. Just like he'd said, "I always wanted to do a dolly shot in an auto factory," he said, "I always wanted to do a chase across the faces of Mount Rushmore." And I thought, "Hey, I really like that idea." And that was the seed of the flower that took eleven months to grow. But I had to ask myself, "Who's chasing whom over the faces of Mount Rushmore?" and "How do they get there?" and "Why?" And that took quite a bit of doing on my part. I remember that I used to squeeze out a tiny bit of the screenplay every day, fully convinced that it would never actually become a movie. There were many nights when I would be driving home from the studio thinking that we were just kidding ourselves—and wondering how long the charade would go on. The truth is, even with all my experience, I really didn't know how to write the script. I'd never written a movie like that before, but gradually I eked it out—or, at least, the first sixty-five pages—and then Hitch went off to make *Vertigo*. So I'd sit there in my lonely office, and many times I'd go home at night having written less than half a page, completely discouraged. And several times I tried to quit while he was away, but my agent wouldn't let me, saying, "You've already quit *The Wreck of the Mary Deare*, you can't quit this one too." So I was kind of trapped into doing it.

Like Roger Thornhill.

LEHMAN: Yes, like my own character, always wondering, "How can I get out of this?" And the only way I could get out of it was to "write" my way out of it. And I think that, despite the unpleasantness of having to work under those conditions, I wound up at the top of my form as a writer, and, later, Hitch was at the top of his form when he directed the picture. In a sense, it's unlike any picture he ever made. And it seems to have legs. They've just rereleased the film in Australia as a feature—all over again.

It's still extremely popular.

LEHMAN: Yes, it's just incredible what endurance it has. It's kind of timeless.

It is. And one of its great pleasures is the ingeniousness of the plot. You can't watch the film without being amazed at how it keeps working itself out, how it keeps progressing. Given all its complications, it's amazing that you were actually writing the script without an overall plan—without knowing where you were going, except to Mount Rushmore.

LEHMAN: And I think that difficulty turned out to be very positive and beneficial. Since I never knew where I was going next, I was constantly painting myself into corners, and then trying to figure a way out of them. As a result, the picture has about ten acts instead of three, and if I'd tried to sit down at the beginning and conceive the whole plot, I could have never done it. Everything was written in increments: moving it a little bit forward, then a little bit more, one page at a time. Saying to myself, "Okay, you've got him out of Grand Central Station. Now he's on the train, now what? Well, there's no female character in it yet, I better put Eve on the train. But what should I do with her? And where should they meet? Well, let's see, I've ridden on the 20th Century, how about the dining car?" That's the way it went, very slowly. Always asking, "What do I do next?" So, in the end, the audience never knows what's coming next, because I didn't either.

It pays off consistently, and most thrillers don't.

LEHMAN: And it's not just suspense. It's not like *Shadow of a Doubt* or *Vertigo*. It's not really a "dark" picture at all.

But it does have definite affinities with other Hitchcock films, and I wonder if you thought about any of them while your were writing North by Northwest? *Like* The 39 Steps *or* Saboteur *or* Notorious?

LEHMAN: Not at all. As a matter of fact, I'd forgotten all about *The 39 Steps,* and I was a little chagrined when somebody reminded me about it. I was a kid when that picture came out, and I'd mostly forgotten it. Then somebody reminded me that there was a helicopter chase in the film.

Well, it's not really a chase. Robert Donat is being pursued over the Scottish moors by the police, and there's a single, cut-away shot of a surveillance hover-craft. On the other hand, there is an extended train scene in the film—as well as the other similarities I mentioned earlier.

LEHMAN: Well, I guess if you write long enough, all kinds of parallel-isms will pop up. And if you've gone to the movies all your life, you're bound to absorb certain things, and then reuse them without realizing that you're doing it. I'm sure that it happens, but when I was writing *North by Northwest,* I had no other films in my mind. I was struggling too much with the one I was working on.

Is it true that the idea of the nonexistent spy, Kaplan, was suggested to Hitchcock by a New York newspaperman?

LEHMAN: Yes. That was back when Hitch and I were bouncing around ideas, and he said, "You know, I was at a cocktail party in New York, and Otis Gurnsey told me that the CIA had once used a nonexistent decoy." Gurnsey, who was a drama writer for the *New York Sun,* was wondering if Hitch could use it in one of his films sometime—and we did.

I didn't know that the CIA actually did it?

LEHMAN: As far as I know, they did.

This may be a bit of a stretch, but I wonder if you were influenced by the 1956 British film The Man Who Never Was, *which told the true story of the extraordinary World War II deception in which the British Secret Service took a corpse, dressed it up, gave it phony papers, and dropped it in the ocean off the coast of Spain? The deception was so effective that Hitler significantly altered his defenses for the Allied invasion of Italy.*

LEHMAN: I'm sure I didn't have it in mind, but, now that you mention it, I do remember that film. I guess you can never be sure where the hell your ideas come from. It's very hard to describe how one "writes," the actual process—unless you're writing an essay or an article, then you've got something specific to focus on. But when you're writing an original screenplay, you can't help but wonder where some of your ideas come from. Often, they just pop into your head in response to the questions you ask yourself. "How do I get out of this?" or "How do I get them to say that?" I decided to make Thornhill an advertising executive so he could talk in a kind of clever repartee, rather than speaking in a straightforward manner. I felt that would be more amusing, and that it sounded like something Cary Grant could do very well. That's one thing about that script that I'm very proud of—the dialogue, the repartee. Nobody ever says anything straight. Yet even though it's rather oblique, it's still perfectly understandable.

It's one of the cleverest scripts ever written, both for its plot and its dialogue. Now, I also wanted to ask you about your on-site research trip for the film.

LEHMAN: Well, I pretty much followed Thornhill's movements, beginning in New York where I spent five days at the United Nations. I was looking for a place where a murder could take place, and when they found out what I was up to, they banned Hitchcock from shooting there. So, he had to build his own sets in Culver City.

They're very convincing.

LEHMAN: Yes, they are. I think Hitch managed to steal one shot at the UN—Cary walking up the steps and into the building—but that was it. Then, I went to a judge in Glen Cove, Long Island, and had him put me through the business of being arrested for drunk driving. I had no idea how to write that scene, and going through the process was a lot of fun.

Didn't you also check out the home of the Soviet ambassador while you were out on Long Island?

LEHMAN: Yes, in Glen Cove. That's where the Russian delegation lived during the Cold War. They rented a mansion out there for the United Nations sessions.

Then, you headed "northwest."

LEHMAN: Well, even though I'd traveled on the 20th Century when I was a New Yorker—and I certainly knew Grand Central Station and all that—I decided to take a trip on the 20th Century Limited just in case something useful stuck in my mind. So, I got off at the LaSalle Street

Station in Chicago, went to the Ambassador East Hotel, and checked things out. Then, I took the bullet train to Rapid City, South Dakota, hired a forest ranger on his day off, and started climbing Mount Rushmore. I wanted to climb to the top and see what was up there. But it was an absolutely idiotic thing to do. Halfway up, I looked down and thought, "God, I'm just a screenwriter. What the hell am I doing up here? One slip and I'm dead!" So, I gave the Polaroid camera to the forest ranger, and I told him to go up to the top and take photos of everything.

Did you wait where you were until he came back, or did you climb down by yourself?

LEHMAN: I came back down by myself. Very, very carefully. It might be more accurate to say that I crawled back down. It was an absolutely idiotic idea.

Were the Polaroids any good?

LEHMAN: Yes, but I was surprised that there's nothing much up there. Then the Department of Parks found out that we were planning to have people fall off the face of their famous monument, and they banned Hitchcock from shooting up there. He was furious. So the whole thing had to be constructed in Culver City. It was a marvelous job of set design. There was only one long shot that Hitch got at Rushmore. It was taken from the cafeteria, and they couldn't stop him from doing that. Looking back on it all, it was a very memorable project. But there was a lot of drama behind the drama—especially trying to get the script finished. There were constant, endless, seemingly insurmountable crises of script, but, somehow, I finished the first sixty-five pages, and I sent them off to Hitch. He was on vacation in the Bahamas at the time, and he sent me back a very enthusiastic, four-page, handwritten letter. He loved the first sixty-five pages—which was high praise from Hitch—and it was very encouraging. So I kept pressing forward, and Hitch, confident that I now knew what the hell I was doing, moved over to MGM from his home base at Universal, and started story-boarding the script with his art director, and casting the roles. And all the time, I'm sitting there in my office sweating the fact that I have no idea whatsoever why the hell they're all going to Mount Rushmore! Why were these people heading to South Dakota? I had no idea! So, the last act of the script was blank. Actual blank pages! Then Cary Grant came on the picture with some astronomical salary, and I was still sitting there in my office with nothing but a partially-completed script. So I called up Hitch, and I told him we were in big trouble. He came rushing over to my office, sat across from me, and the two of us stared at each other. Finally, he suggested that we call in some mystery novelist to help us kick around ideas, but I didn't like the idea. After all, I was getting paid by MGM to write the thing, and I felt that it would make me look pretty foolish. I kept saying,

"God, what'll they say about me upstairs?" and Hitch would say, "Don't worry, I'll tell them it's all my fault. I'll tell them I should've been able to help you, but I couldn't—or something like that."

Then we went to his office—it was about six o'clock in the evening—and we kept talking about his idea, even discussing which mystery writer we should get, and, all the time, the right side of my brain was working, and suddenly, as I was listening to him—not really ignoring him—I said, "She takes a gun out of her purse and shoots him." So where the hell did that come from? It just popped into my head. That's the way it works sometimes: you've got a problem and, no matter what else is going on around you, the right side of your brain keeps working on it and then, suddenly, it pops out of nowhere. And Hitch took it right in stride. Even though I'd completely changed the subject and suddenly blurted out, "She takes a gun out of her purse and shoots him," he didn't miss a beat and responded, "Yes, the Polish Underground sometimes killed their own members, just to prove they weren't in the Underground." And I said, "Yes, but these are fake bullets. That'll convince Van Damm that he has to take her away with him. Now that she's a fugitive, he'll decide to take her on the plane." And, instantly, I had the whole last act.

It must've been quite a relief.

LEHMAN: It sure was. For both of us.

And it's still a very effective scene when she pulls out that gun in the Rushmore cafeteria.

LEHMAN: It's crazy, but it worked.

You've already mentioned Cary Grant a couple of times, but I read somewhere that Jimmy Stewart also wanted the lead, but you were convinced that Grant was right for the role.

LEHMAN: Definitely. Both of them kept calling up Hitch and saying, "When's my picture going to be ready?" So very different from today! Nowadays, they'd be paying Cary Grant twenty million dollars a picture! If not more. And yes, I always felt Cary was right for Thornhill—the Madison Avenue type. Besides, if it was Jimmy Stewart, the picture would've been five hours long.

Because of all the dialogue?

LEHMAN: That's right. All that repartee.

Is there any truth to the old story that the studio wanted Gregory Peck?

LEHMAN: No, not at all.

It's currently listed on the back of the video box under "Facts From the Vault." Another one of the three listed "facts" is the old Hamlet error—which we'll get to later.

LEHMAN: Where do they get this crap from?

From the "vault"—whatever that means. How about the female lead? Was Cyd Charisse ever considered for the role?

LEHMAN: Not that I ever knew of. There might have been some talk about Princess Grace, but we were both delighted with Eva Marie [Saint].

She was excellent—just a few years after her extraordinary, Oscar-winning performance in On the Waterfront. *There are very few performers in cinema history who've starred in two classic films in their whole careers—and she did it in less than five years.*

LEHMAN: That's right. And in such different roles, too. For *North by Northwest,* Hitch made her over into the image of his "cool blonde" type—like Kim Novak, Grace Kelly, or Tippi Hedren—and she was perfect.

Okay, now that the script's finally done, you have this long history of warring with directors and actors who try to alter your dialogue. So it must have been quite a relief to work with Hitchcock, who didn't allow that kind of thing.

LEHMAN: That's definitely true. He never allowed a word to be changed. Just like Billy Wilder. Absolutely. I could be pretty awful about people messing with my lines; I guess I'm a very passive-aggressive person. I remember one time on *From The Terrace,* when they were rehearsing downstairs in New York, and I was up in my apartment at the Plaza Hotel, and the director called me and said, "Paul Newman's struggling. He says he can't read one of his speeches. He doesn't know how to do it." So, I said, "I'll be right down there." I immediately went downstairs, walked over to Paul, took the script, read the speech, handed him back the script, and said, "There, *I* read it. Now, *you* do it." It was very rude. But I was always very protective of my scripts, and Hitch respected that. But Cary Grant would get annoyed with me sometimes. Once on location in Bakersfield, when we were doing the crop duster sequence, we were sitting in the backseat of an air-conditioned limousine while they were setting things up, and Cary started complaining to me that he had to carry the whole story on his back. And I said, "Well, that's the way it's written." And he said, "You think you're making a Cary Grant picture? This is a David Niven picture!"

What did he mean by that?

LEHMAN: Well, I guess he considered David Niven more "road company." Not as "suave." On a lower level.

Could you discuss the metamorphosis of the title?

LEHMAN: As I mentioned earlier, all of Hitch's original ideas—even the ones I didn't use—seemed to be unconsciously moving in a northwesterly direction. So, that's what I called the project for quite a few months, *In a Northwesterly Direction.* Finally, after Hitchcock told them that I was writing an original screenplay instead of *The Wreck of the Mary Deare*, the head of the story department, Kenneth McKenna, heard the title, and he said, "Why don't you use *North By Northwest* as a working title?" So we did. And Hitchcock and I were always certain that it was *only* a working title and that we'd change it later when we came up with something better, but we never did.

What about The Man on Lincoln's Nose?

LEHMAN: That's right, for about a week or so, we used that title. And, one day, Sammy Cahn, the great songwriter, came into my office and said, "I've got the title song." And he stood there in my office and sang "The Man on Lincoln's Nose." It was just like Broadway in the thirties. It was a love song, but it sounded like something from a Kaufman and Hart farce.

Some critics have incorrectly claimed that the title is a reference to Hamlet's remark, "I am but mad north-northwest," and other critics have made much of the supposed "existential" significance of the fact that there's no such actual direction as "north by northwest."

LEHMAN: It's those damned French critics, the *auteurs*. They're always coming up with all kinds of pretentious crap that has no basis in reality. They were always trying to attach deep, serious interpretations to everything that Hitchcock did, and he definitely liked all the attention. But the truth is, it wasn't until after the picture was done, that somebody wrote in and pointed out the quotation from Shakespeare where Hamlet says, "I am but mad north-northwest." And the same thing's true with the direction. When we were making the picture, we had no idea that "north by northwest" wasn't an actual direction. For some reason, it sounded right to us.

One of the most famous and most discussed sequences in American film is the crop duster attack on Thornhill. How did it transform from a cyclone to a crop duster?

LEHMAN: One day, Hitch said to me, "I've always wanted to do a scene in the middle of nowhere—where there's absolutely nothing. You're out in the open, and there's nothing all around you. The camera can turn around 360 degrees, and there's nothing there but this one man standing all alone—because the villains, who are out to kill him, have lured him out to this lonely spot." Then Hitch continued, "Suddenly, a tornado comes along and...." "But Hitch," I interrupted, "how do the villains create a tornado?" and he had no idea. So I wondered, "What if a plane comes out of the sky?" And he liked it immediately, and he said, "Yes, it's a crop duster. We can plant some crops nearby." So we planted a fake cornfield in Bakersfield and did the scene that way. And, like you said, it became a very famous sequence. As a matter of fact, that's how I knew that Cary Grant had died. Every channel on TV was showing that shot of Cary running away from the plane. It's strange, isn't it, that such a distinguished career should be remembered mostly for that one shot?

But it's an unforgettable image.

LEHMAN: Yes, it is.

I wonder if you were surprised at all by the way Hitchcock did the crop duster sequence. I know that you and Hitchcock discussed every shot in the film, but still, not many directors would've had the nerve—or the confidence— to shoot a seven-minute sequence with only a few lines of dialogue.

LEHMAN: Well, that's the way I wrote it, almost shot by shot. I pictured it that way, and I even acted it out for Hitch. But you're right, only Hitch- cock would've had the guts to let all those cars go by with nothing else happening. But taking risks was one of Hitch's trademarks, and, since the audience knew it was a Hitchcock picture, they were willing to be patient.

And the scene grows more and more ominous. You know that "something" is coming.

LEHMAN: Yes, like when the truck is approaching, and you start to wonder if it'll run him down, but, instead, there's just lots of dust. It's very surprising, and very effective. Hitch felt that the longer you can keep the audience waiting, the better.

Over the course of your career, you had a habit of suggesting camera shots to the directors you worked with. How did Hitchcock react to that?

LEHMAN: The only time he ever *really* got angry at me—though I'm sure he got mad at me at other times—was about that very thing. Fed up, he suddenly burst out, "Why do you insist on telling me how to direct this picture?" And I said, "Why do you insist on telling me how to write it?" But that's the way I was. I'd get a picture in my head, and if I had a good idea about how it should be shot, I'd put it on paper. Why not? Some directors, like Robert Wise, who did four of my pictures, appreciated my suggestions. I remember that sometimes I'd go down to the set, and I'd be astounded. I'd see Bob building this huge set, and I think to myself, "God, just because I put those words on the paper, look at what's happen- ing here! Be careful! Be sure it's a good idea!" But Bob always listened, unless it was something really terrible. So on *North by Northwest*, I tried to develop a Hitchcock frame of mind. I became like Hitchcock, and I tried to think like him. And whenever Hitch didn't like something I suggested, he'd simply say, "Oh, Ernie, that's the way they do it in the movies." And then I'd know better, and I'd try to write the scene over again.

When the picture was finished, it was Hitchcock's longest film at 136 minutes, and an anxious MGM wanted to cut out the forest scene at Mount Rushmore when Thornhill and Eve are finally able to talk to each other without the previous lies and deceptions. It's clearly one of the best and most important scenes in the movie. Did you get involved in the arguments over this?

LEHMAN: Actually, they just wanted to cut the scene down, not to cut it out entirely. Because you *have* to have that scene in the film—which, by the way, was very difficult to write. All the deception is gone, and they're very serious, but they're still being clever—because that's the way they are. Anyway, we kept the whole scene. Sol Siegel asked us down to the screening room, and we watched the scene, and he pleaded with Hitch to cut it down. But Hitch said no. He said that "it would spoil the picture," and he was adamant. He knew that he had the final word—given his contract. Besides, the studio people were pretty much in awe of Hitchcock, and they were very afraid of offending him. The scene actually *is* a bit long, but I didn't know how to write it any shorter. And the transition is absolutely necessary. Another scene that was extremely difficult to write was the one in Eve's hotel room after she's just tried to have him killed by the plane. How do you play it? You can't have him get too angry, because then you won't have a relationship. So, I tried having him be angry with her in a slightly affectionate way: "How does a girl like you get to be a girl like you?"

What also helps is his deception in the bathroom. When we realize what Thornhill is up to, we can accept what came before, thinking, "So that's why he contained his anger"—because he's planning to follow her.

LEHMAN: Yes, I'm glad that works.

North by Northwest *is a classic in the thriller genre, but it also has serious underlying themes, and I'd like to ask you about two. The first is Thornhill's "remaking" himself from a smug, slick, self-absorbed Madison Avenue liar into a man who becomes extremely heroic and compassionate at the end. First, his identity is stripped away, and then all the comforts and protections of his easy, shallow life are similarly removed before he can remake himself.*

LEHMAN: Well, this may sound strange, but I wasn't consciously trying to remake him or redeem him. It happened unconsciously.

But he's so glib in the beginning . . .

LEHMAN: I know. He even steals a cab.

That's what I mean. Would he do that at the end?

LEHMAN: I don't think he would.

So he's matured. He's changed himself.

LEHMAN: Yes, as a result of his wild escapade.

But you're *the one who wrote it—the one who made him mature.*

LEHMAN: I know, but it wasn't conscious. I think I have little computers in my head that work unconsciously. And I'm glad they do. Who
knows where this stuff comes from?

*Well, maybe you'll say the same thing about the next question which relates
to the "marriage" theme in the movie. British critic Robin Wood and others
have written quite perceptively about this aspect of the film—which portrays
two shallow people, afraid of commitment, who eventually find love and, at
the very end of the picture, marriage.*

LEHMAN: Well, you know, we were forced to put in that very last line
on the train, "Come along, Mrs. Thornhill." It's actually dubbed over. If
you watch it carefully, you won't see Cary's lips moving. That was the old
production code. What a difference from today!

*Yes, but it's still a logical progression from the previous scene when Thornhill
proposes to Eve on Mount Rushmore. And that scene follows naturally from
their discussion in the woods when Eve explains how sad and pathetic her life
has been, and Thornhill asks, "How come?" and she responds, "Men like you."
But Thornhill, confused, asks, "What's wrong with men like me?" and Eve
replies, "They don't believe in marriage." Then the always-clever, twice-
divorced Thornhill says, "I've been married twice," and Eve responds, "See
what I mean?"*

LEHMAN: Yes, you're right. And that scene in the forest definitely makes
it better—it leads naturally to the ending. But I still can't honestly say that
I would've put that final line in the picture. But who knows? That was forty
years ago. All I can say is that the marriage theme rose naturally out of my
struggles with the plot, and I didn't dwell on it very much when I was
writing the script.

When North by Northwest *was released, it was a tremendous success, both
with the critics and at the box office. Then, sometime later, you and Hitchcock
began planning another film—one set at Disneyland—which had a very
intriguing premise.*

LEHMAN: Yes, and Hitch liked the idea very much. It was going to be
called *Malice in Wonderland*, and it was going to be shot—most of it—at
Disneyland. Then Walt Disney saw *Psycho*, and that was the end of that.

Could you discuss it a bit?

LEHMAN: Well, the project's still alive. Miramax has been considering it
lately. My good friend Mel Shavelson and I tortured out a screenplay called
Dancing in the Dark, based on the same basic idea, but having nothing to
do with Disneyland. We set it on a cruise ship. It's about a very popular jazz
pianist who's been sightless from birth, and he has this double-eye trans-
plant and begins to get hallucinations in which he sees someone holding a
gun that's just been fired. In his subsequent attempts to find out whose eyes

he's been given, he ends up on the *Queen Elizabeth* just as it's sailing on a cruise. It's a very good premise, and you can pitch it quite easily even though it's got a very intricate plot. Back when Hitch and I first started working on it, I felt that I didn't know how to write it properly, and since there were no offices at Paramount at the time, I stopped going to the studio, and I managed to get off the picture. Hitch was very upset that I quit. But I'd quit many other projects over the years—or said "no" to them from the beginning—and, in my opinion, I made very few mistakes.

Eventually, you and Hitchcock collaborated on his last film, Family Plot, *and then, as his health declined, you worked together on another film called* The Short Night. *I've never heard you discuss that film.*

LEHMAN: There's not much I care to remember about it. It was based on a novel called *The Short Night,* which was set in England, although we changed it, and it never got made. We were kidding ourselves that Hitch could make it. He was in no condition to go on location and shoot a film in the middle of a lake in Denmark. And maybe it was a lousy script, too.

Did you complete it?

LEHMAN: Yes, but it has bad memories for me. It's something I prefer to forget. We had a number of arguments about it. He wanted the hero to rape a woman at the beginning of the picture.

He did?

LEHMAN: Yes, and I just refused to do it. I've always wondered why he insisted on that.

That's astonishing. Was it in the novel?

LEHMAN: No. The novel started with an escape from prison. Anyway, as you can see, I have no affectionate memories about that project.

Years ago, before you came to Hollywood, you were a very successful fiction writer in New York, appearing in Esquire, Collier's, *and other prestigious magazines. Eventually, you returned to fiction, publishing your best-selling novel,* The French Atlantic Affair *in 1977. Apparently, you greatly enjoyed the freedom of fiction.*

LEHMAN: Oh, yes! It's like taking off a straitjacket. When you're a screenwriter, you're always constrained and restrained by the demands of the craft. Scenes mustn't be too long, the script mustn't be too long, and so on. It requires a great deal of craft, whereas a novelist is free to go wherever he wants.

But can't those restraints be beneficial as well as frustrating? Many writers feel that formal restraints—say a sonnet or a play—force them to be even more creative—to find new and interesting ways to meet the demands of the form. Think of North by Northwest. *It tortured you for months, but, in the end, all the restraints and requirements of the form forced you to create such an ingenious story.*

LEHMAN: That's true. I was forced into making it a better picture than it would have been if I had more freedom. I was also very fortunate to be working with Hitchcock. He once said to me, "If a director can get eighty-five percent of a writer's intentions onto the screen, the writer should consider himself very fortunate." Well, he got a hundred percent of *North by Northwest* up on the screen! And, of course, everything was enhanced by the way Hitch did it.

You've always been an eloquent proponent of the screenwriter's contribution to film creation. Do you think the status of the screenwriter has changed very much over the years?

LEHMAN: It's gone down. It's worse. We haven't gained one inch. I was the president of the Writers Guild in the eighties, and I've had a lot to say about the lack of recognition given to screenwriters. Just a few weeks ago, for example, someone sent me *The New York Observer*, which is running an essay on a classic film each week. And here's this glowing piece on *North By Northwest*. Absolutely glowing! And the author mentioned *everybody* connected with that picture, except for me—except for the screenwriter. So I wrote him a rather nasty note and told him I was disgusted. Fortunately, the note came back unopened. The post office couldn't find him. The note had been forwarded from the newspaper to his home address, but he'd moved recently and it came back to me. So, I tore it up and threw it away.

You've done it before.

LEHMAN: Yes, most recently, about a review of *Out of Sight* in *People* magazine a few issues ago. It was a rave review, but there was no goddamn mention of the screenwriter, Scott Frank. At least, they published my letter. I've got a long history of trying to rectify these oversights by the media. For my very first movie, *Executive Suite*, *Newsweek* did a cover review of the picture—the movie was on the cover of the magazine, which is very rare. There was a five-page takeout inside the magazine, and *everybody* was mentioned, but there wasn't one word about the screenwriter or the screenplay. Well, I was fresh from having bylines in well-known magazines, and I fired off a blistering telegram. Then *Newsweek* published the telegram, and, two weeks later, they published an apology. How times have changed! I've called critics at their homes. I reduced one woman to tears over *North by Northwest*, and, back when I was president of the Guild, I had a terrific exchange with Vincent Canby. He used to do those terrific Sunday pieces for *The New York Sunday Times*, and he did a piece about the longest-running film series ever, namely the James Bond pictures, and he mentioned every producer, every director, every star who'd ever played James Bond, and on and on and on, but no writers. So I wrote him a fanciful letter complaining that I was trying to watch the weekend football games on TV but my phone kept interrupting me—with writers demanding to know what I was going to do about his article. And I'd tell them, "Well, you can't change Vincent Canby! Just forget about it." So Canby printed most of my letter, and then he ran a piece the next week about all the writers who worked on the series.

Is the neglect intentional? Or, is it just the natural consequence of the focus on stars and directors?

LEHMAN: I think they know better. They know how things work out here. I don't know what their problem is, and I've never been able to figure it out. Maybe it's just writers being jealous of other writers. Underpaid writers not wanting to praise writers who can make a lot of money, or something like that. And, of course, there's always been a very snobbish attitude on the part of the East Coast literary circles toward screenwriting.

Even today?

LEHMAN: Sure. They'll act like they don't know who wrote the film. Well, can you imagine writing a review of a play and not mentioning the playwright? It's *never* happened.

That's a very good analogy. Now, how about your audiences? You've always maintained the highest respect for your audiences, and they've loved your work. What have you figured out about them?

LEHMAN: I first figured out that *I'm* an audience, and that's helped me a lot. First of all, never confuse them. The minute the viewers get confused, they start trying to figure out what they've missed. "What was that?" "What did she say?" And the movie's going by, and they're trying to play catch-up. You can be indirect in a film—as in parts of *North by Northwest*—but you have to be sure that you're getting across what you *need* to get across. Since characters can't always be explaining what they're thinking, you have to make sure that the audience knows what's going on. Maybe it isn't art, but at least the audience is with it. I also feel that audiences have to have a strong desire to know what's coming next. "What's going to happen?" If it's too amorphous and without suspense of any kind—and I'm not talking about Hitchcock suspense—you'll lose your audience. Don't let them get up and buy popcorn in the middle of your picture. They don't want to leave, so keep them there. Always keep them wanting to know what's happening next. That's very important to me. And it's also very important to convey exposition in such a way that it doesn't seem to be "exposition." For example, have characters say things that are *forced* out of them in the heat of a scene—so that it won't seem like the primary intent of the scene is just to get some information to the audience. Sometimes that's done very well, and sometimes it isn't. I've seen movies in the past year where I didn't know a goddamned thing about what I was seeing. It makes you feel stupid, and no one in the audience wants that.

In many contemporary films, there's no real development of character and virtually no backstory. It often seems like a movie actor has suddenly been dropped into a story. You have no idea who the character is or where he came from.

LEHMAN: That's right. And it's such a problem because exposition's so hard to do. It's very difficult. So either the writers don't know how to do it, or else they just say "to hell with it" since they can usually get away with it. Occasionally, I'll see a noticeably well-written picture, but most of them are poorly done.

At the Oscars in 1960, North by Northwest *lost out to* Pillow Talk *for best original screenplay—which seems quite preposterous now.*

LEHMAN: But it only seems so in retrospect. At the time, I actually won a bet about that Oscar, and I bet on *Pillow Talk* before it was even made! While the film was still in production, the columnist Sidney Skolsky came up to me one day and said, "Ernie, you're going to win the Oscar this year." And I said, "No, I'm not," and he said, "I'll bet you fifty bucks." And I said, "Fine, and I'll even tell you what's going to win: *Pillow Talk.*" I just had a gut feeling about it, and I was right.

Even though you've never won an Oscar—which seems quite amazing— you've always been very generous in your comments about the Academy.

LEHMAN: I guess so. Given all the troubles I've seen in my life, it doesn't seem that important. Of course, it's great to be nominated, and I've won more Writers Guild screenplay awards than anyone else in town. The truth is, most people don't even know that I've never won an Oscar. They just assume that I have.

Over the years, you've turned down countless pictures and you've wanted to quit all the films you worked on. You've had wars with directors, actors, producers, and film critics, yet you once said, "I had a charmed life for most of my career."

LEHMAN: Well, I'm not really sure what I meant by that, because it's not exactly accurate. I didn't have a "charmed" life.

Then you're arguing with yourself.

LEHMAN: I know. I'm always arguing with myself. Probably because underneath everything I do is the fundamental fact that I've always feared and abhorred failure. Failure is so terribly painful to me that I've worked furiously and desperately my whole life to avoid it. As a result, I've been able to accomplish many things that I wouldn't have achieved otherwise. So for me, everything was always hard, hard work—endlessly tearing up things and redoing them—doing countless versions of the same scene, over and over again. And at the same time, I was always turning down projects that I suspected didn't have much of a chance for success. I felt like I was a studio head or something—like a producer, writer, and director all rolled into one—constantly making decisions based on my overall estimate of a picture's worth—its final possibilities. I remember imploring MGM not to buy a certain novel—much less having me do it—but they bought it anyway, and made it, and it was a big flop. And, of course, *The Wreck of the Mary Deare* was another big flop when they finally made it. I'm not trying to say that I knew more than anyone else, but I did have a kind of "sense" about things. And there was also in me quite a bit of the show-off. I liked to do projects that people would be talking about while I was in the process of doing them. That's nothing to be proud of, but it's true. Like when I was doing *Who's Afraid of Virginia Woolf?* and everyone was wondering, "How the hell's he going to do that?" And I'd be thinking, "You'll see, you'll see." And people would ask, "Who's in it?" and I'd say, "Elizabeth Taylor," and they'd say, "You're crazy! You're out of your mind! It'll never work!" So, I always liked that kind of challenge—especially when people in the business were waiting to see how the hell you were going to do something.

But it was the fear that really motivated you?

LEHMAN: Yes, I was a person who always felt like he was running scared, and I took on a lot of projects that I was afraid of. I think the fear of failure was the primary motivating force in my life. I absolutely *can't* fail. Failure is terrible, awful. You can't get out from under it. The fear never goes away.

Well, the hard work paid off.

LEHMAN: And that's what counts. But what came along with it was not very pleasant. Often, I couldn't sleep at night. I'd pace back and forth in the kitchen trying to solve the next day's scene. I was a Depression kid, and I watched my father, who'd been very successful, go out of business. But he didn't give up. He got back into business, worked hard, and persisted for fifty-five years on Madison Avenue. So, I knew the benefits of hard work, but, still, the fear of failure motivated everything I've done in my life, and it came with a price—an awful lot of anxiety. So I don't know if I can agree with myself that I've had a "charmed" life, but I've certainly been very fortunate to have worked on so many good pictures and with so many talented people—like Hitch and *North by Northwest.*

Thanks, Ernie.

LEHMAN: Thank you, Bill.

CHAPTER 5

Psycho (1960)

A CONVERSATION WITH JOSEPH STEFANO

Born in Philadelphia, Joseph Stefano (1922–2006) was a musical performer, composer, and songwriter before he began writing for Hollywood and television. His feature films include *The Black Orchid* (1958) with Sophia Loren and Anthony Quinn; Hitchcock's *Psycho* (1960) with Anthony Perkins and Janet Leigh; *The Naked Edge* (1961) with Gary Cooper and Deborah Kerr; *The Kindred* (1986) with Rod Steiger; *Psycho IV: The Beginning* (1990) with Anthony Perkins; and *Two Bits* (1995) with Al Pacino. In 1998, his original screenplay for *Psycho* was used for the remake, directed by Gus Van Sant and starring Vince Vaughn and Anne Heche. From 1963–1964, he was a producer-writer for the television series *The Outer Limits*, and his various television movies include the award-winning *Made in Japan* (1959) with Dean Stockwell. He received both the Robert E. Sherwood Award and an Edgar Allan Poe Award from the Mystery Writers of America.

In his famous interview with François Truffaut, Alfred Hitchcock explained that Psycho *was undertaken as a personal and professional challenge: "Could I make a feature film under the same conditions as a television show?" Others have suggested that Hitchcock also wanted to "out-do" at the box office all those popular, low-budget horror films of the late fifties—like the ones produced by William Castle and Roger Corman—while, at the same time, making a more intelligent and astonishing film in the vein of Clouzot's* Les Diaboliques. *Were these objectives clear to you when you first became involved with the project in 1959?*

STEFANO: In our very first meeting, Hitchcock told me that he'd been impressed by a company called American International which was making movies for less than $200,000 apiece, and he was especially impressed with what the films were doing at the box office. His very words to me at the time were, "What if somebody good did one?" In putting it that way, he wasn't criticizing American International and the other low-budget production companies; he was just issuing a challenge to himself. Since he was already set up as a production company at Universal for his television series, *Alfred Hitchcock Presents,* he was in the perfect position to attempt such a project. So right from the beginning, every single consideration was guided by his idea of doing "a low-budget movie"—not really to prove anything, but simply to make a lot of money. Hitchcock's movies had always made astonishing amounts of money, but he felt that they were beginning to cost far too much to make. *North by Northwest,* which he made right before *Psycho,* starred Cary Grant and had a huge budget, and Hitchcock felt that he wasn't being appropriately rewarded financially for what he was doing. So he decided that a low-budget success would change all that.

When you first became involved with the project and read Robert Bloch's novel Psycho, *you clearly disliked the fictional Norman Bates. He was an unpleasant, obese, and balding drunk—not to mention his other problems. And you felt it was crucial to make him more sympathetic in the movie. You also felt the same way about the Mary character, later renamed Marion. Did Hitchcock agree with these changes from the start?*

STEFANO: Absolutely. My take on how to adapt this book into a movie, which I explained to Hitch in our first meeting, was that it should be about a girl who's in a dead-end love affair with a man who has serious financial problems. She loves him, but she doesn't want things to continue as they are—shacking up in cheap hotel rooms over her lunch hour whenever he can get to town. So I described to Hitch what this woman was going through in her sordid life when a wealthy, smarmy man unexpectedly walks into her office at the bank and hands her $60,000 in cash to deposit. And the temptation is just too much for Marion as she later realizes in the parlor scene with Norman. As she says to Norman, we all dig our own little traps, and when she made the decision not to deposit the money, she sealed her fate. It's a true moment of impulsive madness, but quite different from Norman Bates's madness. Norman's madness is a "convenient" madness which works to keep him out of trouble, and which also works to prevent him from confronting his ghosts. Marion's madness is more like one of those moments when somebody bumps into you on a elevator and you go temporarily mad. Marion irrationally thinks, at that moment, that she can solve all her problems by taking the money, packing her suitcase, and going to her lover and saying, "Look, everything's O.K. now," which is, of course, insane.

Since you wanted the film to begin with Marion—unlike the novel which begins with Norman—you conceived and wrote for Hitchcock the opening sequence in which a wide-angle shot pans over the Phoenix skyline, gradually moves down to a seedy hotel, enters through one of the windows, and finally finds two lovers concluding their lunch break assignation. I understand that Hitchcock was very pleased with the sequence, but that, unaccustomed to praising writers, he used his wife, Alma, as a ploy to let you know how he felt?

STEFANO: Yes, the notion of starting with Marion was my idea. And before I wrote it, I described to Hitchcock how the film would begin from a POV moving over the city, then descending into a hotel room and revealing two people shacking up during lunch hour. Hitchcock liked the idea very much, and he also liked the idea that it was initially a movie about Marion. Eventually, of course, Marion was going to be killed and taken away from the audience, and then the film would encourage the viewers to sympathize with Norman—who would turn out to be the very person who'd actually killed her. So the film, as I'd initially conceived it, had a kind of structural trick going for it that the book didn't have, and Hitch liked it very much. At the time, he was scheduled to take a two-week cruise with his wife, and he asked me to write the opening while he was gone. As soon as he got back, he took it home and read it, and the next day we had a meeting, and he said that "Alma loved it." It just wasn't his way to say it directly.

Subsequent to this, you had several weeks of story conferences with Hitchcock. Could you describe what happened at those meetings?

STEFANO: Strangely enough, we rarely talked about *Psycho* at all, but he always gave me the feeling that he somehow *knew* that I was going to write a good script which he could shoot effectively. This, of course, is the rarest gift that a producer or director can give to a writer: total confidence. So in our meetings, we rarely talked about anything specifically relating to the film. I still have my steno notebook from those meetings with maybe three pages of little odds and ends: notions that I had, or something Hitch might mention about something he didn't like, so I'd make a note of it. But most of the time, we talked about other things. He was extremely interesting, and he was a wonderful person to work with. I was in analysis at the time, and I would go to his office directly from the couch and tell him all about it. He was very interested, and he seemed delighted that I was, I guess, a different kind of animal than he'd worked with before. I was very informal and very expressive, and he seemed to enjoy that.

If, in any of those meetings, Hitchcock ever seemed distracted or disinterested, I would ask him to show me a movie, and when it was over, I'd ask him two-hours worth of questions, and he'd explain everything—even draw diagrams of things. It was quite unbelievable. I remember once asking him why he told the audience the truth about Madeleine halfway through

Vertigo, and he explained that there was nowhere else for the audience to go because they would have gotten bored if he didn't reveal the truth. And that was Hitchcock's greatest bugaboo: boredom. It was about the only thing that he was really afraid of, and I made a note of it. The whole experience was incredible. There was no place else in the world I could have gotten a better education about filmmaking. Yet, despite all that he taught me, Hitch never interfered with me as a writer. He was perfectly willing to tell me everything I wanted to know, but he clearly felt that the writing was my job. A lot of directors don't do that, but he had every confidence that I'd come in with a good script.

Was it the opening that gave him such confidence in your abilities? After all, you were a young writer at the time, a former songwriter, with only one feature film, The Black Orchid—*a family drama about Italian-Americans—to your credit.*

STEFANO: I think so. Fortunately, at our first meeting, he discovered that I had a sense of humor. I know he was a bit concerned about meeting me because he thought *The Black Orchid* was "kitchen sink" drama, and the only other thing I'd done was a *Playhouse 90—Made in Japan*—which had to do with the racial intolerance surrounding a young soldier who gets involved with a Japanese girl in occupied Japan. I guess Hitch thought it was kind of "heavy," and he actually resisted meeting me at first. This was because Hitchcock hated to say "no" to anybody. I later made the mistake of asking him to do something that he didn't want to do, and I was sorry afterwards. I asked him to look at a film that a friend of mine had made, and it was very awkward. His feeling was, "What if I don't like it?" He'd rather leave town than tell someone, even an absolute stranger, that he didn't like his movie. When I realized this, I resolved things and pressed on with the script.

When you began on the full script, were you writing it with Anthony Perkins and Janet Leigh in mind?

STEFANO: Tony Perkins, yes, but Janet Leigh wasn't locked in yet. Hitch had Perkins in mind mainly because Tony owed Paramount a picture and his price for the picture was much less than his normal rate. In one of our earliest discussions, when I was complaining about the Norman Bates character in the novel, Hitch let me go on for a while, and then finally he said, "We can get Tony Perkins." And I was delighted. I'd just seen Tony in New York during the final run-through of *Look Homeward Angel,* and when Hitchcock told me that Tony was Bates, I had this powerful image of Perkins on stage, and said to myself, "That's Norman Bates! That's exactly who I want it to be!"

Did you ever read the earlier screen adaptation done by James Cavanaugh, which Hitchcock didn't like?

STEFANO: No. I never read that screenplay. As a matter of fact, I wasn't even aware that it existed. The general Hollywood policy at the time was that the studio was supposed to inform the writer's agent that there'd been an earlier script. But very often, back then, the agent wouldn't tell the writer, and that's what happened in this case. Only much later, when somebody at Universal told me about it, did I learn there was an earlier version.

Did you know of William Pinkard's Paramount memo that described the novel as "impossible" for film adaptation?

STEFANO: Not at the time, but he was right. The novel opens with Norman having a dialogue with his "mother," and there's no way to shoot that unless you want to show that he's talking to a corpse. So the novel couldn't have been adapted as it was, not without major changes.

Did you ever look into the real-life case of Edward Gein which, in outline, was far more shocking than either the novel or the eventual movie?

STEFANO: At the time I wrote *Psycho*, I didn't know there was such a person. I didn't find out until a couple of years later when William Friedkin told me about it. He had collected all kinds of information about the real case, and he took me into his office at Universal and showed me. I had no idea that Bloch had loosely based his novel on a real person.

What did you think of the odd structural challenges of the story, particularly the peculiarity you mentioned earlier: the murder of the main character before the film's half over, and the subsequent shift from Marion's situation to Norman's problems?

STEFANO: When I first read the book, I didn't have any definite thoughts about how to deal with this. All I knew is that by page three or so, it was clear to me that I couldn't start the movie like the novel. Then on my way over to meet Hitchcock, the idea of making it into a movie about Marion Crane came to me, so I pitched it that way to Hitchcock, and I think that he instantly appreciated that I was solving the big problem with the book. I believe that every audience wants to grab onto somebody almost from the first frame; they want to care about someone. In this film, it was going to be this young woman who steals the $60,000 and then is killed unexpectedly. That was the shocker. My hope was that in the scene between Marion and Norman in the back parlor at the motel everything would be set up right for the audience to deal with the loss. During the parlor scene, when Marion learns about Norman's life, she gets a renewed perspective on herself. She sees this pathetic guy who's stuck in something he can't get out of, and she realizes that she's also in a similar situation. But she remains sympathetic to Norman, and the audience needs to feel the same way. The scene has to properly prepare the audience to like this pathetic guy because they're going to lose Marion very soon and unexpectedly.

In the real world, murders happen all the time, and nobody seems to give much of a damn about the victim, and that's why I felt it was important for the audience to like Marion and sympathize with her before she dies. Then, in the middle of the shock of her death, the audience needs to shift its sympathies to Norman who, we believe, knows that his mother committed the murder. What a horrendous situation for a young man to be in! So the audience, which already kind of likes him from the scene in the parlor—for his shyness and so on—is hopefully prepared to shift its loyalties to Norman. And it worked. If the audience could have gotten on screen and helped Norman get rid of the body, they would have done so. When the car stops sinking in the bog, there was often an audible gasp in the audience because they didn't want him to get caught. I think that's the most magical moment in the movie for Tony Perkins as an actor because of the way he stood there and chewed on that candy corn waiting for the car to go down. It was terrific. You just knew there were a lot of other cars down there!

You developed a great deal of personal sympathy for Marion as a woman motivated by love who finally realizes that she can't buy happiness, especially with stolen money. Did you feel, as Janet Leigh did, that Marion loved Sam more than he loved her?

STEFANO: Janet Leigh thought that?

Yes.

STEFANO: Well, that's right. I wanted it clear that Sam loves to come down to Phoenix and see Marion and have sex with her. But he doesn't seem to think that anything more than that is absolutely necessary. This was not such a strange thought for a man, even in 1959: "Shouldn't we both be happy? We're having sex after all." But I don't feel that Marion stole the money just for Sam; I think she felt she was in a desperate situation, and her sense of morality was giving her ulcers. She didn't think she could go on shacking up anymore—having sex on her lunch hour in sleazy hotels where the people didn't care about her when she checked in, but they wanted her to check out on time. Marion felt disposable and demeaned, and when the chance came, she tried to do something about it.

In the Truffaut interview, Hitchcock described the first part of the movie as a "red herring"—as a way of distracting the audience's "attention in order to heighten the murder." He found the film a "very interesting construction" and felt that the "game with the audience was fascinating." Did he really approach the film in that way?

STEFANO: Well, that's certainly true in the sense that Hitchcock felt that *everything* one does is a game. And he also loved theatricality. He always wanted to stimulate his audiences, and he clearly liked cinematic tricks as so many of his films have shown. He especially liked *Vertigo* because there was a great trick in it, yet, at the same time, I don't think that he was unaware of the psychological or emotional aspects of whatever he was filming. But with a number of his films before *Psycho*, like *To Catch a Thief*, for example, there's not much characterization involved, with the astounding exception of *Vertigo*. He'd gotten into what I call his "marshmallow Technicolor" period in which the characters acted just like the movie stars portraying them. They were big, lush movies—a pleasure to watch—and you could sense the good time they all had making them, but there wasn't much depth. Then just before *Psycho*, with *North by Northwest*, Hitchcock got back to his strengths again. He put a man in such a harrowing situation that it would make you scream if you were in it, and then made the man work through it somehow. In a way, this is what Marion was also trying to do. She was trying to work through this awful situation she was in, but she just happened to end up in the wrong place at the wrong time. So *Psycho* had both the Hitchcock tricks as well as the depth of some of his earlier films.

One of the many themes in Psycho *is voyeurism, most clearly portrayed by Norman's looking through his peephole as Marion undresses for the shower. Many critics feel that the film is not only an indictment of voyeurism in general, but a specific indictment of the voyeurism of movie viewers—what Hitchcock called "Peeping Tom audiences." The film seems to manipulate the viewer into rooting for a thief—hoping she'll escape from the policeman, for example—and then shifts the viewer's allegiance to the seemingly pathetic soul who covers up her murder—going so far, as you've mentioned, to hope that the car with Marion's corpse will sink completely into the swamp. The film's clever manipulation of audience identification seems to make the viewer unusually involved and even complicit in the main characters' guilt. How do you feel about all this?*

STEFANO: That's true right up until the murder, but then the audience, amazingly, forgets completely about Marion. One reason that we're so quick to nullify the victim is because we can't stand the thought of the death and loss, so the best thing to do is turn our attention elsewhere. I became even more aware of this after the film was made, and I watched it with a general audience. Despite our previous concern for Marion, we don't want to worry about her dead body, and we're ready to move on. In a more general sense, I think a fundamental essence of watching films is voyeuristic because we intrude so deeply into the characters' lives—while sitting in the dark. It's not necessarily sexual, although it can be, but its power to involve us with the characters is incredible. The very first movie that I can recall seeing was Greta Garbo's version of *Anna Karenina* where she dies at the end. As a child, I was horribly upset because I thought that Garbo had actually died, so my mother had to explain that she was just pretending to die. That helped a lot, but I was still greatly affected. The intimate situations that we watch movie characters deal with are utterly personal, and the more personal, the more successful the film. Hitchcock clearly understood this basis aspect of film, and he knew how to exploit it.

In adapting the novel, you made quite a few significant changes— beginning the film in Phoenix, eliminating Norman's interest in the occult, showing the shower murder in detail, substituting the telling piece of ripped paper for an earring, having "Mother" confront the insurance detective at the top of the stairs rather than at the front door, and so on. I'd like to ask you about a few others. One was using the voice-overs to let the audience know what Marion was thinking as she was driving away from Phoenix.

STEFANO: One day, when we were talking about the film, I said to Hitch, "It's a shame that we don't have time to show what's happened back in Phoenix," and he said, "Yes, it would really be something to show how they're all reacting back in the city." So I thought, what if we did it— what if I wrote those scenes as *Marion* might have imagined them. This was especially enjoyable because Marion could give her own characteriza- tions of the people she left behind—like the wealthy guy who made a pass at her who she now imagines is saying that he'll get his revenge on "her fine soft flesh," and so on. Of course, it's something we all do. We leave a party, and we wonder what they're saying about us now that we're gone— a kind of fantasizing. So I wrote up those scenes, then cut down the dia- logue, and then we used them as voice-overs. For *Psycho*, as I always do, I wrote many scenes which didn't appear in the final screenplay, and, in this case, they turned out to be especially useful.

In the later parts of the novel, there's clearly a romance blossoming between Marion's lover, Sam, and her sister, Lila, but it's not really there in the movie?

STEFANO: Yes, I felt that would be distracting, but I also didn't want to do that to Marion. I didn't want to show Sam meeting with her, loving her on whatever level he loved her, having sex with her, and then, as soon as she's killed, just turning around and saying, "I wonder if there are any more like her at home?" I felt it was too cheap and crappy, and I always appreci- ated the fact that neither Vera Miles nor John Gavin ever gave any indication of a romantic attraction in their performances. Even though it wasn't actually in the script, actors could still project it anyway—with a look or gesture. But Vera and John didn't, and I was very grateful. Ironically, the only scene that Hitch cut from the screenplay was a three-minute scene in one of the motel rooms between the sister and the lover where they finally realize that Mari- on's really dead. They've both lost somebody very important in their lives, and it's a moving scene, but Hitch felt that it slowed the narrative down too much for the audience. I don't think he would cut that scene today.

At the very end of the movie, the psychiatrist attempts to explain Norman's condition, whereas in the novel, Sam and Lila speculate on Norman's problems.

STEFANO: Yes, I didn't feel that they would know enough to explain things properly. Not only weren't they aware of many things, but where would they get all the technical information? On the other hand, I felt it was absolutely necessary to have things explained to the audience. I never believed the film should end with Norman weeping in the cellar, and the audience going, "Oh, it's Norman!" Then blackout, "The End." The audience, I believe, would feel cheated and unresolved, so I had the film shift quickly to the authorities. I also didn't want Sam and Lila driving off in his truck and talking things over because I wanted to keep the audience within the world of the crimes, and the subsequent legalities as well, in order to help them resolve their feelings.

But that scene, as you know, is probably the most criticized aspect of a movie that's generally considered an overall masterpiece. How do you feel about that now?

STEFANO: My own opinion is that the problem with the scene is the way it was performed by the very actor that I recommended for the part! Simon Oakland orated the scene which wasn't at all how I'd envisioned the psychiatrist explaining things. My feeling was that the police had already given this doctor all the facts, and that he'd talked to Norman, and that he'd put it all together. But Simon did stuff that was a little too broad for the role, and Hitch was always afraid that the scene was what he called a "hat grabber." But I disagreed. No one was going to grab his hat. Everyone wanted to know what happened. It just need to be performed a bit more naturally.

I read somewhere that Hitchcock required only one sequence rewritten from your original screenplay and that was making the highway cop less flirtatious and more threatening?

STEFANO: Yes, I originally had him as a sort of charming guy who was coming on to Marion. Hitch originally liked the idea, but then he felt it wasn't right for this particular movie because he needed the cop to be more threatening. And he was right because we needed the audience to feel frightened that the cop would pull Marion in and catch her with the stolen money. The irony, of course, is that later you realize that you were frightened about something that would have saved her life.

One of the great peculiarities of the script is that Marion goes through with the car transfer even though she knows the policeman is watching her. The English critic Robin Wood suggests the reason is that Marion, in her theft of the $60,000, has lost control of herself—that she's gone a "little mad" as Norman puts it later. Is that correct?

STEFANO: Absolutely. I also used it as a way to show that, at this point at least, absolutely nothing can stop Marion from proceeding with things. If she can't stop the transaction of the car when a cop is watching her, then she clearly doesn't have the sense to get into her car and drive back to Phoenix. At that point in her flight, Marion *should* have turned around, gone home, and deposited the money where it was supposed to be. But she can't. She's lost control. She can only dig herself in deeper and deeper.

After her talk with Norman about the "traps" that human beings get caught in, Marion finally decides to undo what she's done, drive back to Phoenix, and return the stolen money. Then she goes to her motel room and symbolically washes away her guilt in the purifying, baptismal waters of the shower. In the Truffaut interview, the French director asked Hitchcock, "What was it that attracted you to the novel?" and Hitchcock replied, "I think that the thing that appealed to me and made me decide to do the picture was the suddenness of the murder in the shower, coming, as it were, out of the blue. That was about all." But there's very little detail about the shower murder in the novel.

STEFANO: That's right, there's just a few lines at the end of the third chapter. Mary, the Marion character, is in the shower, the door opens, a butcher knife appears, and it cuts off her head. That last part was especially appalling and unbelievable—the murderer cutting off her head. If Bloch had said, "stabbed her and stabbed her and stabbed her," I would have been sickened enough by it, but to cut off her head was way too much, not to mention unlikely, since I'm sure it isn't very easy to cut off someone's head with a single blow.

The shower scene is one of the most famous scenes in motion picture history, and it's probably been analyzed more times than the famous "Odessa Steps" sequence from Bronenosets Potemkin. *On the set, Hitchcock broke from his fast-paced, low-budget schedule, and spent seven full days shooting this single scene, using over seventy camera setups for forty-five seconds on the screen. Were you aware, while you were writing the script, of the attention that would be paid to this one scene by the director?*

STEFANO: Naturally, I knew that it was a crucial scene in the movie, but I also knew that there was no way that I could actually write out in the screenplay everything that we wanted to show on the screen. So Hitchcock and I, despite his usual reticence about discussing the picture, talked about the shower scene at great length, especially the absolute terror of being naked and wet when you're suddenly attacked, completely helpless, and unable to defend yourself. Nevertheless, despite all our discussions, when I actually watched the scene being shot I was amazed that Hitch was doing so many setups. The original shooting schedule gave no indication of a seven-day shoot, and everything had been carefully arranged by Hitchcock to make it look like a single afternoon of filming. Naturally, there was a great deal of secrecy surrounding the scene, and Hitch didn't want anybody to know a damn thing about it—or the rest of the movie for that matter. Very early on, he'd told me point blank that he didn't want me to discuss the picture with anyone. Not exactly in those words, but his meaning was clear. So when people would say, "I hear you're writing a movie for Hitchcock?" I'd have to say, "Well, it's not really settled yet," or something evasive like that.

Since you were on the set almost every day of shooting, I wonder if you could resolve a few long-standing questions about that famous scene? For example, did Saul Bass, who did the storyboards for the scene, actually direct any of it?

STEFANO: I truly don't understand that bizarre story. In all honestly, Saul Bass's claim that he directed the shower scene is the most shocking thing I've ever heard about the making of *Psycho*. We all knew, of course, that he'd been assigned to design the storyboards, which he did and did well. So maybe in some peculiar way, he came to believe that by doing the storyboards, he'd somehow "directed" the scene, which is, of course, nonsense. I was there every day for seven days, and Hitchcock directed every shot. Ironically, one of my favorite memories of the making of the film is Hitch standing next to the shower calmly directing the naked model that he'd brought in so Janet Leigh wouldn't have to perform in the nude.

Were any shots of the body double, Marli Renfro, used in the final cut?

STEFANO: I'm not sure. I don't think that there's anything shown in the scene that couldn't have been Janet Leigh. It seems to me that we were on Janet's face and shoulders most of the time in the scene, so I'm not quite sure where the model is—if she's there at all.

Does the knife actually touch the flesh? Hitchcock told Truffaut and many others that "the knife never touched the body," but Donald Spoto, in The Darker Side of Genius: The Life of Alfred Hitchcock, *claims that one of Hitchcock's two important additions to the Bass layout was "the quick shot of the knife entering the woman's abdomen." The film itself seems to bear out Spoto's contention.*

STEFANO: I don't know, but I never saw that kind of special effect shot being done on the set. I know there's definitely a shot in the film where it looks like the knife touches and penetrates, but I'm not sure. I don't think Hitch would have been satisfied with a retractable knife or a fake torso. He certainly wasn't shy about artificial things, but I don't think he would have done it for this particular scene.

Despite the unforgettable horror of Marion's murder and some critics' musings about its abject meaninglessness, the scene seems to have two important meanings for someone with Hitchcock's Jesuit training. One is that Marion has been punished for her crime in the very way that she imagined earlier in the car—with her "fine soft flesh." Second, and more important, is that Marion dies repentant of her crime and seemingly purified—which makes her even more sympathetic to the audience and heightens her terrible tragedy. How do you feel about that?

STEFANO: Yes, that's true. During her talk with Norman in the parlor, Marion realizes how trapped the young man is, and she decides to escape her own predicament, and I think that's why the audience cares so much about her. At the time I wrote the screenplay, I was very upset by all the supposedly "meaningless" murders that were happening in our society, and I couldn't bring myself to see how *any* murder of a human being could be meaningless. As for Hitchcock's attitudes, I must admit that I've never really thought about it before, but Hitchcock and I definitely came from similar religious backgrounds. I was raised a Catholic, and although I'd left the faith, so to speak, we both had a similar moral sense, and, for both of us, it seemed much more terrible—and affecting—for someone to be killed after she's finally gotten back on the right track and washed herself clean.

I wonder if we could also talk about the other classic scene of terror in the movie: the death of the detective?

STEFANO: Hitch and I had quite a few long talks about that scene too, since it's so crucial that the audience continues to believe that "mother" is mother. In the novel, "mother" comes down the stairs and kills the detective at the front door. So I suggested that we reverse things and follow Marty Balsam *up* the stairs and then keep the camera rising up to a high crane shot before "mother" comes out at the top of the stairs. Then things would happen so fast that the audience would *think* that they'd actually seen the old woman as she stabs the detective and knock him down the stairs. And Hitch liked the idea very much, and he felt that it would work, but he was worried because it would cost him about $25,000 to build the crane into the set. In the end, he finally decided to do it, and the scene was very successful. Many people who saw the finished picture were absolutely convinced that they'd seen Norman's mother in the scene, but, of course, they only saw the top of her head.

Along with these powerful moments of terror, the film is full of many themes and key images that delineate the characters—for example, the notion of secrets (everyone has one), voyeurism, the stuffed birds, and the countless mirrors. Late in the film, when Lila is exploring Norman's room, a number of specific details help define Norman's character. One is a book with a blank cover which Lila opens up and stares at just before the film cuts away from her face. One critic has wondered if it's a "family album," but in the novel, it's a book with "almost pathologically pornographic" illustrations. Was this dropped in deference to the more sympathetic portrayal of Norman in the film, or was it just too hard to relay to the audience?

STEFANO: Well, I wanted the audience to see Norman as a suffocated young man who constantly seeks sexual stimulation, but I didn't want it to come from pathological pornography—maybe just pictures of women in corsets or something like that. So it was definitely muted from the novel. Another detail in that same scene is the record of Beethoven's *Eroica,* which Hitchcock got very excited about. He felt it was a very telling detail. There was, I can remember, a lot of tightrope walking in constructing that scene in screenplay format. I needed to quickly convey a few things about Norman that were further indications that something was quite wrong, but it couldn't be spelled out or overdone.

After the film was edited by George Tomansini and scored with the masterful music of Bernard Herrmann, Hitchcock was apparently worried about Psycho's *commercial possibilities and even considered cutting it down to an hour for his television show. Were you aware of this at the time?*

STEFANO: No, I never heard him say anything like that. As a matter of fact, when he showed me the first rough cut, I was quite disturbed, and he patted my knee and said, "Don't worry, it's just a rough cut." It looked terrible—like all rough cuts look—but this was only the second one I'd ever seen, and the editor had put in absolutely everything. There were tremendously long pauses, and all kinds of crap that was gone by the next time I saw it. When I did see the second cut, I knew it was a good movie, but a "good movie" in the sense that *Laura* was a good movie: just one of those dark movies that it's nice to have in your credits.

Despite some initial panning by a number of film reviewers, Psycho *proved to be an enormous success with audiences—eventually turning an investment of $800,000 into over $20 million in profits. But in the wake of the film, many people felt that the career of the film's star, Anthony Perkins, was greatly damaged by the inevitable stereotyping. Did this happen to you as well?*

STEFANO: Absolutely, throughout the sixties and seventies, I was always being offered the "new" *Psycho,* and I seldom had a chance to write other kinds of pictures. I guess the size of the reaction to that kind of movie is just too huge. It blocks out everything else. Then I also made my own mistake, if any of this can be called a mistake, by becoming a producer and writer for *The Outer Limits* not long after *Psycho.* That put the final nail in the coffin. I remember a few years later, I was able to write a movie for CBS called *A Death of Innocence* with Shelley Winters about a woman who discovers that her daughter, who's been charged with murder, *really* is guilty. It was a deep, heartfelt kind of movie, and about two days after it was aired, I went to a meeting at CBS on some other matter, and everyone there was talking about the fact that the ratings for the movie were fantastic and that everybody thought it was wonderful picture. Then someone said something nice about the script, and I said, "Thank you." But the man looked at me strangely, so I said that I'd written the screenplay, and he said, almost reflexively, "No, you didn't." It was quite a blow to realize that even when I'd done something completely different from *Psycho*—and very successfully—people still couldn't accept it. I really didn't know that people in the industry still had such narrow mind-sets. It was like the casting of the studio movies in the thirties and the forties—where the character actors always did the same thing in every picture. Well, that was how Hollywood continually stereotyped certain established screenwriters.

Aside from Psycho, *you also wrote the original treatment for* Marnie *when Grace Kelly was still involved in the project. But then Hitchcock did* The Birds, *and you began producing and writing the very popular television show* The Outer Limits. *Is that why you were unable to do the script for* Marnie?

STEFANO: Yes, Hitch put it on the shelf when Kelly dropped out, and when he decided to use Tippi Hedren, he called me up, but I was in production on *The Outer Limits*, and there was no way I could get out of it. So Hitchcock went ahead with Jay Presson Allen, and I was very disappointed that she made some key changes from the book which I'm surprised Hitchcock went along with. His original fascination with that book was the triangle among the young woman who steals, her husband, and her psychiatrist. But Allen unfortunately decided to combine the two male characters into one. Nevertheless, I still like the film quite a bit.

In discussing Alfred Hitchcock for Janet Leigh's 1995 book about the making of Psycho, *you said of the director, "I don't think he ever recovered from* Psycho." *Why do you feel this way?*

STEFANO: I think he felt that, in a strange way, he'd made a movie that trapped him inside his TV persona. I don't know this to be a fact, but it's just how I see it. Audiences loved him on the TV show, and they wanted more *Psycho*. So he decided to make *The Birds*, but I felt that the birds themselves were not a good enough killer. Since I still had a two-picture deal with Hitchcock, I turned down the assignment for *The Birds*, and he picked a novelist to do it. *Marnie* was the picture I wanted to write, but he had to postpone it after Grace Kelly backed out of it. He was very angry about that at the time. I never saw him so pissed off at anyone. He was very hurt, and that's the worst kind of pissed off to be when you hurt, too.

What do you make of Hitchcock's numerous remarks that Psycho *was made in "fun." He said that "You have to remember that* Psycho *was made with quite a sense of amusement on my part. To me, it's a fun picture. The process through which we take the audience, you see, [is] rather like taking them through the haunted house at the fairground." What do you make of that? The humorous* Psycho *trailer seems to reinforce the idea.*

STEFANO: That trailer was written by the same guy who wrote all Hitchcock's intros for the TV show. Hitch liked this persona so much because the public liked it, and it made him a star. The truth is, Hitch was not very well treated by the Hollywood establishment, even though he'd clearly found a niche for himself, so he greatly enjoyed the public's adulation—and he wasn't about to give it up. So he did the tongue-in-cheek trailer for *Psycho*, just liked he did with the TV productions. It was all part of Hitchcock trapping himself within his television persona, but the movie itself is another matter. He might have had fun making it, but he took it seriously.

Speaking of humor, is it true that Hitchcock received a letter from a man complaining that his daughter wouldn't take a bath after seeing Les Diaboliques *and wouldn't take a shower after seeing* Psycho, *so Hitchcock suggested that the man have his daughter "dry-cleaned"?*

STEFANO: I've heard the story! But I'm not sure if it's true.

Does it sound like Hitchcock?

STEFANO: It definitely sounds like him, but I can't picture him actually responding to the letter. But who knows?

Despite Hitchcock's well-known sense of humor, Psycho *clearly represents a significant shift in the vision of his films. It's definitely a much darker vision where violence is shown in all its horror and were sexuality is implied in an unprecedented manner. There have been many theories as to why this happened when it did—some critics have even suggested that it was the result of his difficulties with some of his leading ladies—but you once suggested that it was really the result of the famous director's struggle to deal with his own mortality. Could you discuss this?*

STEFANO: Yes. The year before he made *Psycho*, both Hitch and his wife had been quite ill, and he'd had a very serious surgery and lost a lot of weight. At the time we were working on *Psycho*, he hardly looked like the Hitchcock that we're all familiar with. It's very possible that this affected his overall vision, but, at the same time, I've always felt that his primary motive for making *Psycho* was the desire to make a successful, low-budget movie in which he could share heavily in the profits. Despite all his success, Hitchcock had money problems, and he wanted to feel more financially secure.

Whatever Hitchcock's motives, critics have compared Psycho *with the Orestia,* Macbeth, Crime and Punishment, *and Conrad's "The Heart of Darkness." Richard Schickel has described the film as "one of the crucial cultural artifacts of this era," and Donald Spoto has called it "one of the great works of modern American art." Why do you think that this low-budget, unpretentious masterpiece of cinematic horror continually inspires such serious commentary?*

STEFANO: I really don't know. I think it might have been a case of timing. It might have appealed to the public so much because they felt that it was saying something no one else had articulated yet. Important pieces often become so because they say something that no one else has managed to express. With *Psycho*, it might have been a heightened sense of mortality, societal violence, and moral responsibility. It was very unsettling to an audience to see a film where the star—one they'd come to care for—suddenly is killed halfway through the picture. Just a few years after the film came out, Americans were astonished and horrified by the much-publicized death of Kitty Genovese in New York City where she was attacked, yelled out for help, and nobody did anything—even though many people heard her chilling, desperate cries. It was very upsetting, and it made everyone reconsider violence in our society and our responses to it. Maybe *Psycho* did something similar to audiences. Maybe it touched a nerve—and still does. I think the film aroused in the audience some of the guilt we would all later face when we heard about Kitty Genovese and wondered what *we* would have done if we'd heard her calls for help. Maybe *Psycho* makes us think about similar things, even subconsciously, "I heard the girl screaming for help, and I didn't do anything. Then I saw him bury the car, and I didn't do anything. And then I didn't think about her very much anymore—even though she was a human being and one I cared for." Maybe the public was ready for that in 1960. All I know is that people still feel compelled to talk to me about that film, especially Marion's death in the shower. And not only do they talk about it, but they seem to *need* to talk about it. It's necessary somehow, and maybe that's what we're all responding to.

Thank you very much.

STEFANO: Thank you, Bill.

CHAPTER 6

Hud (1963)

A CONVERSATION WITH IRVING RAVETCH AND HARRIET FRANK, JR.

The distinguished screenwriting team of Irving Ravetch and Harriet Frank, Jr., first met as young writers at MGM and were married in 1946. Irving Ravetch, born in Newark, New Jersey, was an aspiring playwright who'd attended UCLA before coming to MGM. Harriet Frank, Jr., was born and raised in Portland, Oregon, but eventually attended UCLA while her mother was working as a Hollywood story editor. After their marriage, the Ravetches worked independently for over ten years before beginning their first collaboration on Martin Ritt's *The Long, Hot Summer* (1958) starring Paul Newman and Joanne Woodward. This experience initiated a remarkable series of collaborations with Martin Ritt that extended over eight films and included: *Hud* (1963), starring Paul Newman and Patricia Neal, for which the Ravetches were nominated for an Academy Award; *Hombre* (1967), also with Paul Newman; *Norma Rae* (1979), featuring Sally Field, for which the Ravetches received their second Oscar nomination; and *Stanley and Iris* (1990) starring Robert De Niro and Jane Fonda. They also wrote various scripts for other directors, including an adaptation of William Inge's *The Dark at the Top of the Stairs* (1960), directed by Delbert Mann and starring Robert Preston and Dorothy McGuire; an adaptation of William Faulkner's *The Reivers* (1969), directed by Mark Rydell and featuring Steve McQueen; and *The Cowboys* (1972), also directed by Mark Rydell and starring John Wayne.

After graduating from UCLA at different times, you both ended up at MGM. How did you actually meet?

RAVETCH: Harriet was in the Junior Writers' Program, and I was writing shorts for the studio, things like "Crime Doesn't Pay." Then one day, I saw this beautiful, radiant, young woman walking down the hallway toward her office. So I went to the guy in the office next to hers, and I said, "I'll give you fifty dollars if you'll trade offices." So we made the deal—he was one of the studio lawyers, not one of the writers—and I immediately went to "work" on L. B. Mayer's time!

And it worked.

FRANK: It *definitely* did! Any man who comes into your office every morning and reads you *The New York Times* is the man you have to marry.

RAVETCH: It not only worked, it's worked for over fifty-five years!

You were married in 1946, but you worked independently in Hollywood for over ten years until you finally collaborated on a script in 1957 when producer Jerry Wald approved your proposal to adapt William Faulkner's novel The Hamlet. *Is that correct?*

FRANK: That's right. Jerry Wald was very serious about doing "serious" films, especially literary adaptations. So we began writing the script using both *The Hamlet* and Faulkner's short story "Barn Burning" as starting points, but, in the end, we created mostly new material, so it wasn't really a true adaptation.

Why did you suggest to Jerry Wald that Martin Ritt be chosen to direct the film, which was eventually titled The Long, Hot Summer *and starred Paul Newman and Joanne Woodward?*

RAVETCH: I'd met Marty in the New York office of Audrey Wood, who was a well-known agent back then. I'd gone to New York for the production of one of my plays, which, unfortunately, had turned out disastrously. Marty had been a member of the Group Theater, and he was one of the founding members of the Actors Studio. Recently, he'd directed his first film, *Edge of the City*, with John Cassavetes and Sidney Poitier. So when I got back to Los Angeles, Jerry asked me to suggest a director for *Long, Hot Summer*. He definitely wanted somebody young and creative and promising, and he finally said, "You pick the director, Irving." So I remembered Marty, and that's how it happened.

After the success of The Long, Hot Summer *(1958), you wrote your second film for Martin Ritt, an adaptation of Faulkner's* The Sound and the Fury *(1959). Then you wrote screenplays for Vincente Minnelli* (Home from the Hill, *1960) and Delbert Mann* (The Dark at the Top of the Stairs, *1960). How did you come upon the source material for your next film, Larry McMurtry's first novel,* Horseman, Pass By?

RAVETCH: I found the book in a bookstore, took it home, and read it. Then I asked Harriet to read it.

FRANK: It's a beautifully written book. McMurtry was very young at the time, and it was clear that he was a very gifted writer.

RAVETCH: And since we'd enjoyed working with Marty and Paul so much, we wanted to do it again, and we thought the book could be adapted in such a way as to create a leading role for Paul. So we acquired the rights to the book.

Before we get to the specifics about writing Hud, *I'd like to ask you about your approach to literary adaptation and literary collaboration. First, let's talk about adaptation. In the past, you've referred to your scripts based on other literary sources as being more like "hybrids" than adaptations.*

RAVETCH: Yes, very much so. *The Long, Hot Summer*, for example, was probably 95 percent ours and only 5 percent Faulkner. *The Hamlet*'s a marvelous book—brilliant and hysterical—and Faulkner's "Barn Burning" is one of the great American short stories, but in actually writing the film, we basically took one of the characters from the novel, altered him drastically, and then created a new story around him. On the other hand, *The Reivers*, which we did many years later, is almost entirely from the book. It's 100 percent Faulkner because we found it readily adaptable to film. So our approach to adaptations, whether it be Faulkner or someone else, really runs the gamut because it's always crucial to focus on what's best for the film.

Faulkner, who was a screenwriter himself, seemed to understand that approach since he called The Long, Hot Summer *a "charmin' little movie."*

RAVETCH: Well, I'm glad to hear that. Faulkner is absolutely our favorite novelist of all American novelists, and we always worried that he might have hated what we did in *The Long, Hot Summer*.

FRANK: Faulkner's definitely America's glorious writer, but you're right. He knew all about screen adaptation. He'd worked with Howard Hawks, and he worked on the screen adaptation of Hemingway's *To Have and To Have Not*, so he knew from personal experience that film and fiction are two very different mediums.

So how do you collaborate? How do you actually go about creating a script together?

FRANK: First, we talk out an outline, and since we want to stay married, we talk it out very amiably. At that point, we're not laying out an absolute chapter-and-verse for every single moment in the screenplay; we're, instead, creating large blocks of organization, so we can visualize the line of the story, and get ready to go. We usually start with a one-page outline listing about thirty-five to forty-five major scenes.

Irving once said that "The script is not so much written as it's talked onto the page."

FRANK: That's right. That's how we do it. Once we're ready to begin, we start "talking" the screenplay to each other. Out loud. It's a line-for-line conversation. In truth, we get so involved that we can't even tell who starts a line or who finishes it. It's a very animated, running conversation where we act out the lines—Irving's a very good actor and I'm not!—along with a running commentary like, "That's good," or "That's lousy," or "Why not try this?"

RAVETCH: And there's *no* ego involved. None. Over the years, we've heard about a number of other collaborators who do a lot of screaming at each other, but we never raise our voices.

FRANK: We want to stay married!

RAVETCH: Yes, but as conscientious writers, we can't let our egos get in the way; otherwise, it will start to interfere with the work and ruin it.

FRANK: And from many years of experience, I can tell you that Irving is *never* a man of ego. He's *never* aggressively critical, although, if he hates something, he's very honest and plainspoken. So we have none of that push-me-pull-me business. We work things out amicably, and we don't waste time arguing.

RAVETCH: Who was that married couple at Metro who collaborated on so many scripts? They did *The Thin Man* and *It's a Wonderful Life.*

FRANK: Hackett and Goodrich.

RAVETCH: Yes, Frances Goodrich and Albert Hackett. Apparently, they also had a seamless and unegotistical collaboration.

So who types the script?

RAVETCH: I do. I sit at the typewriter, and Hank paces around. We always work in the mornings, nine to one, five days a week. Usually, we'd get about three pages done each day, and those pages are *finished* pages. We'd polish them as we go, over and over again, doing our revising as we proceed. So when we're finished, we're *really* finished. We very seldom do any revising.

How long does a script usually take?

FRANK: About ten weeks.

Now the McMurtry project, which was eventually titled Hud, *was the first film in a three-picture deal for the newly-formed Salem Pictures, which was established by Martin Ritt and Paul Newman in agreement with Paramount and Columbia. Were you partners in Salem Pictures?*

RAVETCH: No, we weren't.

But Irving was listed as a producer on the film?

RAVETCH: Well, you know that Hollywood is always pretty loose with the term "producer." All I did was find the source material.

But I think you're being too modest. The whole idea for the picture came from the both of you. Weren't you involved in the casting?
RAVETCH: Yes, Marty always kept us with him, from the beginning to the end.

FRANK: Yes, he truly embraced us as collaborators. It was a very unusual relationship. Just glorious!

Let's talk about that relationship.
RAVETCH: We made eight films with Marty Ritt, and on every single one of those pictures, we were with Marty from the preproduction and casting to the final advertising campaign. We were also on the set every single day, and he invited us to the rushes every single morning. It was a *true* collaboration, and we always had a marvelous time. Marty Ritt was an extraordinary man in many ways, and unlike most directors, he never insisted on a vanity credit.

FRANK: That's right, Marty's films never opened with the credit, "Film by Martin Ritt." Never. He was a class act, and he was never concerned with ego.

RAVETCH: And he was always willing to try something new, something "difficult."

Well, Hud *was certainly a unique picture in many ways, but, most significantly, it dared to portray a central character who was a "pure bastard"—and who remained totally unredeemed and unrepentant at the end of the picture.*
RAVETCH: Yes, we sensed a change in American society back then. We felt that the country was gradually moving into a kind of self-absorption, and indulgence, and greed—which, of course, fully blossomed in the eighties and the nineties. So, we made Hud a greedy, self-absorbed man, who ruthlessly strives for things, and gains a lot materially, but really loses everything that's important. But he doesn't care. He's still unrepentant.

FRANK: In our society, there's always been a fascination with the "charming" villain, and we wanted to say that if something's corrupt, it's still corrupt, no matter how charming it might seem—even if it's Paul Newman with his beautiful blue eyes. But things didn't work out like we planned.

It actually backfired.
RAVETCH: Yes, it did, and it was a terrible shock to all of us. Here's a man—Hud—who tries to rape his housekeeper, who wants to sell his neighbors' poisoned cattle, and who stops at nothing to take control of his father's property. And all the time, he's completely unrepentant. Then, at the first screenings, the preview cards asked the audiences, "Which

character did you most admire?'' and many of them answered, ''Hud.'' We were completely astonished. Obviously, audiences *loved* Hud, and it sent us into a tailspin. The whole point of all our work on that picture was apparently undone because Paul was so charismatic.

Paul Newman actually took much of the blame on himself, feeling that he'd portrayed Hud as far too vital and appealing and charming. But Martin Ritt disagreed, saying that the film clearly revealed Hud for exactly what he was, and denying that any of the film's creators could have possibly anticipated the rising cynicism of the baby-boom generation. How do you feel about that?

RAVETCH: I think they were both right, and both innocent. We could have never anticipated the reaction of those audiences, especially the young people, and if we *had* known beforehand, we would have definitely done things differently.

That was a time when young people were looking for rebels to emulate.

FRANK: That's right.

RAVETCH: That's true, but Hud's more than just a bit rebellious. He's truly villainous. But, of course, that's the way things have gone in our society. In many movies today, there's a stream of endless violence and murder and high-tech fireballs, and the young audiences are eagerly clapping, and laughing, and banging their feet. They love it. So what have we created? What kind of society is that? Back in the early sixties, we knew something was in the air, but we never could have anticipated what's come to pass.

In McMurtry's novel, Hud's a minor and infrequently seen character, so one of the key changes in the script is the expansion of Hud's role. Was that alteration made to accommodate Paul Newman?

RAVETCH: Yes, we were specifically trying to create material that would interest both Paul and Marty. So we enlarged the character of Hud and wrote the part with Paul in mind.

Many critics have drawn comparisons between Hud *and* Shane *since, in both films, a young boy is attracted to a charismatic man. Shane, of course, despite his past, is an admirable Western hero, but Hud is not, and young Lon must decide whether he will be lured into the immoral but seemingly exciting lifestyle of Hud, or whether he'll eventually side with his grandfather, Homer Bannon, a man of high integrity and old-fashioned values. Was it a complete coincidence that the role of Lon was played by Brandon de Wilde who'd also played the part of Joey Starrett, the young boy in* Shane?

RAVETCH: I never thought about that before.

FRANK: I don't think it ever crossed our minds.

RAVETCH: I can certainly see that there's lots of parallels in the two stories, but the casting of Brandon in *Hud* was just a coincidence. He was the
only young actor we could find who we felt was right for the part.

FRANK: Brandon was a very gifted young actor and an elegant young
man, but he died soon afterwards. He was killed in a car accident on a slick,
rainy road. It was dreadful.

*As you were tightening up McMurtry's novel, you made a number of other
significant changes. For example, Hud is now the son of Homer Bannon, not
just his son-in-law; Homer is still a widower, eliminating the role of Lon's
grandmother; and the role of Jesse, the former rodeo rider, is greatly diminished.
An even more important change is the metamorphosis of Halmea, the black
housekeeper, into Alma, the laconic, worldly-wise, and very sensual white housekeeper played so perfectly by Patricia Neal. Why did you make that change?*

FRANK: We would have loved to keep her black for the movie. She has
moral strength, she's benevolent, she's tough-minded, and she's secure in herself. So we would have loved to say to the world, "Look, here's a hell of a
woman, and she's black," but in those days you simply couldn't do it, and not
because the talent wasn't there, there were at least a half-dozen powerhouse
black actresses who could have played that role. But the times weren't ready
for it yet, and it was, of course, further complicated by the attempted rape.

RAVETCH: We also wanted to enrich the character by making her more
of an antagonist for Hud—a protagonist, really—than she was in the novel.
And we wanted to do that by creating a kind of romantic possibility
between them, a dark romantic possibility. And neither American film nor
American society was quite ready for that back then.

FRANK: But fortunately for us, we had this extraordinary actress, Patricia
Neal, waiting in the wings. Until then, everyone thought of Patricia as special-
izing in those mean-spirited, raffish, high society ladies she'd played in most of
her pictures—with fox furs and bourbon—like her role in *Breakfast at Tif-
fany's* with Audrey Hepburn. But I told Irving and Marty, "Believe me, she'll
be absolute hell-on-wheels in this movie." And they said, "But she's too elegant," and I said, "Trust me." And they did, and Patricia came in, kicked off
her shoes, rolled up her sleeves, took off her makeup, and instantly transformed into Alma—generous, intense, womanly, earthy, and intelligent.

She was perfect.

FRANK: Yes, she was, but when she first read the script, she said, "Well,
it's not a very big part." Then later, when she won the Academy Award,
she sent us a wire saying, "It's big enough!"

*Alma's an excellent counterpart to Hud, who, as his father clearly states, is
an "unprincipled man." But in the novel, Hud's even worse, and I'd like to
ask you about two important changes that you made in the script. The first is*

the fact that in the novel, Hud actually rapes Halmea, whereas in the script his assault on Alma is thwarted by Lon's intervention.

RAVETCH: Well, the change highlights Lon's significance in the film, and it also helps to keep Hud human. We didn't want to create a character who was totally and simplistically evil, so Lon's intervention prevents the drunken Hud from going too far.

FRANK: Also, in the film, Alma's definitely attracted to Hud. There's a real chemistry between them—there's clearly something in the air—and the two of them are playing a very sophisticated, sexual "card game." But when Hud gets drunk, he ruins everything, and his attempted rape both insults and violates Alma, and she decides to leave. But up to that point, things *might* have worked out if Hud hadn't been so crude and vile. At the bus station, Alma clearly admits it, saying, "You want to know something funny? It would have happened eventually without the roughhouse," and Hud's final comment to the departing Alma is: "I'll remember you, honey. You're the one that got away." So thwarting the rape in the film allowed for much more subtlety in their relationship.

Similarly, at the end of the novel, Hud actually shoots his wounded father-in-law, claiming it to be a mercy killing, and he ends up indicted for "murder without malice"—although he expects to get a suspended sentence. In the script, however, Hud doesn't kill his father, who dies of his injuries and a broken will.

RAVETCH: That's another attempt to humanize Hud, so he wouldn't be one-dimensionally evil. In that scene at the end, with his father dying in his lap, there's a subtle sense of unspoken grief. Hud's a villain, but he's a villain with seeds of something worth preserving.

FRANK: What? Leave the room! We'll have none of that, Mr. Ravetch!

RAVETCH: But he's human; he's not all dark.

FRANK: We can discuss that tomorrow morning in divorce court!

RAVETCH: But in that crucial scene with Lon and his dying father, Hud tries in some way—a very laconic way—to give the young boy some kind of consolation. There's something decent going on.

FRANK: But not nearly enough. There's something in the American psyche that's sadly attracted to the dangerous, the flamboyant, and the immoral. And that's exactly what we were trying to show in that film.

RAVETCH: Well, now you can see how we collaborate!

FRANK: Yes-no, yes-no, back-and-forth.

Let's try another important topic. One of the most famous scenes in the film is the killing of Homer's herd of cattle to prevent the spread of hoof-and-mouth disease. The scene is expertly directed by Martin Ritt and powerfully shot by

James Wong Howe. A number of critics have suggested that the scene, in some way, recalls the terrible human genocides of the twentieth century. Was that on your minds when you were writing the scene?

RAVETCH: Yes, we certainly had that in mind when we were writing that scene.

FRANK: Yes, the undertone was clearly intended.

RAVETCH: Definitely.

Let's talk about the end of the script. Just like in the novel, young Lon leaves the ranch to get away from Hud, and he hitches a ride with a trucker who recalls Lon's grandfather, Homer, and refers to him as the "old gentleman." But this scene was eventually cut from the movie. Do you know why?

RAVETCH: It was too much of a dying fall. Marty always had a gutsy, muscular attack on life in general—and, in his films, he would always opt for the punchiest moments he could get. And it definitely seemed more dramatic to end the film with Hud shutting the door and making his "the hell with you" gesture.

Was the script ending ever shot?

RAVETCH: No, Marty was satisfied with closing on Paul, and so were we.

Let's talk some more about that final scene. The film ends with Hud completely alone on the deserted ranch. He goes into the empty house, gets a beer, and comes back to the screen door. Then he looks out, as if wondering if he should go after Lon, but then he shrugs, makes a dismissive hand gesture—as if to say, "the hell with it"—and shuts the door. It's a very powerful ending— reminiscent of the Greek tragedies and so many of Faulkner's novels— illustrating the fall of a once-great household. Did you think about that larger theme as you were writing the script?

RAVETCH: Not specifically, although it's clear that the film is about the fall of Homer Bannon and everything he'd built and stood for. But in writing the very end of the film, we relied more on a gut instinct that that's *exactly* how Hud would have reacted under those circumstances. He'd be consistent. He'd be Hud. It's an odd movie in a way because Lon is the central character in that he's the one who has to make the crucial choice, but Hud's also the main character since he's always at the center of everything. So Marty decided—we all did, in fact—to end the film with Hud.

In the script, you added a very effective and funny greased-pig contest which reveals both Hud's aggressiveness and his popularity. Originally, you'd written the scene as a baseball game. Do you remember where the pigs came from?

RAVETCH: Isn't that in the novel?

No, it's a baseball game in the book, and you originally wrote it that way in the script.

RAVETCH: I don't remember where that scene came from.

FRANK: Me neither, not the faintest idea. But it's a good piece of small-town America.

And very effective. I wonder if you ever discussed the script with Larry McMurtry?

RAVETCH: No, we never even met Larry McMurtry until he visited the set one day in Texas while we were shooting the movie.

Did you ever talk about the film after it was finished?

RAVETCH: Not really, but he definitely liked the film. He even sent us his second novel called *Leaving Cheyenne*, which wasn't very successful, and we eventually visited him down at Rice University to talk about it. Unfortunately, we had to tell him that we weren't interested in adapting the book, and he was quite disappointed.

FRANK: But we've always been deeply indebted to Larry for *Horseman, Pass By*. We were very fortunate that Irving stumbled onto it in that bookstore.

As mentioned earlier, you had a very special relationship with Martin Ritt who stayed very close to your scripts and dialogue. But he did suggest a number of changes over the course of your eight collaborations, and I wonder if you can remember any about Hud?

FRANK: In general, Marty would ask us to cut a scene, a subtext, or a line. For example, in *Hud*, we originally wrote a scene between Lonny and his girlfriend who lived on the adjoining ranch. But Marty felt it was unnecessary, and we agreed, so we cut it out. Marty never altered our scripts, but he would suggest small cuts, and they were always carefully thought-out suggestions. It was never arbitrary, and it was never a command. It was never a "You *have* to do this" kind of thing. It was rather, "Let's sit down and discuss this scene," or "How can we tighten it up?" or "Let's think about taking that one out." As a director, Marty was, remarkably, without ego, which was extremely attractive, and he was one of the great defenders of writers in Hollywood—if not the greatest. He was always your friend and advocate—tough-minded, but always fair—and he truly considered his films a collaboration. He couldn't have been more devoted to his writers. It was a marvelous relationship.

RAVETCH: I don't know of any other director in Hollywood who was more respectful of his writers than Marty was. What other Hollywood director kept his writers with him from the very beginning to the very end? And on the set every single day of shooting? I don't know of any.

What did you do on the set?

RAVETCH: Very little!

FRANK: Have fun! Marty always rehearsed the film very carefully, like a theater director, for several weeks before shooting began. So by the time we were actually on the set, everything was fully prepared, and there were very few changes. So, we had a great time sitting around and shooting the breeze.

RAVETCH: Sometimes we might cut a line or two, but not much more. Mostly, I think Marty wanted us there for support. It gave him a certain comfort to know that we were always with him on the set.

FRANK: And his sets were always great fun, just like a big family. On _Hud_, Paul was always professional, but also great fun, and Pat was extremely maternal—which everyone loved—even James Wong Howe who was usually rather austere, but he loosened up on _Hud_ and had a really good time. It was perfectly pleasant and congenial.

You shot the whole picture down in Texas?

FRANK: Yes, we did, and we were very lucky to have such a brilliant cinematographer as James Wong Howe to shoot the film. He wasn't afraid to capture the bleak Texas landscape, and he did it with a stark, yet beautiful quality that no one else would have even dared to attempt.

What was Martin Ritt like on the set?

FRANK: Patient and punctual. Marty loved actors, and even though he was so volatile in his own life, he was remarkably patient with his performers. He truly loved them, and it always amazed me. I remember when he first said that he wanted to be a director, and I said, "You'll never be able to do it. You're too demanding. You'll force the horse to drink the water whether he wants to or not," but I was wrong. Marty was always the soul of patience with his actors.

And punctual?

FRANK: Yes, he was punctual to the point of insanity about food and actors and everything else. I'm also a bit fastidious that way, so on _Hud_, the two of us started showing up at the rushes a little bit earlier each morning just to see who was _more_ punctual! At first, we'd both show up at 5:00, then Marty would start arriving at 4:45, so then I'd start coming at 4:30, and so on. Finally, I said, "For God sakes, Marty, just stay in bed! Enough of this! Let's just watch the rushes at six o'clock." So we did, but he was always there and ready-to-go right on time, and he expected everyone else to do the same.

RAVETCH: Yes, and he was always quite the perfectionist. I remember when we were shooting the scene where the cattle are being guided through the chutes to be injected, and the wranglers were having some trouble moving the cattle into the right position. So Marty got right down in the dirt behind one of the cows, and started pushing it forward, when, suddenly, it "let go" all over him. He was filthy, completely covered with manure, and one of the wranglers came over and said, "Don't worry about it, Marty, it's only grass and water," and we all laughed about it. But it shows you the kind of guy he was.

After the filming was complete, were you in the editing room?

RAVETCH: Always. And I can still remember watching Marty trimming a little bit more each day, day after day, and finally, I knew he was going too far, and I actually screamed. So Marty stopped, turned to me, and asked, "Does it hurt, Irving?" and I said, "Yes, it hurts!" And he said, "Okay, that's it," and he wrapped the movie there.

FRANK: Is that a man or is that a man?

RAVETCH: He was just terrific.

Now, once the film was cut, did you attend any of the early previews, which apparently made the studio quite nervous, and even convinced several of the Paramount executives that the ending should be changed?

RAVETCH: We were present at a number of the early previews, but I wasn't aware that they were talking about changing the ending. Of course, I can easily imagine how some of those executives might have said, "Well, why not have a happy ending?" On the other hand, I clearly remember that, earlier, after the shooting was done, Paramount was actually thinking about dumping the whole picture because they felt it wasn't commercial enough.

FRANK: But Marty Rackin saved it.

RAVETCH: Yes, he did. Marty, who was the overall "godfather" of the project, immediately got on the plane to New York, arrived at five in the morning, and went to the executive offices of Paramount—way up in one of the skyscrapers. Then he sat there for four hours until the big boss arrived for work. Then he collared the guy, and screamed and shouted and pleaded and cried and wept, and finally convinced the man to go ahead with the project. It was very touch-and-go, believe me. They came very close to abandoning *Hud*, but Marty saved it.

I read somewhere that Marty Rackin wanted to change the ending?

RAVETCH: Not that I ever knew.

Of course, the studio had messed with the ending of your previous film, The Long, Hot Summer.

RAVETCH: They sure did! You know, we've *never* watched the end of that film. Never. We can't bear to look at it. We had a terrific ending in the script—where Varner goes out on the balcony and screams down at the departing lovers—but the studio said, "Nah, that's not good enough. It won't work." So they changed it, but Marty Rackin had nothing to do with it, and he stood by *Hud* all the way.

Hud was nominated for seven Academy Awards, including Best Adaptation. Melvyn Douglas, Patricia Neal, and James Wong Howe all won Oscars, but, unfortunately, John Osborne was given the writing award for Tom Jones.

FRANK: Yes, sigh!

RAVETCH: I could give you an opinion about that.

FRANK: Maybe you shouldn't. What do *you* think, Bill?

I always thought Tom Jones *was overrated, but I will say in Osborne's defense that it's a very hard novel to adapt—with all its peculiarities.*

FRANK: That's true. And now we don't need any of Irving's opinions!

Did you go to the ceremony?

FRANK: I didn't. I went to Paris with my mother, but Irving went. So I'm over in France, out of touch with everything, and I get a telegram from Irving: "Oscar loves Pat. Oscar loves Melvyn. Oscar loves James Wong Howe. And I love you."

RAVETCH: Can you imagine her not going to the Academy Awards?

FRANK: Well, I knew damn well we weren't going to win.

RAVETCH: Oh, how could you know that?

FRANK: Well, I did, and I was right. Irving's more brave than I am, so he went alone. But I'm smart. I went to Paris instead!

Well, it's better to get a telegram that says "I love you" anyway.

FRANK: Absolutely! Much better!

But you should have won the Oscar too.

FRANK: You're welcome to come to dinner anytime you want!

As for the critics, the film received extraordinary reviews, and the picture did very well at the box office. But critics did raise a number of questions, and I'd like to ask you about a few. One, which I don't fully understand, is the complaint that the animosity between Homer and Hud was not clearly delineated. Yet, you purposefully added the telling backstory about Hud's drunken car accident fifteen years earlier which resulted in the death of his older brother, Norman. And you also had Homer make the shocking revelation, in the film's most powerful scene, that he was sick of Hud "a long time before that"— because Hud was so selfish and didn't "give a damn" about anybody but himself. So why do you think some people weren't satisfied with that?

RAVETCH: I'm not sure. Most of the critics felt they "understood" Hud, but a few didn't care for Homer because he was so rigid.

FRANK: Yes, so unyielding. And so judgmental. There's a very reasonable point of view about *Hud* that growing up in the home of a man like

Homer Bannon might seriously damage a young man like Hud, and I accept that. It was a *very* dysfunctional family.

But Homer's firmness is also admirable. He actually stands for something.

FRANK: Yes, but he's too uncompromising. I grew up with a mother who gave me encouragement and lots of freedom, and it was very nourishing. But growing up in a household where the standards were as impeccable as those of Homer Bannon would have been very difficult. All your failures would naturally engender resentment and anger—even contempt.

RAVETCH: That's right, without the understanding, uncritical love of a parent, a child can become emotionally crippled. Also, in *Hud*, there's clearly the sense of parental favoritism—that Homer favored Norman over Hud. So those are interpretations of the film that we're comfortable with.

But doesn't that run the risk of making excuses for Hud? Surely, Homer has his flaws, but that's because you made him a real human being, but there's quite a bit about him that's admirable.

FRANK: Yes, his standards were certainly admirable.

RAVETCH: I agree. Homer's standards, which don't exist very much anymore, were definitely admirable, even if he was too inflexible in dealing with his son. In a way, Homer was a lot like Marty Ritt who was such a principled man that even if you threatened to kill him, he'd never budge from his ethical beliefs.

FRANK: And Paul Newman's a very principled man himself—and very generous.

RAVETCH: We were certainly fortunate to work with men like Paul and Marty.

Let's return to some of the critical commentaries on the film. Although Hud *is clearly set in contemporary Texas, it's often cited as one of the films that began the "demystification" of the American Western. It came out a year after* The Man Who Shot Liberty Valance, *in which John Ford began to reexamine the Western hero, and it predated the so-called "revisionist" Westerns of the later sixties, like* The Good, the Bad, and the Ugly *(1966) and* The Wild Bunch *(1969). I wonder how you feel about that?*

RAVETCH: To be perfectly honest, I never thought of *Hud* as a Western. Never. I always thought of it as a domestic drama. Whenever I see *Hud* listed with other Westerns, I wince. Not because I don't admire Westerns—I wrote a number of them in my earlier days—but because I don't feel the film is appropriate to that category.

The film's become a classic of the American cinema, and it remains a devastating indictment of individual greed and selfishness. At the time of Hud's *release, Penelope Gilliatt in* The London Observer *called* Hud: *"American writing at its abrasive best."*

FRANK: We love that quote!

RAVETCH: Yes, we do!

Well, you earned it. Similarly, Bosley Crowther wrote in The New York Times *that the film's characters "behave and talk so truly that it is hard to shake them out of your mind." He also claimed that* Hud *was "as wide and profound a contemplation of the human condition as one of the New England plays of Eugene O'Neill." That's high praise indeed, and fully justified. I'd like to finish up today by asking you about your own personal favorite moments in the film. When you watch* Hud *these days, after all these years, what do you most appreciate?*

RAVETCH: Well, we have to admit, Bill, that we don't watch the film anymore. In fact, once our films are finished, we never watch them again.

Never?

RAVETCH: No. For us, it's over and done.

But you don't know what you're missing!

RAVETCH: Well, that's very kind of you to say that, but it's an experience that we lived through once, nurtured, and watched come alive. So it's very hard afterwards to go back and look at the movie again.

FRANK: But thinking back to when we did see it last—and trying to answer your question—I'd say that the last scene is one of my personal favorites. I feel that it has a powerful punch that resonates—as Lon leaves and Hud slams the door. Also, I have to admit, I loved every single scene that Patricia was in. She was always perfect, and always affecting. She never missed a moment.

RAVETCH: I have to agree that I'm partial to all those scenes with Pat—like when she's leaving at the bus station. It's very touching. Her whole performance is very moving. But Paul was impeccable as well. I still remember standing on the set and watching him perform, and, in my mind, I was always acting out the scene right along with him, and, almost invariably, he would play it exactly the way we'd envisioned it when we wrote the script. Paul completely understood that role, and he completely embodied the character of Hud. He was just terrific.

FRANK: Well, you're a very good actor yourself—you always were.

RAVETCH: Yes, I would have been a terrific Hud, if only I'd had the talent! Like Edna May Oliver said in *Pride and Prejudice*, "I would have made a marvelous musician, if I only had the talent."

Well, both of your talents are perfectly obvious in your masterful writing of the American film classic Hud. *Thanks for your time.*

FRANK: Thank you, Bill, it was fun!

RAVETCH: Yes, thanks, Bill.

CHAPTER 7

The Sound of Music (1965)

A CONVERSATION WITH ERNEST LEHMAN

Ernest Lehman (1915–2005), one of the most acclaimed screenwriters in Hollywood history, was born in New York City. After graduating from City College of New York, he worked for a publicity agency that specialized in a Broadway/Hollywood clientele. His early short stories, often related to theater and film, began to appear in prestigious journals like *Collier's* and *Esquire*, and his short novel *Sweet Smell of Success* was first serialized in *Cosmopolitan*. After moving to Hollywood in 1953, his first screenplay was *Executive Suite* (1954), directed by Robert Wise and starring William Holden. His subsequent films include: Billy Wilder's *Sabrina* (1954), starring Humphrey Bogart and Audrey Hepburn; *The King and I* (1956), with Yul Brynner and Deborah Kerr; *Somebody Up There Likes Me* (1956) and *From the Terrace* (1960), both starring Paul Newman; Alfred Hitchcock's *North by Northwest* (1959), with Cary Grant and Eva Marie Saint; *West Side Story* (1961), starring Natalie Wood, which received the Academy Award for Best Picture; Robert Wise's *The Sound of Music* (1965) with Julie Andrews, which also received the Academy Award for Best Picture; Mike Nichols's *Who's Afraid of Virginia Woolf?* (1966), which was produced by Ernest Lehman, starring Elizabeth Taylor and Richard Burton; Gene Kelly's *Hello, Dolly!* (1969), with Barbra Streisand; *Portnoy's Complaint* (1972), which was produced and directed by Ernest Lehman; and Hitchcock's final film, *Family Plot* (1976). In 1995, his cowritten screenplay for *Sabrina* was adapted for a remake, directed by Sydney Pollack and starring Harrison

Ford and Julia Ormond. Ernest Lehman was also the author of a number of successful novels, including *The French Atlantic Affair,* which was a national best seller in 1977. His various screenplays received five Writers Guild Awards and were nominated four times for Academy Awards. In 2001, he became the first writer in film history to receive a Lifetime Achievement Award from the Academy of Motion Picture Arts and Sciences.

In 1962, 20th Century Fox reported a loss of $39.8 million, due primarily to the tremendous failure of their $31 million picture, Cleopatra. *In the after-math, Darryl Zanuck took over from Spyros Skouras, he put his son Richard Zanuck in charge, and they promptly shut down the studio. Everyone was laid off; the lot was an empty shell; and, eventually, you were hired to adapt* The Sound of Music. *What was it like?*

LEHMAN: It was a most peculiar experience. Not long before, when I was working on *The King and I,* 20th Century Fox was a very active, bustling studio, and now I was startled to find this empty wasteland—a ghost town. When I met on the lot with the studio manager, he said, "We need to give you an office space," and I said, "Well, which one can I have?" And he said, "You can have *any* office you want. Just name it!" So I found myself in the amazing position of having my choice of any office on the whole lot, even Darryl Zanuck's old office. So I settled into a small office on the second floor of the Administration Building and started working, and the very next thing I knew, my "signing" to write the screenplay for *The Sound of Music* was emblazoned across the front page of both of the Hollywood trade papers because the studio wanted to let everyone in the industry know that there was no truth to the rumor that 20th Century Fox had gone belly-up.

How did that make you feel? After all, you were being asked to revive a moribund studio?

LEHMAN: I felt good about it. I felt challenged, and I liked the challenge, and, for the time being, I had absolutely no distractions since no one was on the lot.

Were you confident the film would actually be made?

LEHMAN: No, not at all. But something happened very early on that gave me a sense of confidence. After I reported to the studio, I was sched-uled to have lunch at Romanoff's with the young head of the studio, Richard Zanuck. I arrived at the restaurant first, and while I was sitting at my table, I saw Dick coming in. But he was stopped by a well-known agent named Irving "Swifty" Lazar, and Swifty kept Richard standing there for about five minutes before they finished, and Dick finally came over to my table and sat down. "Guess what?" he said, "Irving Lazar just offered me two million dollars if I'll sell him the rights to *The Sound of Music* for an 'unknown' buyer. That would be a clear profit of 750,000 dollars." I was both astonished and concerned, so I said, "Well, does that mean we're finished, Dick?'' And he said, ''Absolutely not. I turned him down—that's how certain I am about this picture.'' Then, later that same afternoon, when I got back to my office, I got a phone call from Swifty, and he said, ''Look, Ernie, what are you doing over there? Don't let them pull the wool over your eyes. They're never going to make *The Sound of Music*, and they probably won't even pay you.'' So I said, ''Irving, I know that Dick Zanuck just turned you down for a 750,000 dollar profit about an hour ago,'' but Swifty ignored me completely. He just kept talking like he'd never even heard what I said. So after that day, I felt pretty confident that Fox was serious about the picture.

Given the film's remarkable success, it's easy to forget that making The Sound of Music *was quite a gamble in 1962, especially for a studio in crisis. The budget was a huge $8.2 million, the film was based on one of the ''lesser'' Rodgers and Hammerstein stage plays, and the cast was virtually unknown when hired—since Julie Andrews's first film,* Mary Poppins, *hadn't been released yet. But you'd always been confident about the story's filmic possibilities ever since you first saw the play on Broadway.*

LEHMAN: That's right. It was a gamble because nobody wanted it. Part of the deal for *The King and I* was that Fox had the first option to purchase any subsequent Rodgers and Hammerstein plays, but when *The Sound of Music* came along, the studio hesitated to buy the rights. Now, long before I was actually involved with the project, my wife and I were in New York—I was there on business related to another picture—and while we were there, we just happened to see *The Sound of Music* in the second week of its run. By that time, it had been taking a lot of abuse from the critics, and there was ''disaster'' talk in the air. But at intermission, when my wife and I rushed next door to a restaurant to get a bowl of clam chowder, I said to my wife, ''I don't care what *anyone* says, someday this will make a very successful movie.'' So when I got back to California, I told my opinion to David Brown, who was Dick Zanuck's right-hand man, and David said, ''Ernie, I want you to tell that to Dick.'' So I did, and the studio exercised its option and purchased the film rights to *The Sound of Music* for an unprecedented $1.25 million. So, in a very significant way, I was responsible for Fox's ownership of the rights, but then the whole project sat on the shelf for over two years until the studio was shut down and they hired me to write the screenplay.

Then getting a director proved very difficult.

LEHMAN: That's for sure! Zanuck first approached Bobby Wise because he'd so successfully directed my script for *West Side Story* and we'd also worked together on *Executive Suite*. But Bob turned it down cold, saying it was too ''saccharine'' for him, and that he was more interested in making a picture in Taiwan with Steve McQueen called *The Sand Pebbles*. So there

I was, working hard on the screenplay, even though my agent had strongly recommended that I refuse the assignment, and it was clear that *The Sound of Music* had developed a very bad odor about it in the industry. One day, I ran into Burt Lancaster in the cafeteria at 20th Century. He was there to dub a picture called *The Leopard*, and he was sitting at a table all by himself. When he saw me come in, he said, "Ernie, what the hell are you doing here?" And I said, "I'm working on the screenplay for *The Sound of Music*," and he gave me a look, and he said, "Damn, you must really need the money." So that was the reputation the project had at the time—all over Hollywood.

Weren't other directors, like Stanley Donen and Gene Kelly, offered the picture?

LEHMAN: They were, and that thankless job fell to me. On *The Sound of Music*, I was in the very rare position of being the only one hired for the project. There was no producer, and there was no director, just me— working on the screenplay. So one of my assignments was to personally go out and find someone to direct the picture. So after Bobby Wise turned it down, I called up Stanley Donen in Switzerland, where he had a home at the time, and Stanley said, "Look, Ernie, I've already invested in the Broadway show, and that's enough. I don't want to have anything else to do with *The Sound of Music*." So then, I went to Vincent Donehue who'd directed the stage version of *The Sound of Music* on Broadway, but he said he wasn't interested. Then I went to George Roy Hill, and he said, "Thanks, Ernie, but no thanks." Finally, I tried Gene Kelly. I went over to his house, and I said, "Gene, we need a producer and a director for *The Sound of Music*, and he took me by the elbow, and he ushered me out of the house, saying, "Go find someone else to work on that piece of shit." Isn't that amazing?

It certainly is. So how did you get William Wyler involved?

LEHMAN: At one point, Dick Zanuck and I flew to New York to confer with Dick's father, Darryl F. Zanuck, who was the president of 20th Century Fox but who was living in his suite at the St. Regis Hotel in New York. Darryl, who'd recently retaken over the studio in a huge proxy battle with the Skourases, couldn't come to Los Angeles because of the possibility of divorce proceedings against him if he showed up in California. Now, the purpose of this meeting was for me to "report" on the project to Darryl— who'd, of course, approved Dick's purchase of the picture on my recommendation! Primarily, we wanted to talk about who the hell we could get to direct the picture, and, while we were in the conference, I said, "You know, William Wyler is one of the greatest directors in the world. I have no idea whether he's seen the Broadway show, but I'd love to have him direct the picture." So Darryl said, "Ernie, when you get back to Hollywood, I'd like you to call up William Wyler and try to get him interested." So I said,

"Well, why wait? Why don't I pick up the phone right now and call him up?" So Darryl said, "OK," and I called Wyler in California, and Willie said, "Well, I've never seen the show, but I'll tell you what, if you'll wait for me there, I'll fly to New York, and we can go see it together." So I stayed in New York, Willie flew in, and we went to the show. But when it was over, and we walked out of the theater into the lobby, he just kept shaking his head, saying, "God, how I hated that show!" I was naturally discouraged, and I reminded him, "Well, Willie, we have to go meet Darryl now. He's waiting for us at the 21 club. There's a car waiting outside with a chauffeur." But he said, "Ernie, I can't go meet with Darryl now. I hated this show!" So when we arrived at 21, he sent the chauffeur inside to tell Darryl he wasn't coming in, and then he said, "Come on, Ernie, let's take a walk, it's only midnight." So we walked the streets of Manhattan together talking about the show, and all Willie could say was how much he hated it. Finally, I stopped him at one point, and I said, "Willie, just tell me this, what did you think of that scene when the Baron hears his children singing inside the house, singing, 'The hills are alive with the sound of music'? Then he goes into the house, starts humming, then finally joins in the children's singing, as they all rush around him and hug each other? What did you think of that?" And Willie said, "Well, it's funny you mention that moment because, when I saw it, I felt like I was going to cry." And I said, "Willie, *that's* why this'll be a very successful movie." And that's what sold Willie Wyler on the picture. He made a deal with Dick Zanuck, and he moved himself and his brother—as his associate producer—into a separate building on the 20th Century lot.

But you were suspicious, right?

LEHMAN: Yes, I was. Willie was well known in the business for being a guy who played all the different studios against each other, making each of them think he was going to do their picture, while he was really trying to make up his indecisive mind. So I quickly got suspicious that he was using us, until he could find something he was more excited about. Now, Willie was hard of hearing—he was deaf in one ear—and one day Marty Ransohoff from MGM called him up, and Willie asked me to take the call and serve as a go-between, which I did. At the time, Ransohoff was producing a picture called *The Americanization of Emily,* and I suddenly found myself helping Willie dicker around with some other studio while he was supposed to be producing and directing *The Sound of Music.* So I had my doubts, and I told Dick Zanuck, and he told me to keep an eye on things. He also suggested that I write the first draft as fast as I could, so we could try and smoke out Willie's intentions. So I did a very quick draft of *The Sound of Music* and turned it in to Willie, and then, one day, he stopped by my office. Now, you have to remember that Willie Wyler was a great director, and great directors don't go to their writers' offices; it's the other way around. Also, Willie was very well known for being extremely hard on writers and their screenplays—and actors as well. So he walks into my office, and he says, "You know, Ernie, I'm quite embarrassed. Never in my whole career have I ever read a first draft of a screenplay that's *so* good that I haven't got a single suggestion to make." So, I was very suspicious. Then he said, "And now, Ernie, if you don't mind, I have a date to play hearts with David Lean." And he left.

Was that before the beach party in Malibu?

LEHMAN: Yes, it was right before Malibu, and that, of course, settled everything. So one day, Willie calls me up, and he says, "Ernie, this Sunday I'd like you to come out to the beach house and meet Rex Harrison. He'll be there with his wife, Rachel Roberts, and I want you to talk him into playing Baron von Trapp. But I said, "Why me, Willie? I'm just the writer." And he said, "Rex'll be more impressed if it comes from the writer." So I showed up, and I went swimming with Rex, and I did my best to talk him into playing the Baron, although I never got a commitment. And all the while I was there—out on the beach or sitting in the sundeck chairs—I noticed that Willie was never really with us. He was always off in a corner of his property talking in an animated huddle with Mike Frankovich, the head of Columbia Pictures. So later, when no one was in the beach house, I slipped away, and roamed around Willie's big living room facing the ocean. Everywhere I looked, there were scripts, and on every one of them I could read the title on the front page. But there was one script that was turned over so that the title couldn't be seen, so, surreptitiously, I turned it over and read the title. It was *The Collector* from Columbia Pictures. Now, totally by coincidence, I knew that Jud Kinberg and John Kohn were mutually producing *The Collector*, because I'd run in to them in London, and they'd told me that they were desperately looking for a director. So that night, I called up Dick Zanuck, and I said, "Dick, I've got bad news. Willie's planning to do *The Collector* for Columbia." So Dick said, "OK, thanks for the warning, now I'm ready for him." And sure enough, the very next day, Willie's agent, Paul Kohner, arrived at Dick's office unannounced, and he asked him to postpone *The Sound of Music* because Willie wanted to direct *The Collector*. And Dick said, "You tell your client, Willie Wyler, to go make *The Collector* and forget about *The Sound of Music*. I'm not postponing this picture 30 seconds—for Willie or anyone." And that was it for Willie. He disappeared from the picture, and he went off to make *The Collector*, which was a financial disaster for Columbia.

So what changed Robert Wise's mind?

LEHMAN: One day after working on the screenplay, I came into the Fox cafeteria, and I saw Bob Wise sitting there all by himself. He was looking rather forlorn, and I said, "What are you doing, Bob?" And he said, "A huge monsoon hit Taiwan, and they've postponed *The Sand Pebbles*. So

I've got nothing to do, but wait." Now, as we discussed earlier, Bobby had already turned down *The Sound of Music* because he'd read all the negative reviews of the play that tore it apart and said it was too "saccharine." So I left him in the cafeteria, and I called up his agent, Phil Gersh, and I said, "Phil, I'm going to send you a copy of my screenplay for *The Sound of Music*, and I want you to slip it to Bob. Don't ask any questions." But he said, "Ernie, how can I do that? Willie Wyler's directing the picture," and I said, "Look, Phil, just don't ask any questions." So he slipped the script to Bob Wise, and Bobby read it, and he was very impressed. So he sent a copy to Saul Chaplin, who'd worked with us on *West Side Story* as Bob's associate producer—in charge of all the musical aspects of the picture. So, as I learned later, Saul and Bob started talking about the script, and they were both saying the same thing, "This is a really good screenplay. I had no idea it could be so good after all the negative stuff they said about the play." Finally, they came to a decision, "Well, if you'll do it, I'll do it." So one day, Dick Zanuck calls me up, and he says, "Come over to my office, Ernie, I have some interesting news." So I walked into his office, and he looked up at me, and he said, "Ernie, what would you say if I told you I can get Bob Wise to direct this picture?" and I said, "That would be marvelous, Dick. What a wonderful idea!" Then he stared up at me, grinned, and said, "You son-of-a-bitch, you slipped that script to Bob, didn't you?" And I said, "Who me?" And to this day, I've never actually admitted it, but that's how Bob Wise became the producer/director of *The Sound of Music*, which made him tens of millions of dollars and became the number one picture in the whole world for many years to come.

When did you take your scouting trip to Salzburg?

LEHMAN: That was earlier, when Willie Wyler was still on the picture. Willie had hired Roger Edens as an associate producer. Roger was a wonderful guy, who'd had a long career at MGM with the Arthur Freed unit, and he'd also been crucial in the amazing career of Judy Garland. So after Roger was hired, we made a list of possible locations in Austria, and then Willie, Roger, and I flew to Salzburg, by way of London. Incidentally, it was during our stopover in London, that I ran into Jud Kinberg and John Kohn who were sitting at a resort on the river Thames complaining that they had no director for their pet project, *The Collector*. Then we went on to Salzburg, and I combed the area, feeling that it was a wonderful place to open up such a stage-bound musical and make a real movie out of it. So, I actually picked all those terrific locations that we used to stage the film's musical numbers even before Bob Wise was on the picture. So, when Bob was finally signed, he sent me off on a one-month, paid vacation, so that he and Saul Chaplin could visit Salzburg and catch up on all the locations I'd picked out for Willie Wyler. So I went off to Palm Springs and had a very nice vacation.

When you were still writing the script, I wonder if you watched either of those earlier German films about the von Trapp family?

LEHMAN: Well, that leads to another curious anecdote that happened many years before the writing of the screenplay for *The Sound of Music*— and even before the writing of the stage play. At the time, I was working on an earlier picture at Paramount, and the studio had signed an open contract—a one-picture deal—with a New York stage director named Vincent Donehue, the man who would later direct *The Sound of Music* on Broadway. So one day, when Vincent was at the studio, the head of the story department showed him a German film that Paramount had taken an option on. It was called *The von Trapp Family Singers*. Since it was German made, no one had ever heard of it before, and when the lights went up in the projection room, Vincent Donehue said, "You have to do me a big favor. Don't do anything with this picture right now. Let me go back to New York and talk to Richard Halliday. I think this story could make a great Broadway musical." Now, of course, Richard Halliday was the New York producer who happened to be the husband of Mary Martin, and that's how the Broadway musical starring his wife came into being. It was first written by Howard Lindsay and Russel Crouse, and then it was transformed into a musical when Rodgers and Hammerstein were brought in on the project. Interestingly enough, years later, Paramount still kept a small percentage of 20th Century Fox's movie production of *The Sound of Music*. This was because Paramount had agreed to turn over to Fox all their rights to the German films, and once that legal matter was resolved, Fox could take the project off the shelf and make the picture.

Now, when you eventually saw Die Trapp Familie, *was it of any use to you?*

LEHMAN: None whatsoever. It had nothing to do with *The Sound of Music* because it all took place in New York City after the von Trapps had escaped from Austria.

But that's the German sequel, Die Trapp Familie in Amerika. *The first film,* Die Trapp Familie, *came out in 1956, and it was set in Austria. Later Paramount edited them together for a dubbed composite.*

LEHMAN: Then I never saw either the original or the composite. I don't even remember hearing about them. So the German films had absolutely no influence on the screenplay, except for the fact that they inspired the Broadway play.

Eventually, you met with Maria von Trapp.

LEHMAN: That's right. Maria von Trapp was all over the place. She'd written a book called *The Story of the Trapp Family Singers*, and she was very visible and full of advice. I remember the first time I saw Mary Martin in the stage play, and when the curtain came down, Mary came out to take her bows and, suddenly, up stood this lady from her seat in the front row, and she turned around to the audience and bowed. It was Maria von Trapp! Later, when we had lunch together at the St. Regis Hotel, she gave me one line, which I used in the picture. It's in the love scene when Maria tells the Baron one of the Mother Superior's favorite sayings: "When the Lord closes the door, somewhere he opens a window." So I'm very grateful for the line, but that's all I was able to use from my meeting with Maria von Trapp.

Now, by the time you got back from Palm Springs, had the casting begun?

LEHMAN: Yes, they'd cast Chris Plummer, and that proved to be quite a big problem for Bob Wise. Chris got very upset when he learned that Bob intended to dub his voice. The idea that his own voice wasn't good enough insulted Chris's pride, and he kept threatening to walk off the picture. Finally, Dick Zanuck made an agreement with Chris Plummer's agent over the telephone, and I happened to be present when the deal was made. Dick promised that Chris would have the right to hear the finished picture and if he still thought his voice sounded good enough, they would leave it in. So the choice would be left up to Chris. Naturally, his agent agreed, and when Dick hung up the phone, he turned to me with a grin and said, "Don't worry, Ernie, we're not going to use Chris's voice no matter what he says." In the meantime, Chris was also dissatisfied with the role of von Trapp as I'd written it. Chris was a very bright guy, and when he said he wanted "time with Ernie alone," we gave him five days. So, for five intense days, Chris was in my office all day long, and we went over every single line of dialogue and every single movement he had in the entire picture. As a result, he helped me rewrite his entire role, and it helped the picture enormously.

How was the Baron changed?

LEHMAN: In general, we transformed him from a "stock" musical-comedy character into a real, living human being. And it worked beautifully. Also, as a result of Chris's help, I was forced to rewrite the role of the Countess into something much more meaningful than a simple stock character. So Chris was enormously helpful.

How about the crucial casting of Julie Andrews? Weren't you the first one to propose her as the lead?

LEHMAN: Well, I'm glad you brought that up, and I'll tell you why. All the time that Willie Wyler was still "on" the picture—with his own building at Fox and his own brother on the payroll—I kept saying, over and over, there's only one person who should play the role of Maria, and that's a young actress named Julie Andrews. By coincidence—or good luck—I was over at Disney one day, and I happened to see some rushes for their uncompleted picture, *Mary Poppins*. At that point, Julie Andrews had never been seen on screen before, but I immediately said to myself, "She's *got* to be Maria von Trapp." So I told Willie Wyler, and he said, "Never, never,

I'll find someone else to play the role." So when Bob Wise officially became the producer/director of *The Sound of Music*, the first thing I did was take Bob to Disney and show him the rushes, and he said, "Let's get out of here quick and sign her up before anyone else sees this film. She's going to be a huge star!" So that's how we signed Julie Andrews to the role, even though Willie Wyler said he'd never even consider using her. Incidentally, when I went to New York to meet with Richard Rodgers about *The Sound of Music*, he said, "Who are you guys going to use in the movie to play Maria?" And I said, "Well, we haven't cast it yet, but there's only one person I want in that role and that's Julie Andrews." And he gave me a kinda sour look, and he said, "So what else is new?"

What did that mean?

LEHMAN: He was clearly displeased. Julie had starred in his "television special" version of *Cinderella,* and he didn't feel she was right for Maria.

What about the rumors about Doris Day?

LEHMAN: You know, that same day, when I walked into Richard Rodgers' beautiful apartment in New York City, the very first thing he said to me was, "I suppose you're going to use Doris Day to play Maria." And he said it with a very sarcastic tone, and I didn't even know what he was talking about. Then, not long after that, Marty Melcher—Doris Day's husband who swindled her out of all her money—showed up at my office one day and gave me a big, long pitch about his wife. But I lucked out; Bob Wise responded immediately and completely nixed the idea. Fortunately, we wound up with exactly the right person for Maria.

What about Audrey Hepburn?

LEHMAN: At the time that Willie was still on the picture, and all the time we were in Austria, I kept saying "Julie Andrews, Julie Andrews." And Willie would say, "Why don't you stop bothering me about that, Ernie. I'm either going to use an unknown, or I'm going to use somebody like Audrey Hepburn." Which, of course, I didn't think was such a terrible idea, since we would have dubbed her voice with Marni Nixon. But in the end, we lucked out. We got rid of Willie! By the way, I'm convinced that if Willie had done the picture it would have been a disaster because his desk at Fox was piled high with books on the Anschluss. Willie was an Alsatian who'd lost some family members during the war, and he was obsessed with the whole business of the Nazi invasion. I'm convinced he would have ruined the picture with too much heavy-handed Nazi and invasion stuff.

Didn't Billy Wilder, your old friend and collaborator on Sabrina, *worry about Nazis in musicals?*

LEHMAN: Yes, one time at a party at Jack Lemmon's house, Billy said to me, "So Ernie, I hear you are working on *The Sound of Music*. Don't you realize that no musical with swastikas in it can ever be a success?'' But he was wrong, and he admits it to this day, and he even inspired me to write that scene where the angry Baron rips up the swastika flags.

You once said that any writer who's doing the screen version of a Broadway play has to be "merciless," but you've also pointed out that he has to have enough self-confidence to leave the good parts alone.

LEHMAN: Absolutely, in my opinion, that's one of the secrets of being a successful screenwriter. You have to be smart enough to realize that if something's good in the original work, and if it'll work well in the movie, then you have to keep it. That's the challenge: to be smart enough to know what needs to be retained from the original—and what needs to be rewritten.

I'd like to ask you about various scenes in the film—either additions to the play or alterations from the play—starting with the famous opening sequence in the Austrian Alps. In Julia Antopol Hirsch's book about the film, she says that Robert Wise was hesitant to open the film with the aerial shots.

LEHMAN: I don't think that's true. I certainly know nothing about that, and I never did. Every single draft of the screenplay began exactly that way, and Bob shot it exactly as I wrote it. I remember absolutely no hesitation on his part. As a matter of fact, *no one* ever objected to that opening, and the way Bob shot it, it's one of the most beautiful openings in musical film history.

I agree, and you'd previously used another very successful aerial opening in your script for West Side Story.

LEHMAN: Yes, that's *exactly* where I got the idea. I was stealing from myself! I felt that the aerial opening had worked very well in *West Side Story*—which, of course, Bob had also directed. As a matter of fact, a few years later, I felt quite stymied when I was writing the movie version of *Hello, Dolly!* because I had no city to glide over! The New York of the 1890s was long gone, so I had to devise an entirely new device for the opening of *Hello, Dolly!*: the frozen frames that suddenly came to life.

One of the two songs you added to The Sound of Music *is "I Have Confidence," which the anxious Maria sings on her way from the Nonnberg Abbey to the Captain's house. Is it true that you and Associate Producer Saul Chaplin wrote down some suggested lyrics and that Richard Rodgers completed the song?*

LEHMAN: Yes, I wrote them down with Saul Chaplin, standing at his piano, writing on a yellow pad. They were "dummy" lyrics that we sent Richard Rodgers so he could get the feel for what we needed. You have to remember that by that time Oscar Hammerstein had died. So Richard wrote us a song that was still lyrically incomplete for what we needed, and Saul and I ended up writing a good portion of the song's lyrics that were actually used in the movie. In fact, we did it without telling anyone, including Julie Andrews. So, to this day, she still thinks she was singing Richard Rodgers's lyrics.

Didn't Rodgers mind?

LEHMAN: I guess not. He never said a word. And since we later worked together on another idea for a musical, I don't think he really cared about those additional lyrics in "I Have Confidence."

You once said that the only scene in the movie that you'd like to change is when the children, sitting at the supper table, begin crying after Maria makes them feel guilty for putting the frog in her dress.

LEHMAN: Yes, I wrote that scene as a complete original because I felt we needed a transition after Maria's first arrival and the rather rough and unfriendly attitude of the children when they're all introduced. So, I decided to create a scene that would show the beginnings of her friendly relationship with the children. I thought to myself, "Make the kids feel guilty about how they've been treating Maria," and I wrote the scene. But I always felt—and I still feel—that, in the film, it's over-directed. In my opinion, the kids started crying much too easily and unrealistically. Now, I've never explained my opinion about this before, and I certainly hope it won't hurt Bob Wise to hear it. It's the *only* moment in the entire picture that I wish we could do over again.

Well, that's an amazing tribute to Robert Wise. How many screenwriters have ever felt satisfied with every single scene but one?

LEHMAN: Not many, if any. On every single picture I've ever made, no matter how much the critics might have liked it, there've always been scenes that I wished I could buy back—and have a chance to rewrite. That's the strange thing about the craft of screenwriting: the writer never gets a chance to really "see" his work until the picture's done. A playwright can sit in on rehearsals, and change things as he goes along. He can even change things after opening night, but not with film. Once it's done, it's done. So, yes, it's truly amazing to say of one of your pictures that there's only one scene you'd like to have back, and that's because of the great talents of Bobby Wise.

In the play, the famous but lengthy "Do Re Mi" song is sung in the living room, but, in the film, you moved it out into the streets and surroundings of Salzburg. Using such a montage technique to visually and thematically advance the story was considered quite innovative in the mid-sixties.

LEHMAN: Well, I hate to pat myself on the back, but I felt that it was very effective when I wrote it because it accomplished so many things in terms of the story. It displayed the marvelous Austrian scenery and local color; it revealed the passage of time by changing the costumes of the children for the various scenes; it portrayed the developing relationship between Maria and the children; and it made it clear that she was *really* teaching the children how to sing.

Yes, it's crucial that the audience believes that the children have really learned to sing together before the Captain returns from Vienna.

LEHMAN: Absolutely, very few of the millions of people who watched the film version of *The Sound of Music* had seen the stage play. So they had to be convinced that Maria really had enough time to properly teach the children to sing because, only then, would they be able to believe the crucial scene when the Captain comes home, hears them all singing, and is so moved he joins in the singing.

Another great addition to the film was the Bil Baird Marionettes, which were used in "The Lonely Goatherd" number. Who came up with that idea?

LEHMAN: Roger Edens suggested the idea. We knew we needed something special at that moment in the film, and the marionettes were marvelous.

Not only are the roles of the Captain and Maria greatly deepened in the screenplay, but the Baroness becomes much more significant. Underneath her witty self-absorption is a sad, intelligent woman who's ready to fight for the Captain. In the film, it's the Baroness, rather than the child Brigitta, who tells Maria that she's fallen in love with the Captain—thus driving her anxious rival back to the abbey. Also, in the play, rather astonishingly, it's the Baroness who breaks off with the Captain over the political issue—and she does so even before Maria comes back from the abbey. But in the film, she's still trying to make things work when the Captain points out that their relationship is futile: "It's no use—you and I."

LEHMAN: Yes, as I mentioned earlier, Chris Plummer got me thinking very seriously about the role of the Baroness while we were working on the character of the Captain. We wanted to make her more integral to the conflict, and to make her more "real"—to move her beyond the stock character of a musical comedy. So I'm very proud of those scenes in the movie, and they were played impeccably by Eleanor Parker. That whole section of the movie up to the love scene between the Captain and Maria, which leads to their singing "Something Good," is very beautiful and masterfully directed by Bob Wise.

That particular song, "Something Good," was the second new song written exclusively for the movie by Richard Rodgers. It's sung after the Captain, having broken off his engagement with the Baroness, tells Maria that he loves her. It's a much more romantic and effective song than the one it replaces from the play, "Ordinary People," which never really made much sense since there's obviously nothing very "ordinary" about either of them. It's also not very romantic. But, at first, you resisted replacing the song?

LEHMAN: Yes, I have to admit it. I clung to that song way too long, even though "Ordinary People" is probably the weakest song in the play, and even though it creates a very dull moment in the story. I still don't know why I was so stupid, and why I didn't realize it at the very beginning. Finally, thank goodness, it was Bob and Saul who were smart enough to talk me out of it. As I always like to say, "Being successful means being lucky enough to lose the right battle."

One of the most powerful scenes in the movie is the crucial moment earlier in the film when the Captain and Maria dance the Austrian folk dance, the Laendler, and Maria clearly recognizes her romantic feelings for the Baron. It's very beautifully done in the film, as choreographed by Marc Breaux and DeeDee Wood.

LEHMAN: Absolutely! DeeDee and Marc did a marvelous job arranging the famous Laendler. There was a short, little version of it in the stage play, of course, but it was perfectly staged and performed in the film.

The most criticized element of the original story is the subplot with Liesl and Rolf. Here you also made some important improvements over the play, but I wonder what you think of the performance. Rolf seems to be the one serious piece of miscasting in the film. He's stiff, and unbelievable, and he often seems in over his head. How do you feel about that?

LEHMAN: Well, he was a bit stiff, especially in the scenes with Liesl. But, of course, it's not up to me to criticize the work of an actor or director.

At the end of the Broadway play, a much more sympathetic Rolf protects the Trapp family and helps them escape. In the film, however, after the Captain remarks, "You'll never be one of them," Rolf calls out to his fellow Nazis and betrays the family. It's a very effective shocker in the film, but didn't it seem quite risky when you were still writing the screenplay?

LEHMAN: Not really, I didn't hesitate at all. I felt that the audience would accept it, and I felt that it gave a bit more character to the role of Rolf. It made him much more real and human. Also, it allowed me to use an effective gimmick to allow the von Trapps to escape—when the nuns remove the carburetors. Audiences love that moment, and it was pure lucky invention on my part. It left everyone with a nice feeling at the end of the film, and it helped get the audience back after Rolf's betrayal.

One thing that you never minimized in the film is the strong religious nature of Maria and thus of the whole film. Not only did you keep all the key aspects of this important theme from the play, but you even added a few significant religious touches—such as the early scene when Maria sits down for her first meal with the Baron and his children and, realizing that they haven't said grace yet, she leads them in prayer. Were you and Robert Wise in full agreement on this approach to the film?

LEHMAN: Absolutely, I felt it was crucial to the substance and reality of the film, and I also believed that it added stature to the story. I felt that way right from the start, and I never wavered, and when Bob Wise came on the picture, he agreed entirely.

When the picture was finished, did you attend that amazing preview of the film in Minneapolis where a paying audience stood and cheered not only at the end of the film but at the intermission as well?

LEHMAN: I'm so sorry I wasn't there for that. Unfortunately, I was already working on my next picture over at Warner Bros. I was writing and producing *Who's Afraid of the Virginia Woolf?* so I had no time to attend any of the tryout screenings for *The Sound of Music.*

Then came the reviews, most of which were dreadful. Bosley Crowther, Judith Crist, and Pauline Kael, among others, attacked the film as too manipulative and "sugar-coated." The film was called The Sound of Muzac, The Sound of Marshmallows, *and, eventually,* The Sound of Money. *It became quite unfashionable among a small group of people—called the "snobs" by Richard Zanuck—to admit liking anything about the film.*

LEHMAN: Yes, we were stunned. And given that the first two reviews were very lukewarm and that *My Fair Lady* had opened so successfully just a few weeks earlier, we all felt we were doomed—overshadowed, finished, and doomed! But then, despite all the bad reviews, the picture's grosses just kept climbing higher and higher every single week until it finally dawned on us that, in spite of everything, *The Sound of Music* was going to be a hit.

Well, the audience response was, of course, quite different from the film reviewers. It was truly astonishing, and, with the possible exceptions of The Birth of a Nation *and* Gone with the Wind, *entirely unprecedented. It ran in many first-run theaters for well over a year, its attendance in many cities exceeded the population, and it eventually dethroned* Gone With the Wind *as the all-time biggest box office hit. But, apparently, no one involved with the film ever expected it to be more than moderately successful. So did it take you totally by surprise?*

LEHMAN: It sure did! We'd all naturally hoped for a successful film, but we had no idea it would become the blockbuster it became. Then one day, my agent came to visit me, and he said, "Ernie, you own a piece of this picture, and you're in big trouble. You're going to get a huge amount of money at the end of the year, and, if we don't do something fast, it'll all end up with the federal government. So we need to rewrite your contract so that the studio can defer payment over the next ten years." Wow! The picture was doing so well, I was being pushed up into some huge tax bracket if we didn't rewrite my contract—which we did immediately. Not only was the film breaking all kinds of box office records, but the studio had also sold the picture to NBC for $10 million for four television screenings. And it seemed, all across America, as though the audiences would never stop coming. In some places, the film ran for over a year, and in some small college towns, the students started protesting because there was nothing else they could see in their theaters. To this day, I still draw large checks for *The Sound of Music,* which, of course, is now on videocassette and DVD. It just keeps going and going and going, and it still shows a profit every single year even though it's over thirty-five years old.

Not all the critics were so blind about the film. One perceptive critic, Roy Hemming, said that "such [negative] judgments usually tell more about the people voicing them than about the film itself."

LEHMAN: I think that's a very wise observation. For a while there in the beginning, it was very "fashionable" to attack the film, but the huge audiences eventually put an end to that. Usually, I never go on the record criticizing critics, but we all know what happened to Pauline Kael.

Yes, she attacked the film in a rather vicious review in McCall's *magazine—calling the film a "sugar-coated lie that people seem to want to eat"— and the readers were so outraged that they wrote a million letters to the editor, and Kael was fired. Her editors felt she was completely out of touch with their readers.*

LEHMAN: Yes, they fired her even though she was so famous. It's one thing to be critical, but most readers felt she went too far. She not only attacked the movie, but she also attacked the audiences who liked the film.

Unfortunately, the astonishing success of The Sound of Music *inspired a glut of high-budget musicals in Hollywood, which all, for the most part, failed at the box office.*

LEHMAN: That's right. Our huge success ended up costing a lot of other studios quite a bit money. They all jumped right in. They all said, "Look what *The Sound of Music* is doing! Let's make a musical!" But it's not that simple.

No, it's not, and everyone was trying to analyze the astounding success of The Sound of Music, *including* The New York Times, *which ran a long article in 1966 asking, "How Come?" Every possible "reason" was suggested: kids, nuns, music, the Alps, and, of course, Julie Andrews. When* The Times *asked you about the reasons for the film's success, you weren't entirely sure yourself. You discussed the popular "escapist" theory, and also your own opinions about the crucial "father–children" aspect of the film. How do you feel about that now?*

LEHMAN: I think that's right. I think it's a universal yearning. I think in all of us—no matter who we are, or where we are, or what age we are— there's always a secret yearning on the part of parents to be closer to their children and vice versa. It's what almost made Willie Wyler cry when he saw the play, even though he hated the show overall. So, I still believe that that's at the very heart of the picture, along with the beautiful love story. But, of course, with *The Sound of Music*, everything else came together as well: the scenery, the beautiful score by Rodgers and Hammerstein, the casting, the marvel of Julie Andrews's performance, the children, and the extraordinary direction of Bobby Wise.

Well, you've left out the writer! And one of the things that made that musical come together so perfectly is how you, very skillfully and naturally, managed to integrate the songs into the film.

LEHMAN: Well, I've worked on four pictures with Bob Wise, and he always says that one of the things he likes best about my musicals is how the scripts lead into—and out of—the songs. I must admit that I work very hard on that. I try to introduce each song in such a way that the audience doesn't know—or doesn't care—about the artificiality and staginess of a performer suddenly bursting into song. You want the audience to be already enjoying the song and the musical moment before they realize what's happening. So I'm very pleased with how it all worked out on *The Sound of Music*. We had many talented people working on that picture, and we were very lucky.

I wonder if you've heard what's been going on over in England. British theaters have been showing the film with interactive audiences.

LEHMAN: I know, sing-alongs.

And a lot more than that! People are dressing up as the characters; they boo whenever the Baroness enters a scene; and they sing along with all the lyrics, which are actually subtitled at the bottom of the screen. How do you feel about that?

LEHMAN: I think it's a hell of an idea! It's a wonderful new exploration of the film, and everyone's having fun. I don't feel that it demeans the overall reputation of the film in any way. It's all in fun, and I'm all for it. Besides, maybe it'll rake in some more dough and give me more tax problems!

Over your long and distinguished career in Hollywood, you've always been reluctant to say anything very favorable about your own films, but you once told a story about a conversation that you had with Richard Zanuck. You were walking back from the Fox commissary together talking about The Sound of Music, *and he forced you to admit that it was "a great picture." Do you remember that?*

LEHMAN: I do.

Tell me about it.

LEHMAN: Well, Bill, you may not think so from this interview, but usually I'm very wary of blowing my own horn, and the idea of coming out and saying that *The Sound of Music* was "a great picture" was anathema to me. It made me very uneasy, and I kept saying to Dick, "No, I won't do it. No, I won't do it." And he'd say, "Come on, Ernie, we're standing here outside the commissary, and there's no one else around, and I want to hear you finally admit it. Just say it once: '*The Sound of Music* is a great picture.'" "And, finally, he just wore me down, and I said, "OK, damn it, *The Sound of Music* is a great film."

   And it is.

LEHMAN: Yes, I think it really is.

CHAPTER 8

The Wild Bunch (1969)

A CONVERSATION WITH WALON GREEN

Although raised in Los Angeles, Walon Green attended both the University of Mexico and Göttingen University in Germany. His early work in films was as a documentarian at David L. Wolper Productions, where he did numerous documentaries, including *The Search for Vengeance* in 1966. He also served as a dialogue coach on several Hollywood features in the mid-sixties, including Martin Ritt's *The Outrage* starring Paul Newman. His first produced screenplay, *The Wild Bunch* (1969), starred William Holden and Ernest Borgnine, and the script, for which he shared credit with the film's director, Sam Peckinpah, was nominated for an Academy Award. In 1971, he produced and directed the documentary, *The Hellstrom Chronicle*, which received the Academy Award for Best Documentary. Subsequently, he wrote two films directed by William Friedkin, *Sorcerer* starring Roy Scheider and *The Brink's Job* starring Peter Falk. Other screenwriting credits include Tony Richardson's *The Border*, starring Jack Nicholson (cowritten with Deric Washburn and David Freeman), and Stephen Frears's *The Hi-Lo Country* featuring Woody Harrelson. Walon Green has also been a highly successful writer-producer for such television series as *Hill Street Blues*, *Law & Order*, *NYPD Blue*, for which he won an Emmy Award in 1995, and *ER*.

In 1964, you were working as a dialogue coach on Saboteur: Code Name Morituri, *a World War II picture starring Marlon Brando and Yul Brynner, when you began writing for one of the picture's stuntmen, Roy N. Sickner. How did it happen?*

GREEN: Roy had purchased the rights to Warren Miller's *Wine, Women, Warren, and Skis,* a book about skiing, and, since I was rewriting scenes on the set as the dialogue coach, he assumed I could write. Back then, he was one of the few people in the business who trusted me to write anything, and he asked me to do the adaptation. But I told him, "I don't know anything about skiing, Roy. I've never even been skiing." Then he said, "Well, I've got a producer who'll pay you to write the script," and I said, "Well, I'd sure like to try. I could sure use the money." So, one day, while I'm in the midst of trying to figure out this skiing book, Roy suddenly shows up and says, "We don't have to do the skiing project. I've just pitched a Western idea that I've always had, and you can write the Western instead." So I said, "Great." I was delighted. Back then, I hung around with a lot of cowboy stuntmen, and I had a horse, and I rode quite a bit. I knew a lot of those guys out there in the river bottom who were real horsemen—guys who worked in the stockyards, were around horses all week, and then got drunk and beat each other up on Friday and Saturday nights.

What was the story line?

GREEN: It was about a bunch of guys who rob a bank, get away with it, and then go down to Mexico and gamble their money away. Then, when they're really getting desperate, a Mexican general approaches them about stealing some guns from a train in the United States, and they decide to do it. But when they get back to Mexico, the general betrays them, and they end up in a big shoot-out with the army. As you can see, if you look at just the basics, that was essentially *The Wild Bunch.* So I thought, "Yeah, I can make something out of that." I'd lived in Mexico, and I knew the country very well.

Didn't you readjust the time period?

GREEN: Yes. Roy's original idea was to set it in the 1870s—or something like that—and I said, "Roy, that's not a very interesting period in Mexican history. Mexico's more interesting in 1913 during the Revolutionary period, just after the death of Madero." So Roy agreed and said, "Sure, do anything you want with it." So I wrote up a treatment, and then our producer got fired, which is a pretty funny Hollywood story. The guy went into the barbershop on the Columbia lot, and there was another guy in a chair with a towel over his face, so our producer starts sounding off about what an idiot the head of the studio was, and, naturally, the guy with the towel on his face *was* the head of the studio, Mike Frankovich. So our producer got fired immediately, and Roy started shopping the treatment around again, and he found a guy who was willing to put up the money to write the screenplay. His name was Tony Ryerson, and he wasn't really a movie guy; he owned a ski resort or something like that. So I did the script for scale—about $5,000, at the time. In the meantime, I'd begun a career

making documentary films, and I got so busy that I didn't pay much attention to Roy's shopping around the script.

Didn't he take it to Lee Marvin?

GREEN: Actually, we'd taken it to Lee Marvin earlier, in the treatment
stage, and Marvin was the one who suggested using the doughboy uni-
forms in the opening sequence. He said, "If you're in that period, why
don't you *use* the period?" But he wouldn't do the project since he'd just
committed to do *The Professionals* with Burt Lancaster. So I kept working
away on my documentaries, with few thoughts of my Western, and then,
one day, I read in the trades that Sam Peckinpah was planning to do *The
Wild Bunch*.

You had no idea?

GREEN: I knew that Roy knew Peckinpah because he'd been a stuntman
on *Major Dundee*, Sam's Civil War film with Charlton Heston. But I had
no idea that things had progressed so far, and my first confirmation was
reading it in the trades. So I called up Roy, and he said, "Yeah, we're making the film," so, naturally, I said, "Will I get any more money?" and he
said, "No," since I'd already been paid. So I didn't argue, and I signed the
papers that Warners sent, thinking, "Well, if I can actually get a movie
made, then it's worth it."

*Is it true that when you wrote the script you knew nothing about the real
Wild Bunch, also known as Butch Cassidy's Hole-in-the-Wall gang?*

GREEN: That's right. I didn't find out about Cassidy until after I'd written
the script, and I heard that there was another Western script being sold about
the "Wild Bunch." And I thought, "The Wild Bunch? What the hell is that?"
Actually, I was never crazy about the name; the title was Sickner's idea.

Why didn't you like it?

GREEN: Because of *The Wild One* with Marlon Brando. I thought
people might assume that *The Wild Bunch* was another motorcycle movie.
Then I heard about the real-life Wild Bunch from Wyoming, but, by then,
it was too late to get all my treatments back and change the title.

It's very ironic that, at the same time Sickner was circulating The Wild
Bunch, *Warner Bros. was considering William Goldman's script for* Butch
Cassidy and the Sundance Kid.

GREEN: That's right. Although it was Fox who ended up buying *Butch
Cassidy.* When Goldman wrote that screenplay, he knew it was a terrific
script, and he put it out for a studio bid. I think more money was paid for
that script than any other up to that time.

That's right, $400,000.

GREEN: But the real reason that *The Wild Bunch* was done at Warner Bros. was that the studio had been in a weird sort of doldrums, and this guy, Ken Hyman, came in as the interim studio head, and he decided to try various projects from people who'd never done anything before. So there was this little burst of odd movies done at Warners for a while, and *The Wild Bunch* fit right into that category. Besides, it was ready to go, and it had a script, a producer, and a director. Maybe they owed Sam a film—I'm not sure. But, honestly, I don't think that movie would've ever been made, except for the persistence of Sickner and Peckinpah, and the flukey situation that existed at the studio. The script had already been turned down everywhere in town, with all kinds of really nasty rejection notices—which I wish I'd saved.

What upset people the most?

GREEN: It was a single shot: when the young boy smiles after picking up a shotgun and shooting a guy in the face as the gang is riding out of town. That was the most condemned and criticized moment in the script.

But, in the film, Peckinpah shoots it differently. There's just a bunch of kids playing and going "bang-bang."

GREEN: That's right, but it definitely stood out in the script. People would say, "You can't have children doing such a thing and enjoying it," and I'd say, "But the tragedy is, people *do* take joy in such things, and children do as well."

It's a boy who shoots Pike at the end of the film, and, given the context, it doesn't seem unreasonable.

GREEN: That's the tragedy of violence. It infects everyone.

Sam Peckinpah had made a number of films before The Wild Bunch, *but this was the film that made him internationally famous, and he seemed to sense it right from the beginning. He once told producer Phil Feldman, "Of all the projects that I've ever worked on, this is the one that's closest to me." Why do you think he felt that way?*

GREEN: We never actually discussed it, but I think it was the themes—the contagion of violence and the comradeship between the men—as well as the Mexican setting. He loved the story, and he told me it was a terrific script. Years later, he hired me again to rewrite a script he'd been working on about diamonds, but I found him impossible to work with.

So what happened after you signed the papers for Warners?

GREEN: I went back to my documentaries, full-time, and then one day, somebody called me from Peckinpah's office and asked where I'd gotten a lot of the local color in the script. So I told him about these two amazing Mexican documentaries, one of which was *Memorias de un Mexicano*, that were made at the time of the Revolution. Eventually, I showed them to Roy, and he took them to Sam.

So you still hadn't met Peckinpah?

GREEN: That's right. Then I took off to Southeast Asia where I was making a film about reptiles and amphibians, and when I got back to Los Angeles, they were already in production, and they called me up and asked me to come down to Mexico to do some polishing on the script while they were shooting. So I went down to Mexico, and I finally met Sam Peckinpah. I was down there for a few weeks, and I did some adjustments on the script, changing a little of this and a little of that. I also rewrote the bridge-crossing scene, which was originally a cable car sequence over the river, but Sam wanted to change it to a bridge.

Apparently, you weren't very happy about it.

GREEN: I wasn't, and we had quite an argument about it. Finally, I said, "But, Sam, blowing up a bridge? I've seen that a million times." And he said, "You've never seen a bridge blown up the way *I'm* gonna blow it up." And he was right, of course. He made an incredible scene out of it.

It's amazing. The riders seem to drop straight down—like through a trap door.

GREEN: It *was* like a trap door. They had the thing rigged so the bottom swung down and dropped out. And they did it perfectly.

How did you get along with Peckinpah? He was legendary for being a pretty tough character.

GREEN: We got along fine. He was surly, no doubt, but he wasn't particularly difficult. Oddly enough, at Wolper Productions, we had some very difficult people. So it was actually a good place to start out because, for the rest of my career, I've never run into anyone as tough as some of those old documentarians. Wolper was an incredible place, just like a film school, but some of those "professors" were mighty tough, so, by comparison, Sam didn't seem so bad.

I'd like to ask you about a few of Peckinpah's script changes. Mostly, he sharpened dialogue, but he also made some plot changes.

GREEN: I hope I can remember everything; sometimes it's hard to separate the writing from the film. Fortunately, I recently read over the original script with Sam's changes. It was the first time I'd looked at it in over thirty years. We were moving, and cleaning up the house, and I found the script, and I thought, "What the hell, I ought to read it." So I sat down, and I read it through, and it was quite a sobering experience to look at it again after all this time. There were parts of it where I thought, "Wow, this is really great," and there were parts of it where I was thinking, "God, this is just awful."

In general, how did Peckinpah's changes look to you now?

GREEN: Excellent. From beginning to end. It was one of the best examples I've ever seen of a writer taking another writer's script and making it better. After all this time, I could really look at it with a detached eye, and it was quite an experience. *The Wild Bunch* was the second script I ever wrote and, as I read it through, I thought, "Boy, if all of them could only be like this!" I was also surprised to discover that a number of lines that I always thought I'd written, Sam actually wrote, and vice versa. For example, I thought that Pike's line, "If they move, kill 'em!" was my line. But it was Sam's. And there's another line when Angel's girl is sitting on the general's lap and one of the Gorch brothers says, "Just look at her licking inside that general's ear," or something like that, and I'd always thought that Sam added that line, but he didn't.

Well, one part of the script that I'm sure you remember is how Peckinpah reconceived Angel's visit to his Mexican village. Originally, you had Angel returning home alone—with the whole sequence spoken in Spanish.

GREEN: Yeah, that was really moronic. I wrote the whole six-page sequence without a word of English. But when I recently reread that scene, I realized that Sam hadn't just tossed out the whole thing and rewritten it, he actually used a lot of the stuff that I'd originally written in Spanish.

How about the flashbacks that Peckinpah added? Especially the ones that show Pike's abandonment of his best friend, Deke Thornton, and Pike's ill-fated romance with a married woman? Did these events come from the dialogue in the original script, or did Peckinpah originate them?

GREEN: They were only touched on in the dialogue, and when I went to Mexico Sam said, I want some new scenes where this happens and that happens, and I wrote them in a day.

At the very end of the film, Peckinpah decided to let Deke Thornton stay in Mexico with Sykes to help Pancho Villa.

GREEN: Yes, he changed the ending, and I think it was a great idea. Perfect for the film.

Another small but telling addition by Peckinpah was the ants killing the scorpions, which he got from Emilio Fernandez, the Mexican film director who played the role of General Mapache.

GREEN: Yes, and Emilio got it from *The Wages of Fear*, which opens with a close-up of a small kid torturing cockroaches.

Which makes the scene doubly ironic, since most people would naturally assume that the insect idea came from your documentary experiences. And later, you were the writer who adapted Clouzot's Wages of Fear, *retitled* Sorcerer, *for William Friedkin and Roy Scheider.*

GREEN: That's right. It's strange how things work out.

Now, when Lee Marvin decided against the picture, William Holden was cast in the lead. How did you feel about that at the time?

GREEN: I was delighted, but I learned about it in a funny way. Naturally, at the beginning, I'd given a copy of my script to my boss, David Wolper, who'd recently made his first feature film, *The Devil's Brigade*, a *Dirty Dozen* rip-off, starring William Holden. Anyway, David never read my script, probably thinking, "Oh, it's just something from one of my documentary guys." So he passed it off to one of his assistants to read, and the guy told him, "You definitely don't want to get involved with this." So, one day, I get a call from Wolper's office that he wants to see me. So I go into his office, and he says, "What's this? What's this movie you've written that Bill Holden's starring in?" And I said, "I don't know." I didn't know what he was talking about. So he said, "Well, here it is," and he handed me a copy of *The Wild Bunch*. "Bill gave me this script, and he says it's terrific, and I looked at the cover, and I saw your name on it. Did you write this on my time?" And I said, "No, David, I wrote it before I worked for you." And he said, "Well, why didn't I see it?" I said, "You did. I gave it to you, but you never read it." So that's how I found out Holden was starring in *The Wild Bunch*.

The casting of Holden as Pike looks particularly brilliant now. He was at the exact right moment in his career for that role.

GREEN: He was. I knew Bill from all my trips to Africa for the documentaries, and after *The Wild Bunch* came out, I was in Kenya, and I ran into Holden in Nairobi, and we went out and celebrated.

Had you both seen the final cut of the film?

GREEN: He had, but I'd only seen an earlier cut. Until the rerelease, I'd never actually seen the film in a theater with an audience.

Was there anyone in the cast that you were worried about? Peckinpah was a bit concerned about Ernest Borgnine.

GREEN: I felt the same way. He seemed to me a very unusual choice for Dutch. I'd always pictured Dutch as somebody like James Coburn—a lean western-type guy—and I'd always pictured Borgnine as being rather urban. But he was great in the role. He added lots of warmth to the film.

And his rapport with Pike was crucial to the movie, especially on those occasions when they'd talk about more serious things. How about some of the other casting decisions? Like the Gorch brothers.

GREEN: I wrote the Gorch brothers for Ben Johnson and Warren Oates.

You had them in mind?

GREEN: Absolutely. Right from the beginning, Sickner and I had them in mind, and I wrote it that way. I also wrote the part of Mapache for Emilio Fernandez because I knew him from the Mexican movies.

But wasn't he a director?

GREEN: He was, but he'd also acted in a number of films, and I thought he'd be great in *The Wild Bunch* even though I didn't know him at the time. But everything worked out.

What about the fact that there was no significant female role or romance in the film? Was Warner Bros. concerned about that?

GREEN: The studio wasn't, because it was in that unusual period I described earlier, but everybody else had something to say about it. It was probably the third most common criticism of the script when people wrote us their unpleasant rejection letters to say how much they hated the screenplay. The first reason was, naturally, the violence—the "inhumanity" of it; the second was that it had no hero, or maybe that was the first reason; and the third reason was there was no girl and no romance. But one of my favorite films back then was *The Treasure of Sierra Madre*, so I wasn't convinced that you had to have a romance to have a great film. Incidentally, there's a little homage to *Sierra Madre* in *The Wild Bunch* when they come in the wagon with all the stuff, and the guy rides out to meet them, and there's a confrontation.

Apparently, Kurosawa's The Seven Samurai *also affected your writing of* The Wild Bunch *and was even responsible for your inclusion of the slow-motion violence in the screenplay.*

GREEN: Up to that time, *The Seven Samurai* was the best film that I'd ever seen, and, even today, it's still in my top ten. I can still remember seeing it for the first time and discussing it endlessly with all my friends, like Jack Nicholson and other people my age. We were all young nobodies back then, and we'd go watch the foreign films, and we'd talk about them all night, and I still remember how the slow motion in the movie just blew us away. So I started thinking, "Hmm, I wonder what a whole sequence in slow motion would be like? That would really be something!" So I told Sickner my idea, and he agreed immediately. He was originally a stuntman, and he thought it could really highlight the key moments of action. So we got all excited about it, and I put it in the script. And one of the first things Sickner told me, when he told me that Peckinpah liked the script, was that Sam wanted to do the action in slow motion.

It's quite interesting because you're writing the script before Bonnie and Clyde, *but Peckinpah's making the film after* Bonnie and Clyde. *I wonder if* The Seven Samurai *put that idea in a lot of people's heads?*

GREEN: Maybe it did, but it was certainly in the air back then.

I wonder if your experience as a documentarian had any affect on the film? Two years later, in 1971, you received an Oscar for Best Documentary for your apocalyptic nature film, The Hellstrom Chronicle. *You also knew Latin America very well, and did a famous Wolper documentary called* The Search for Vengeance *in which you documented for the first time, from credible secondhand sources, the presence of Josef Mengele in Paraguay.*

GREEN: Well, except for my love of Mexico and my knowledge of useful historical footage from the Revolution period, I don't think it had very much effect on the film. I was just getting my documentary career going at the time, but I did see *The Wild Bunch* as a kind of love letter to Mexico. When I was younger, I went to college in Mexico for a year, and when I finished school, I worked down there for two years for a construction company. I was a site manager on various jobs—building small pumping stations and setting up irrigation projects—and I traveled everywhere, all over the country. There were only three of us, and we hired local people, and I was the only gringo.

So you knew some of the isolation that the gang felt in the film.

GREEN: I did, but I still loved it down there—the country, the culture, the people, the music, everything. And Sam felt the same way. It was a very strong connection between us. Do you know the story about Parras, the place where they filmed the picture?

No, I don't.

GREEN: Well, I picked the town of Parras because it was the birthplace of Madero, even though I'd never been there, despite my many travels all over Mexico. So when it was time to make the picture, the production company looked all over Mexico for the right location, and they finally decided on Parras, thinking, "This town is perfect, the script must've been written with it in mind." So when I was called down there to work with Sam on the rewrites, he had a big barbecue the first night I was there. Sam had ordered all this beef sent down there to be barbecued for the crew, but the cook chopped it up and made chili out of it. Which made them all a bit surly, although I thought the chili was great. At any rate, I was talking to Sam, and he was complaining about the fact that they'd spent several weeks looking for the right location, and he said, "Well why the hell didn't you tell them it was written for a specific town?" And I said, "But I didn't write it for this town. I've never even been here before. I just picked the name because Madero was born here." And Sam said, "Oh, you know about that, huh?" And he was impressed, and we started talking about Mexico. And he said, "You really got all the Mexican stuff right." So I told him that I'd lived down there for a few years, and we talked about how much we both loved Mexico.

When you finally saw the film, what was your reaction?

GREEN: I saw it right here at Warner Bros. in a screening room, and it was very exciting, and I enjoyed it very much. But I saw it with a very rough dub, and I remember complaining about the sound effects. Eventually, I got them to bring in the guy who did the effects on my reptile and insect documentaries.

They redid it?

GREEN: They did. I explained that the sound effects, as they were, were just "real," and that what we needed was a more impressionistic approach. They had all these amazing visuals, but they were using the same old gunshot sounds that had been in the Warners library for sixty years.

Peckinpah apparently felt the same way, and he said that he wanted every gunshot to sound different—and to be appropriate to the person who was shooting.

GREEN: That's right. And right here in this office at Warner Bros., either Sam or Phil Feldman said to me, "Well, who do you think's good enough?" And I said, "The guy who did my reptile show." And they gave me some very doubtful looks. So I said, "Come on, this guy did fifty different frogs, and he built up a chorus of hundreds of frogs, and he did this and he did that," and they started getting interested, and, eventually, they brought the guy in, and he did a great job.

What did you think of the zooms and the swish pans?

GREEN: It looked all right to me at the time. It was kind of a new look, and it was very interesting to me as a filmmaker. I was amazed that Lucien Ballard, who did *True Grit* the same year in the old forties Hollywood-style, could make the adjustment so easily. But he did. So I liked all those swish pans and zooms in *The Wild Bunch*; it made it look, from my point of view, like they were trying to "grab" the story as it happened, and it created a nice feel.

Well, Peckinpah and Ballard didn't overdo it, like some of the films from that period.

GREEN: Right, and they worked the shots into the context.

How did you feel about the cutting. One critic has claimed that there were 3,642 individual cuts in the film—more than any color picture ever made. Some have claimed that it has more cuts than any other picture in film history.

GREEN: I liked it. It didn't look much different to me from the way I'd originally conceived it. Kurosawa cut a lot. At the beginning of *Rashomon*, when the woodcutter's walking through the forest, we see his feet moving along, and his ax, and the trees, and so on. So, yes, it was a stylistic departure from the typical Hollywood film—very much so—but, to my mind, that was the whole idea. There was definitely a whole new sensibility in the air, and *The Wild Bunch* was part of it. Peter Biskind discusses this in his book *Easy Riders, Raging Bulls*. We were all ready to try new things, and it was amazing to me how naturally Lucien Ballard was able to shift into the new style. It looks like he'd always shot that way, and it was wonderful.

Were you at the disastrous preview in Kansas City where a number of people walked out, and, supposedly, some actually got sick in the alley outside the theater?

GREEN: No, I wasn't there, but I certainly heard about it.

Apparently, Warner Bros. didn't mind the violence, but Peckinpah felt that there was too much, and he cut out six minutes. Later he claimed, "If I drive people out of the theater, then I've failed." What's your opinion about that controversial aspect of the film? Clearly, both you and Peckinpah intended The Wild Bunch *to be an examination of the seduction, even attractiveness of violence, and Stanley Kaufman claimed in* The New Republic, *"The violence is the film."*

GREEN: Absolutely, that was the intention. I don't know where it came from for Sam, but I know exactly where it came from for me. When I wrote the script, I was hanging around with a bunch of tough guys that I liked very much. They were real "guys' guys," and they had this intense loyalty to each other—you could never feel that you were ever alone. You could call any of these guys at 3 AM and say, "My car broke down in Pomona," and he'd bail out of bed and get out there and help you. But, at the same time, their idea of fun was to hit the bars like the Palomino or the Cobblestone on a Saturday night and snatch a stool out from underneath somebody and start a fight. And sometimes things would get worse, like the time one of the guys robbed an unemployment office and shot two people, and all the other guys went into court and perjured themselves, saying that he was with them all night. Even the guys who didn't really like him, and thought he was a stupid asshole, and felt that he deserved to go to jail, went into the court and lied for him anyway. I also noticed that in all of our conversations, everything always came back to some aspect of violence. If we're talking about dogs, we'd end up talking about which was the most badass dog there ever was. And if we were talking about people, we'd always end up talking about who was the meanest, toughest guy that ever kicked the shit out of everybody. It was always like that.

So I'm sitting there listening to all this, and I'm kind of enjoying myself. I wasn't doing the bad stuff, per se, although I got in a couple of fights alongside them, which was a necessity. And it started me thinking about this bizarre appeal that violence has for us all—that excites us, that fascinates us, and that runs through all our classical literature. Even in the most controlled of ages, like the Victorian era, there's always an undercurrent of violence. I can remember Margaret Mead once telling me about the Balinese and pointing out that beneath the soft, rather ephemeral tranquility of their society, there was an extreme of violence, and that all of their legends are about people tearing each other apart and devouring each other, stuff like that. So I was thinking a lot about the disturbing appeal of violence when I got the chance to write *The Wild Bunch*. And I thought, "If I can write a movie showing that when these guys start shooting up the town, a young kid will pick up a gun and start shooting back—with a smile on his face—then that'll get the point across."

But that raises a problem because anyone can claim that the violence in his film is just an exploration of human nature?

GREEN: That *is* a problem, and a danger, but you have to remember that, at the time, no one was making films like *The Wild Bunch*. It was pre-*Clockwork Orange*, and the only movies that explored that level of violence on the screen were the Japanese films. In American films, like the Westerns, there was always a "justified" violence. If Indians or outlaws were behaving badly, then they could be shot down with a sense of justice. But I wanted to do a film where it would be very hard to say exactly who's bad and who's good in the story. In *The Wild Bunch*, there are definitely people who are innocent and people who are guilty—the townspeople, for example, are essentially innocent—but who's really good and who's really bad? The truth is, most people are generally rounded in such a way that even if you explore the bad people, you'll sometimes find good in them, and if you examine the good people, you'll often find bad stuff. Now, of course, there *are* monsters in this world who are totally evil, but I'm not talking about them, I'm talking in a more general sense.

When the film came out, the reviews ran the gamut. Roger Ebert called it a "masterpiece," but William Wolf in Cue Magazine *called it an "ugly, pointless, disgustingly bloody film." Yet Wolf's charge of pointlessness isn't a frivolous one, and Robert Culp, in his famous, rather self-important essay on the film really does approach the heart of the matter when he writes, "The Wild Bunch is about the discovery by these witless, limited men (which means all of us) of the difference between Right and Wrong." Then he continues, "they have it all now, the gold, the stake to go on with, but it's no good because they let the kid down." So the film's not really just an exploration of violence, it's also about a group of evil men who finally find some kind of personal redemption. The gang's decision—to help Angel—moves them out of the "gray" area because it's pretty much categorically right.*

GREEN: That's true. They look at something that seems wrong to them, and they decide to take a stand on it. I suppose it's also related to the secondary theme of the film which, like *The Hellstrom Chronicle*, is essentially apocalyptic. These guys know that time has passed them by, and that they really have no place to go. They don't sit around and wax lyric about it, but it's clear enough in the script and the film that they might as well take a stand now. As Lyle Gorch says, "Why not?"

But they've still got the gold. They could forget Angel, leave the town, and have their retirement, and all the other things they talked about around the campfire that night. But now, there's something that means even more to them than the gold and the future, and that's loyalty to their friend.

GREEN: Well, that theme of doing the right thing—regarding a friend—had a lot to do with attracting Peckinpah to the script. *The Hi-Lo Country,* which Peckinpah tried to make for five years but never succeeded, is, essentially, about the same thing—doing what's right on the basis, not of the law or anything else, but on the basis of loyalty.

It's another irony that Peckinpah could never complete the film, and then, when Scorsese revived the project, he hired you to write the script.

GREEN: It's very odd, and yet I was drawn to the story for the very same reason that Sam was: the theme about honor and loyalty between buddies. It's not even an action picture; it's a love triangle.

As The Wild Bunch *was about to be released, the studio cut approximately ten more minutes from the film. Apparently, they lied to Peckinpah, who was in Hawaii at the time, and claimed that the cuts were for a two-theater experiment. But, instead, they cut down all the versions of the film and released it across the country. Peckinpah was outraged and called it a "disaster." Were you involved with any of that?*

GREEN: No, I was in some other part of the world, Africa or Southeast Asia, and I was gone for about four or five months, and by the time I got back the hoo-hah was over.

Have you seen the film recently?

GREEN: I saw the rerelease in 1995, and it was really my first viewing of the film, except for that time in the Warners screening room with the rough dub.

As you know, the studio cuts have all been restored in the video widescreen release. The primary scenes that were cut were the two flashbacks we discussed earlier and a sequence in which General Mapache, showing remarkable courage, is driven from a town by the forces of Pancho Villa. Peckinpah's irritation is certainly understandable, but looking at the scenes today, none of them, despite their good intentions, are particularly effective. Both of the flashbacks seem contrived and unnatural, and the key dialogue in the Mapache scene is, inexplicably, done entirely in English.

GREEN: Visually, that's a nice looking scene, but Sam had to shoot the flashbacks very quickly, and the English in the Mapache scene doesn't make any sense. Incidentally, that scene is taken right out of one of those Mexican documentaries. Like everyone else, I really resent it when people come in and mess around with the editing, but I have to admit, the flashbacks are poorly done.

The one plot flaw in this very carefully crafted film is the fact that Bishop sends Angel along with Dutch to trade with Mapache. Since Angel has previously killed Mapache's mistress, it seems too illogical that Bishop, who's not a stupid man, would allow him to go. Did you struggle with that?

GREEN: It's probably just a bad plot point. I don't remember struggling with it when I wrote it, and maybe I just missed it. But I think I remember some of my friends pointing it out.

Given your admiration for The Treasure of Sierra Madre, *you've woven another "gold" theme into* The Wild Bunch. *But the ending of Peckinpah's film is so completely overwhelming that the audience actually forgets the irony that the gang has buried the gold and no one knows where it is.*

GREEN: Originally, I wanted the gold to be hidden out there somewhere, but the gang had no real interest in going to get it. They just didn't care about it. Then I toyed with the idea that the Mexican peasants got a hold of it, and I fooled around with a number of other ideas as well. Then, finally, I just decided, "The hell with it!"

Well, it's better this way. It's still sitting out there in the desert.

GREEN: That's right. It is.

When you wrote The Wild Bunch, *you definitely set out to write a harder, meaner Western. Are you comfortable with the term "anti-Western"?*

GREEN: I don't mind what they call it, but, to me, it's not really an "anti-Western." From what I've read about the old West, I think it was probably a lot like the way things were portrayed in the film—both in terms of the atmosphere and how the characters behaved. That side of the old West was pretty mean and corrupt and sordid. It's a fact that the railroad barons and other people like that were lording it over a lot of poor people who'd arrived from various places in the hopes of trying to scrabble a life together. As for the Mexican aspects of the film, I feel very comfortable with that. That's how things were during the Revolution.

Besides, the film's about outlaws, not about homesteading families who say grace before meals. The critics tend to forget that.

GREEN: They do. So, I don't really see the film as an anti-Western, although I did write it in rebellion against what I felt were the commercial aspects of the Hollywood films of the time, which I felt were quite boring, and endlessly regenerating the same clichés over and over—and a little worse each time. In those days, I wasn't a very polished or professional

Hollywood writer, so I had no qualms ignoring and rejecting the commercial and redundant clichés of the films of those times.

At the end of the film, it's quite ironic that Pike Bishop is first shot by a woman and then is finished off by a young boy.

GREEN: I liked the idea that in the play of violence nothing is sacred. Once everything breaks down, the woman, just like everyone else, gets caught up with the idea of killing someone—even shooting him in the back.

What did you make of all the commentary that the film was a statement about Vietnam?

GREEN: That it wasn't. At the time *The Wild Bunch* was written, Vietnam hadn't really accelerated yet. This was actually fortunate for the script, because if I did have Vietnam in mind, I probably would have gone overboard and written a lousy script. Like so many others, I became very disturbed by what eventually happened in Vietnam, and I was ready for any type of activism. I doubt that it would have helped the script.

Many activists had trouble relating to the film, and when it was previewed at USC, a lot of the students were openly hostile.

GREEN: Yes, I caught a lot of shit from the students, and from my friends as well. They'd say, "How could you do something like this? How could you write a film that exalts violence when we're trying to stop the war?" And it got worse. Students started calling it a "Fascist statement about violence," and Richard Brooks, on a TV talk show at the time of the Manson killings, said, "Well, who can be surprised when films like *The Wild Bunch* are playing?"

So you created Charles Manson?

GREEN: I guess so. At first, I tried to point out that they were all missing the point, that the film was about the deadly attractions of violence, but no one paid any attention. It was all very difficult. When I'd voted for Johnson, I thought, "Oh, he's the peace candidate. I'll vote for him, and he'll end the war." Then a few years later, things were much worse, and the film was under attack for all the wrong reasons.

Before the film came out, the Screenwriters Guild arbitrators decided that Peckinpah should get no screenwriting credit, but you actually wrote them a memo on his behalf, claiming that he deserved partial credit. Eventually, it was decided that the film credit would read "Screenplay by Walon Green and Sam Peckinpah. Story by Walon Green and Roy N. Sickner." This was, of course, quite significant, since the film was nominated for Best Original Screenplay, losing out, ironically, to Butch Cassidy and the Sundance Kid. *Your support and appreciation of Peckinpah is certainly admirable, but you must have been quite irritated that he demanded first credit on the screenplay?*

GREEN: I sure was. I was furious. I thought, "This guy's a bastard." There, I've said it on record. But Sam was a talented bastard. And he really did, to my mind, contribute enough to get partial credit. I didn't want to have someone say to me that the ending was fantastic, and then have to sit there and pretend that I wrote it. I wanted the credits to reflect the reality of the situation. Sam may not have added that many pages to the script, but he improved it greatly.

It's not uncommon for directors to overestimate their contributions to the script.

GREEN: That's true. On the other hand, a person shouldn't become a screenwriter unless he's willing to accept the fact that film is the director's medium—it's not a writer's medium. If they can't accept that fact, they should write plays or novels or something else. And let's face it, actors can also make a tremendous contribution. I've scripted stuff that was just "okay" and seen actors make it five times better than it was. Unfortunately, there's a general animosity that exists between writers and actors, but I certainly don't feel that way. When I see an actor put a twist or a spin on my dialogue and try to improve it, I'm thrilled. I don't resist it. And I don't resist the fact that people come to the movies to see the actors and not to hear the writer's words. I don't believe that the writer should always be out there vying for preeminence. It's too collaborative a medium for somebody to come in and say, "Well, I'm the writer and I'm not getting enough credit."

Warner Bros. always claimed the picture was a box office failure, although it clearly made over $30 million. It wasn't until after Peckinpah's death that they finally admitted the film was in the black. Were you affected by any of this?

GREEN: Not really. I got nothing from the picture except for some residuals. Occasionally, I still get some checks from cassette sales and things like that, but nothing substantial. But the fact is, the movie *did* make money, and it wasn't a failure by any standard, despite the fact that there was always a strong resentment against the film in the industry. I can still remember somebody telling me that they'd run into Mervyn LeRoy at the track, and he said that the film was a "financial disaster," and that was the very same week that *The Wild Bunch* hit $30 million national gross. So there was always this animosity towards the film because it was so different and because of all the controversies about the violence. I think it was a generational thing. Most of the old-timers didn't like it. A lot of them hated it, in fact.

Now that the dust has settled, The Wild Bunch *is considered a landmark, classic Western extolling the virtues of loyalty and obligation, and the film's even been compared to Sophocles and Camus. What's your reaction to the film after all these years?*

GREEN: I think it's a terrific film. It was one of those rare times when the chemistry of the script, the directing, the performances, and everything else magically coalesced and created something totally unique. It certainly doesn't happen very often in this business. After *The Wild Bunch*, I thought, "Great, I'll just write another film, and it'll be terrific too." But I was very naive, because things don't work that way. Since then, I've had maybe three or four other pleasant experiences in film, like *The Hi-Lo Country*, but most of them have been very unpleasant. So looking back, I feel very lucky to have been part of *The Wild Bunch*.

Thanks, Walon.
GREEN: Thank you, Bill.

Gene Kelly, *Singin' in the Rain*, 1952. (Courtesy of Photofest)

Rod Steiger and Marlon Brando, *On the Waterfront*, 1954. (Courtesy of Photofest)

Corey Allen and James Dean, *Rebel Without a Cause*, 1955. (Courtesy of Photofest)

Cary Grant, *North by Northwest*, 1959. (Courtesy of Photofest)

Anthony Perkins, *Psycho*, 1960. (Courtesy of Photofest)

Brandon de Wilde and Paul Newman, *Hud*, 1963. (Courtesy of Photofest)

Julie Andrews, *The Sound of Music*, 1965. (Courtesy of Photofest)

Ben Johnson, Warren Oates, William Holden, and Ernest Borgnine, *The Wild Bunch*, 1969. (Courtesy of Photofest)

Candy Clark and Charles Martin Smith, *American Graffiti*, 1973. (Courtesy of Photofest)

Robert Redford, *The Sting*, 1973. (Courtesy of Photofest)

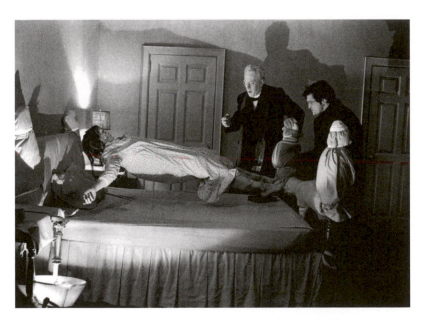

Linda Blair, Max von Sydow, and Jason Miller, *The Exorcist*, 1973. (Courtesy of Photofest)

Roy Scheider, *Jaws*, 1975. (Courtesy of Photofest)

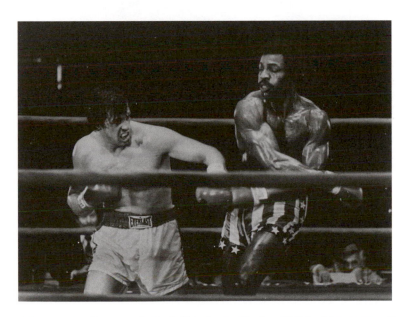

Sylvester Stallone and Carl Weathers, *Rocky*, 1976. (Courtesy of Photofest)

Robert Duvall, *Tender Mercies*, 1983. (Courtesy of Photofest)

CHAPTER 9

American Graffiti (1973)

A CONVERSATION WITH GLORIA KATZ
AND WILLARD HUYCK

The versatile filmmakers Gloria Katz and Willard Huyck were married in 1969. Gloria was a graduate of both UC Berkeley and UCLA's graduate Motion Picture program, and Willard was a graduate of USC's School of Cinema. Aside from various films that they've either produced or directed, they've also collaborated on numerous screenplays including George Lucas's *American Graffiti* starring Richard Dreyfuss and Ronny Howard, for which they received an Oscar nomination for screenwriting; Stanley Donen's *Lucky Lady* (1975) featuring Gene Hackman and Liza Minnelli; Steven Spielberg's *Indiana Jones and the Temple of Doom* (1984) starring Harrison Ford and Kate Capshaw; and *Radioland Murders* (1994), executive produced by George Lucas, featuring Ned Beatty and Mary Stuart Masterson.

In the late sixties, Willard was part of that extraordinary group of students studying film at USC—George Lucas, John Milius, Robert Zemeckis, Randal Kleiser, Caleb Deschanel, Walter Murch, John Carpenter, and many others. Verna Fields, the famous film editor, once said, "I've never seen so many people with so much talent in one place at the same time." What was it like in those days?

HUYCK: Oddly enough, nobody realized that anything was happening. When I first came to USC as a freshman, I'd told my parents that I wanted to study journalism since I'd been my high school newspaper editor, and it sounded very legitimate. But I immediately started taking film classes, and, back then, it was very easy to become a film major, even though USC and UCLA were considered the best cinema schools. The film major wasn't as popular as it is now, and there were very few of us.

Was there a belief that film majors could really get jobs in the industry and make an impact? Something that had never been done before?

HUYCK: Not at all. It was just like art school. We were told that there wasn't a chance we'd ever work in the movie business—maybe commercials or documentaries, but nothing else. We didn't even have role models. I can remember driving up to the San Francisco Film Festival to see Irvin Kershner's *The Luck of Ginger Coffee* because he was the only successful graduate we knew about. He seemed like a really big deal to us because he'd graduated from USC and *actually* made a movie. So we didn't have any big professional hopes at the time—being a film major was kind of a lark—and great fun!

What about the teachers?

HUYCK: We had a lot of terrific professors, but most of them had no feature experience. Some were people who'd had union problems, and others had worked in documentaries. So Verna Fields, who was really a guest lecturer, seemed truly extraordinary to us because she'd actually cut *real* features. So even the backgrounds of most of our teachers gave us little hope that we'd ever work in the movie business.

At the same time, Gloria was across town at the other famous film school, UCLA.

KATZ: Yes, I started UCLA in history, but it was an awful lot of work. Then I noticed a group of students who never carried any books around, and always seemed to be having a great time—and I definitely wasn't. So I finally said, "What's your major?" and they said, "We're film students." So I said, "Don't you have any homework?" and they said, "No, we don't do anything but watch movies." And I thought, "This is for me!" So I started out in film history, and then moved into the film production courses, and I did very well. But, at the time there were very few women, maybe five, in the program, and the professors never gave us any encouragement— certainly no hope that we'd ever work in the film industry. At best, we might work on documentaries or USIA [United States Information Agency] films, and that was about it. If you were a woman, it was as though film studies was a total waste of time. They never gave any of the women fellowships or scholarships or recommendations to the American Film Institute. So it was all quite negative in that sense, but, on the other hand, it was the sixties, and nobody cared very much about jobs anyway. Nowadays, that's all the students think about, but, back then, we weren't very practical. At the time, there was this great wellspring of creativity at

UCLA—even though nobody made a big deal about it—and we were all having fun, and that's all that mattered. It was a big party time, really, and we even had our own band—*The Doors*! They played at all our weekend parties.

Was Jim Morrison still in the film program?

KATZ: He was, but when he'd screened his film project, everyone said it was the worst thing they'd ever seen, and he crushed. His life was "destroyed," so he focused on the band.

Is it true that you and Willard met at a Roger Corman lecture at UCLA?

KATZ: Yes. It was one of the big events of the school year—a shred of hope for the film students. Corman came, lectured, and showed *The Wild Angels*. Then he talked about how it was possible to make a movie for $2 million or less, and, of course, he was everyone's hero because he was working outside the system. By coincidence, Willard and I sat next to each other at the screening.

Then after film school, Willard managed to get a job at American International Pictures (AIP).

HUYCK: I worked as a reader for Larry Gordon, and, for a while, I was the *entire* story department. Eventually, Larry gave me my first writing assignment, and he did the same for John Milius.

Then you went to work at American Zoetrope for Francis Ford Coppola.

HUYCK: Yes, George [Lucas] was working at Zoetrope, and he introduced me to Francis. I ended up working on a project called *The Naked Gypsies*, but after the disastrous screening of *THX*, all of the Zoetrope projects that Francis was planning to put into development were canceled. We called it Black Tuesday. It was very grim; everything was canceled.

Was one of those projects Apocalypse Now, *which began as an idea that Milius and Lucas had in film school?*

HUYCK: I can't remember. The idea had been kicking around for a long time. At first, George was planning to make it, but later, of course, Francis took it over. But I'm not sure if it was one of the six pictures that Francis presented to Warner Bros. on that disastrous day when George first screened *THX*.

And when did you first hear about American Graffiti?

HUYCK: That was back in film school.

So how did things finally get rolling?

HUYCK: George originally had a deal with Warner Bros., and he asked us to help him with the treatment for his "rock and roll" movie. At that point, George didn't have very much set in his mind, except that the film would be about high school cruising in a small town like the one he'd grown up in. He also wanted the film set in 1962 when George was a high school senior and I was a junior. So we sat down for two or three days, and the first treatment we wrote was about fifteen pages. Anyway, Warners and some other studios passed on the film, but United Artists [UA] found it kind of interesting. They wanted a longer treatment, but they didn't offer any money. So when George came back and said UA was interested, we didn't really believe him because we always thought that George was a little naive in those days. But he talked us into it, and the second treatment was about twenty-five pages—which is pretty long—and very well structured. Then George took it back to UA and got the deal, just before he took off on his first trip to Europe.

The Cannes trip?

HUYCK: Right. He was taking *THX* to Cannes. But as soon as he and Marcia [Lucas] left, my agent called and said he'd gotten a hundred thousand dollars from some rich Texans, and we could make our own film. So we didn't know what to do. It wasn't much money to make a feature, but we hadn't been paid anything for *Graffiti* anyway. So we called George in Venice—or was it Cannes?

KATZ: He'd gone to Cannes, but he was in Venice when we called him.

HUYCK: That's right. So we told George what happened, and he felt we shouldn't miss the opportunity, so we made our low-budget horror film. In the meantime, George hired a guy we knew from film school to do the first draft of *Graffiti*, and George insisted that he follow the treatment.

This is Richard Walters?

HUYCK: Yes. So Richard wrote a draft, which we've never read, and George hated it. He kept saying, "This isn't the movie at all!" and he refused to give it to the studio.

Why did he dislike it so much? I read somewhere that he felt it was overly sexual—in poor taste.

HUYCK: I don't know about that, but I do know that George felt the script had gone off in a totally different direction. For example, I remember him complaining about the "chicken" scene in the Walters script.

KATZ: Like *Rebel Without a Cause*.

HUYCK: So instead of the quarter-mile drag, Walters put in a "chicken" scene, and George hated it. He said that nobody he'd ever grown up with would do that kind of thing—no one in his right mind anyway. So I guess what happened is that Richard—and I can't blame him for it—just went off and wrote his own version of things, and George said, "Wait a minute, this isn't what I want at all." So George finally decided to go back to the treatment, and he seemed very happy about it.

Then what happened?

HUYCK: We sat down with George and wrote the script for nothing. Richard's contract had a rewrite guarantee, so all the rewrite money— $10,000—went to Richard even though he never wrote another word. Then George took the script to UA around the same time that *THX* was bombing, and they backed out. So George did another draft by himself and took it all around town—*everywhere*. He pushed the script for about a year, and nobody wanted it.

What were the studios most nervous about? I know that they were uneasy about the wall-to-wall rock and roll and the fact that the film had to be shot entirely at night. Was there anything else?

KATZ: The multiple stories. It hadn't really been done before. Nowadays, of course, it's done all the time, especially on television, but back then it was structurally unique. Also, the film didn't have any well-known movie stars associated with it, and it was about a youth subculture that the studio executives didn't fully understand.

Couldn't they see the appeal the film would have?

HUYCK: Not yet. In those days, they were still making big pictures like *Butch Cassidy and the Sundance Kid*—big studio movies.

Then AIP took an interest.

HUYCK: Yes, George got very close at AIP where I'd worked for Larry Gordon, but they naturally saw the film as a cheap, Sunset Strip "car" movie. Then, when George was finally ready to go with AIP, fate stepped in and Francis made *The Godfather*. Suddenly Francis was hot again, and so was American Zoetrope. So George went back to Universal, and they said, "OK, we'll give you $750,000, but *only* if Francis produces the movie, and it's rewritten." They insisted that Francis *really* produce the film; he couldn't just executive produce it. Then George came back to us.

KATZ: Without any money.

Nothing?

KATZ: Not much. A minimum rewrite fee of $5,000.

HUYCK: But Francis did guarantee us a Movie of the Week since he'd just made a deal with NBC. And he also offered us a percentage of the picture—two points.

Then what happened?

KATZ: We took the script that George had done by himself—which was really just an expanded version of the original treatment—and we rewrote the whole thing. A lot of the stuff in George's script just didn't work, and a lot had to be added.

HUYCK: You have to remember that George had only twenty-eight nights to shoot the whole picture, and you've probably heard about all the disasters that took place in the first few days of shooting—with the lighting, the change of locations, and all the rest of it. So time was very tight, and George was extremely dependent on the script. He shot it as we wrote it.

KATZ: Even though the script was one-hundred-sixty pages long—although we did "shorten" it for the studio executives by retyping it in the smaller "elite" typeface. *American Graffiti* was a long, dialogue-heavy script, and impossibly hard to shoot in twenty-eight days. It's a miracle that George pulled it off.

I've heard you wrote the script very fast.
HUYCK: It didn't take long.

I heard ten pages a day.
HUYCK: That's about right. It didn't take us long because we followed the original treatment.

KATZ: And we went back to the cards. George was very big on 3x5 cards in those days. Each card represented a scene—along with an appropriate song. Structure was extremely important because of the multiple stories.

I understand that you really enjoyed writing the script, even though you had very little faith that it was going to be anything more than a little low-budget film.
HUYCK: Yes. We had an amazing amount of freedom writing that script since the only person we had to deal with was George. Nowadays, you sit around in rooms with eighty studio people, but, back then, it was just us and George thinking out loud, "Hey, I remember one of my friends doing this" and so on. We even started naming characters after friends we'd gone to high school with. It was great fun. George especially liked all the weird stuff—the Goat Killer, for example, or Toad vomiting.

KATZ: That scene with Toad came directly from *The Naked Gypsies* script. We just lifted the scene.

HUYCK: It was great fun to write, but a nightmare to shoot because of the time and budget constraints, and all the technical problems.

What's your method of collaboration? How did the two of you work together? And was Lucas with you when you were actually writing the script?
KATZ: No, we never sat with George and wrote, but we did sit with George and think.

And how did you do the writing?
KATZ: Together, always together.

Did one of you type?

KATZ: Willard typed. We'd just sit together and talk it through.

HUYCK: So much of screenwriting, before you get to the dialogue, is …

KATZ: Structure.

HUYCK: "How do we get out of this hole?" or "What's needs to happen next?" and so on. The dialogue was easier.

George Lucas once said that he's not a very good storyteller, and he's always given you the bulk of the credit for American Graffiti—*especially regarding the characterization of the four main characters. He's admitted that "They were cardboard cutouts in my script, non-people," and that "Bill and Gloria made it one hundred percent better with a combination of wit, charm, snappy one-liners, and punched-up characters." Could we discuss this a bit? For example, I've heard that Lucas had great difficulty with the Steve character— the class-president-athlete-honor-roll guy.*

HUYCK: Well, Steve was a problem for all of us because he's the straight man, and Ronny's a very straight-edge guy. So, while the other characters were great fun to do—all very eccentric—you had this one guy who was Mr. Clean and much tougher to write. Since he had to be used as the straight-man type, we tried to balance him out with the Cindy [Williams] character.

KATZ: That's the key. In a way, Cindy's the crucial character in the script, and since she needs to balance out Steve, we made her very feisty.

HUYCK: And George went along with it—just as he did in *Star Wars*. He had the nerve to make the main female characters in both movies very outspoken, not the usual dumb blondes. He wanted women who were full of life and willing to speak their minds, and he had to resist a lot of studio pressure on both pictures to make Cindy a blonde cheerleader-type and Princess Leia a blonde bimbo. But he made them both tough and more interesting.

In Graffiti, *of course, you have further balance with the Candy Clark character, the spacey blonde.*

KATZ: Yes, a real space cadet.

But you take, even her, far beyond the blonde bimbo-type, because she's an amazingly appealing character—she's quirky, and she's not stupid. She actually enjoys the vomiting and the Goat Killer and watching Toad get beat up. She's very unique.

KATZ: And Candy Clark did a great job.

HUYCK: She fit the role so well because she was kind of daffy herself.

KATZ: It's one of those rare pictures with almost perfect casting.

It's truly amazing. Fred Roos, who'd just cast The Godfather *for Coppola, was called in to help Lucas cast* Graffiti. *Were you involved in the process?*

KATZ: Very involved. We were very influential in casting Rick and Cindy.

You're talking about Richard Dreyfuss?

HUYCK: Yes, George was very good about casting because he listened to other people's opinions. The tests were shot in a commercial house here in Los Angeles, and we watched them all with George, Fred, and some other people. Fred pushed very hard for Harrison [Ford]—just as he did later when George wanted Christopher Walken for Han Solo in *Star Wars*. So if we thought George was really missing something, we'd work on him, and he'd listen.

KATZ: And Francis forced him to work very hard on the casting. Originally, George wanted to use certain "known" actors for *Graffiti*, and Francis insisted that they weren't strong enough.

Who did Lucas want?

KATZ: He wanted Gary Grimes, who'd become big after *Summer of '42*, and Desi Arnaz, Jr.

For Graffiti?

KATZ: Yes, but they both turned him down. To them, *Graffiti* seemed like a dopey little car movie, and it was only three or four weeks work, anyway. So George couldn't get any name actors for the film—no one that anyone had ever heard of. So he had to go out and find his own, and Francis encouraged him. He said, "We're going to look, and we're going to look, and we're going to find the right people." And they did.

How did you feel about casting Ronny Howard—the only known actor due to his TV background?

HUYCK: To be honest, he was our least favorite choice.

Because of the TV association?

HUYCK: That was part of it. Since everyone had seen Ronny before, he was the least "fresh" of all the characters.

KATZ: And I always thought we needed someone more charismatic than Ronny.

HUYCK: He was very straight, and he tended toward the dorky.

KATZ: I thought the Steve character should have been more sensational-looking, more compelling physically. Sorry, Ronny.

How do you feel now?

KATZ: I think Ronny did a very good job. He seemed very "real" in the role.

He seems to transcend the scholar-athlete-politician type. He's got heart.

HUYCK: He does.

KATZ: He certainly does. But I always saw the character in a very different way.

Was there anyone else you were worried about?

HUYCK: Well, we were all kind of nervous about Rick Dreyfuss because he was a little too old for the part.

KATZ: I'd seen him in an Israel Horovitz play called *Line*, and I thought he was a fabulous actor. But when he tested for *Graffiti*, George had a very lukewarm response, and I felt we definitely shouldn't overlook this guy. He clearly had loads of talent, so we really pushed for him, even though he was a bit old for the part.

Wasn't there also some concern that he was a New Yorker and Jewish—and not very Californian?

HUYCK: Yes, but Rick pulled it off. He did a great job.

He did. He seems perfect now.

HUYCK: Rick recognized another layer in the film beneath the very naive surface of things. *Graffiti* wasn't just *Rock Around the Block*, which Universal liked to call it; there was something much more serious about it. Gloria and I always loved Fellini's autobiographical film *I Vitelloni*, and we showed the movie to both George and Francis who'd never seen it before. It's about four guys in their thirties, who've never left their small, Italian town, and, although, the town kind of laughs at them and the film's full of humor and high spirits, it's quite serious as well. One other important thing about *American Graffiti* is that Gloria and I saw the film as being very strange and surreal—with all these amazing things happening in one night, like Wolfman Jack, and the Goat Killer, and all the rest of it. Then George shot it in a low-budget documentary style which, I believe, complemented all the strangeness. He shot it very fast—put 'em up against the wall and shoot—and the film was scoped so he could get more people into the frame at once and not have to worry as much about coverage. It gave the film a very strange quality—it became a very lyric, very visual thing, especially the cruising shots.

KATZ: They're beautiful shots.

HUYCK: George is the absolute master of montage, as compared to Spielberg, for instance. We've worked with them both, and it's very interesting to see the differences. Steven is very mise-en-scène. He does all kinds of things *within* the frame—with people shifting around—but George is all shots. And lots of close-ups.

Let's talk about cruising. Lucas apparently saw Graffiti *as a feel-good recreation of his high school days in Modesto, California—and also a way to shed his cold, techno image from* THX-1138. *Much of* Graffiti *revolves around the phenomenon of high-school "cruising," and many critics have described these scenes as an "auto-ballet." Did you both, like Lucas, grow up in the California cruising culture?*

KATZ: Yes, cruising was a very big phenomenon, even in Los Angeles. Everybody used to cruise a place called Dolores's Drive-In on Wilshire. So, it was something in our vocabulary.

HUYCK: That's right. I was driving at fifteen, and the day I turned sixteen, I got my first car—a fifty Ford. It was a very big thing, and George captured the phenomenon under the most horrible circumstances—especially the time pressure and the lighting problems. In those days, there wasn't much shooting done at night; nothing like nowadays where they can light up a mile. Back then, they really didn't know how to do it, and George was using what was essentially a blow-up process because he was shooting in Techniscope, a half-frame process. So you need even more light than usual, and that was George's problem from the beginning, because he couldn't get much of an image on the film. There just wasn't enough light, and they didn't have enough money to bring in big arcs lamps. So they had to invent a method on the spot in just a few days.

I understand that Haskell Wexler, who was working on a film in Los Angeles, flew north every night?

KATZ: Yes, he helped George quite a bit.

HUYCK: And, in the end, it contributed to our vision of the film. We never saw *Graffiti* as being realistic, even though people would later say, "That's my story!" or "You've really struck a nerve!" and so on.

KATZ: We always saw it as more mythic.

HUYCK: And odder.

Dale Pollock agrees. In his book Skywalking, *he claims that there were very few artistic disagreements between you and George Lucas, except that you envisioned the long night of the film in a more surreal manner, and Lucas wanted it more firmly grounded in reality.*

KATZ: Exactly.

HUYCK: But, in the end, you get plenty of both.

That's right. Now what about the wall-to-wall music? Were you ever concerned about overkill?

KATZ: We were concerned that George was *too* focused on the music, while we were focused on the dialogue. We were also concerned that the audience wouldn't be able to hear the lines. Then, when we finally saw the first cut, we said, "Oh no, he's cutting for the music! He's not cutting for the dialogue!" He'd even removed some of the payoffs in various scenes to accommodate the music, but we finally convinced him to put everything back.

HUYCK: Sometimes we'd say, "Why'd you cut that, George?" and he'd say, "Well, I've got this great song," and we'd say, "But you can't cut there, or you might as well cut the whole scene!" For example, he wanted to trim down the scene near the end of the movie where Candy's relating what happened during the night, and I said, "George, you can't cut that! It's an incredible moment, and she did a terrific job!"

It's also part of her quirkiness.

HUYCK: Yes!

KATZ: So when we saw the first cut, we were hysterical.

HUYCK: We kept yelling, "You can't cut that, George!"

KATZ: But, in the end, he listened, and he put everything back. Then Universal took the picture away and recut it during the writers' strike, when he couldn't cross the lines. It was really low.

HUYCK: Especially since the cuts they made didn't really change the movie very much. It was just vindictive and petty.

The studio cut four-and-a-half minutes—the used-car salesman, Steve's confrontation with an elderly teacher, and Harrison Ford singing "Some Enchanted Evening."

HUYCK: That's right.

Then after the film's success, Lucas was able to reincorporate the scenes back into the movie. But I must admit, trying to be objective about it, those three scenes seem among the weaker moments in the film.

HUYCK: It could be. It happens many times when you see the director's cut of a movie, and you say, "Well, I can understand why they cut those scenes out." I remember a while back when they showed Cukor's version of *A Star is Born.* Since they no longer had the cut scenes, they showed the old production stills and played the original soundtrack. And when I saw it, I had the same reaction as everyone else, "No wonder they cut those scenes out!" It was very clear they shouldn't have been in the movie.

KATZ: They were totally extraneous.

HUYCK: So you never know. When you're making a film, some scenes become very dear to the director, and George felt that cutting those scenes was just another example of getting screwed by the industry.

KATZ: It was very mean-spirited, and George was very anti-Hollywood anyway.

HUYCK: So his victory was being able to put them back in.

Yes, he won in the end. Incidentally, back to the music for a minute, why were there no Presley songs on the soundtrack?

HUYCK: I don't know. Maybe they were too expensive. George was on a really tight budget, and, many times, fifteen or twenty-five dollars made the difference between what he could afford to buy and what he couldn't.

I wonder what that soundtrack would cost today?

HUYCK: Astronomical. Prices went up immediately after *American Graffiti*. It really started a trend.

It was the first film with wall-to-wall pop music, not to mention rock and roll, and, nowadays, it seems that most Hollywood films use old rock songs from the fifties and sixties.

HUYCK: It certainly set a style. George knew what he was doing.

How about the role of Wolfman Jack? Was he involved right from the beginning?

HUYCK: Yes. Wolfman Jack was somebody we all listened to in California, and we grew up hearing him on the radio.

And when you were writing the script, were you sure you could get him to be in the movie?

HUYCK: We had a pretty good idea that he was available. George had made a documentary film at USC called *Rock Emperor* about a local DJ, and he was confident he could get the Wolfman. Right after we wrote the Wolfman's speech, which is longer than what's in the movie ...

KATZ: And it's much better than what's in the movie—only the last half remains.

HUYCK: Yes, and George said take it to the Wolfman, and it turned out that he was broadcasting two blocks away from where we were living in Echo Park. So we drove over, gave him the pages, and he read it with tears in his eyes. He said it was absolutely wonderful and that he'd love to do it.

You've made him a legend.

HUYCK: I guess so.

How do you feel about the scene now?

HUYCK: I don't think Wolfman quite pulled it off. But the feeling's still there, and Rick found ways to make it work.

It does seem like Dreyfuss is carrying the scene. Wolfman seems uncomfortable, except when he's pushing the studio buttons.

KATZ: That's right, but Rick helped. He ad-libbed things and tried to loosen up the Wolfman.

HUYCK: Incidentally, the popsicles are an homage to Kurosawa's *Stray Dog*. There's a heat wave in that film, and Shimura, the older detective, is always licking popsicles. A little homage for a few film buffs!

Since we're talking about specific scenes, what are your personal favorites in the movie?

HUYCK: I like the sentimental scenes, especially the dance scene where they're arguing in the spotlight. It's a wonderful moment.

One of the best scenes in the movie.

HUYCK: And I like all of the Rick Dreyfuss stuff, maybe because he was always the character I felt closest to. I especially like his "initiation" into the Pharaohs—which was George's idea from the beginning and based on something that actually happened. I just love it when the cop car comes off its axle, and all the stuff about Rick being initiated. I also think the liquor store scene's very funny—and very strange.

The first time you see it, you have no idea what's happening when that paper bag comes flying through the air.

KATZ: I still like the Goat Killer.

A very funny and creepy scene. Any others?

KATZ: All the car montages and the roller-skating at Mel's.

HUYCK: Those opening night shots at Mel's, with "Sixteen Candles" playing on the soundtrack, are beautifully done. George really understood scope, and he used it perfectly.

Now for a longer question. One of the greatest achievements of American Graffiti *was its portrayal of a culture that was about to undergo an extraordinary transformation—a radical shift from the fifties' greaser culture to the sixties' hippie revolution. In the script, strangely enough, it's the greaser hero, John Milner, who seems to sense that things are changing. In his conversation with the exuberant Toad after Milner's victorious race on Paradise Road, the greaser hero actually claims that he was losing the race before the crash, despite the evidence of the film, which shows him to be wrong. But Milner seems to have some acute awareness that he and his youthful world of cruising cars and dragging hot rods is passing away. He doesn't express it explicitly, and, eventually, he humors Toad's conviction that Milner can race victoriously forever, but Milner seems to know better. He also seems the most perceptive character in the film—like a prescient cowboy aware that he's living at the end of the Wild West era. How intentional was all this in the writing of the script?*

HUYCK: *Very* intentional.

KATZ: You got it exactly.

HUYCK: We always saw Paul Le Mat—the Milner character—as a cowboy who sees his era ending. He knows things are changing, and he knows that there are kids coming along who'll be able to draw faster than he can.

And I prefer it that way, but many other writers would have let the Curt character—the intellectual and aspiring writer—sense what was happening.

KATZ: But he's wasn't really part of the culture. He's an outsider in the California car culture. Look at his car—it's a two-horsepower Citroën!

HUYCK: That's right. And we reversed another expectation with Curt since the intellectual spends the whole night frantically obsessing over the blonde in the T-Bird.

And all these balances and reversals become even more poignant with the epilogue which reveals the eventual fates of the film's main characters. Is it true that you were originally opposed to the idea as too depressing?

KATZ: Yes, and too corny and obvious.

HUYCK: And too heavy-handed.

But I remember when I first saw the movie when it opened in New York. The place went absolutely nuts during the film, but when those titles came up at the end, you could hear a pin drop. It seemed to give even more depth to everything that came before.

KATZ: Yes, and now everyone tells us how terribly wrong-headed we were back then!

HUYCK: People would come up to us and say that the epilogue "made" the movie for them. That it was "chilling." That it was a sudden shock to be faced with the future, "My God, look at what happened next!"

Some people have claimed that you were concerned that the female characters weren't included in the epilogue?

KATZ: It's not true. At the time, we didn't have enough feminist awareness to be concerned about that. But later, we did get a lot of static about not including the women characters. But, at the time, we were so focused on getting rid of the titles that we never thought about the women characters.

HUYCK: We just wanted to scrap the whole thing.

KATZ: That was our biggest disagreement with George, and we were wrong. If I remember correctly, Marcia also felt that the titles were too depressing and too manipulative. But I'm glad George did what he did.

In a way, those titles force you to rethink everything you've seen—all the fun you've had.

HUYCK: That's right.

KATZ: You know, it's amazing to realize that *that* was our biggest dis-agreement with George—especially when you think about all the problems you have to go through producing a script these days.

Pauline Kael was one of the people who took Lucas to task for not including the girls in the final titles, and, apparently, he's now come to regret his deci-sion. But at the time, he responded to such criticism by reminding people that "It's a movie about the four guys." I wonder why that still isn't true? The guys were close friends, and they were the focus of the movie, not the girls. If the film had focused on a crucial night in the life of four teenaged girlfriends, would everyone have insisted that the guys they spent time with during the night be included in the final titles?

HUYCK: No, they wouldn't.

KATZ: That's true, it's just that the female roles turned out so well in the film—they're such strong characters—and you're likely to say to yourself, "Well, what happened to them, too?" On the other hand, the film really *is* about the boys, and it's tough enough, at the end of the film, to reveal what happened to them, without having to give the fates of the girls as well.

HUYCK: Yes, like Candy's now a stripper, and so on.

We could do without that.

HUYCK: Yes, and, eventually, they had to deal with all those problems when they did the sequel. It was a disaster.

And you both saw it coming.

KATZ: We did. We refused to do it. George wanted us to write the sequel, and he wanted Willard to direct it.

Let's discuss that a bit. You'd sharpened the dialogue for Star Wars, *and you eventually wrote* Indiana Jones and the Temple of Doom *for Lucasfilm. But you refused to be part of the* Graffiti *sequel, which Universal released in 1979 as* More American Graffiti. *What were your reasons?*

HUYCK: You have to remember that, in those days, sequels were always pathetic, and, within the industry, the most pathetic thing of all was to do the sequel to your own movie. Eventually, Francis and Steven changed all that, but it made us very nervous back then. Another problem was that the sequel moved into another era—with Vietnam and all that—and we just didn't want to deal with it. We didn't particularly like what happened to those people we'd created.

KATZ: It was so unpleasant and sad. It would be like destroying our wonderful characters.

Yes, and they'd actually become different *people in the new era.*

HUYCK: That's right.

KATZ: And since we were working on other things at the time, we just told George we'd rather not do it.

Now let's discuss the legendary preview of American Graffiti *at the Northpoint Theater in San Francisco. Even after this extraordinary screening, Universal still didn't like the film.*

HUYCK: Even after the audience at Northpoint went wild!

KATZ: Bananas! We weren't there that night—we were too scared to go—but George called afterwards and told us it was fantastic. People were bouncing off the walls. But, amazingly, right after the screening, Universal's Ned Tanen had this bizarre, violent reaction to the film. Everyone else was saying the film was a "ten," but Tanen had decided it was a "one"! It was very, very depressing. He didn't even want to release the movie, and he considered giving it to television. Fortunately, Francis had an absolute fit and offered to buy the movie on the spot.

Tell me about that—the legendary, post-screening, shouting match between Francis Ford Coppola and Universal's Ned Tanen.

HUYCK: Tanen's behavior was truly unbelievable, and particularly nasty for George and Marcia who'd just spent a whole year editing the film at their house for no money. Ned's attitude at the screening was, "Well, you haven't done much to improve it," which was absolutely untrue. And that's when Francis made his famous, flamboyant gesture, "Where's my checkbook? How much do you have on the movie? I'll buy it from you right now!" But, of course, Tanen backed down, and, to this day, he denies what happened that night.

KATZ: He even denies criticizing the film—which is ridiculous.

Finally, the film was released, and the critical and box office success was phenomenal. Ticket sales eventually exceeded a hundred million, and Dale Pollock claims that it was "The most profitable investment a Hollywood studio ever made," given its more than 50 to 1 ratio of investment dollars to profit dollars.

HUYCK: They made quite a return off their little, low-budget movie.

And the critical success was equally sensational. The New York Times *called* Graffiti *"A lasting work of art!"* The Los Angeles Times *described it as a "Masterfully executed and profoundly affecting movie!" And* Newsweek *called it "brilliant." The film eventually won "Best Screenplay" from the New York Film Critics Association and also from the National Society of Film Critics, and was nominated for five Oscars, including Best Picture and Best Screenplay. Were you at the Oscars that night?*

KATZ: Yes, and, strangely enough, it was incredibly boring.

HUYCK: Yes, so we were joking around a bit, and this woman leaned over and asked us to be quiet, and I turned around and thought, "Oh no! It's Lew Wasserman's wife!"

So that's who's always talking in the movies, the writers?

HUYCK: That's right.

The uniqueness of American Graffiti *was obvious at the time it came out: the music, the unusual narrative, the night shooting, and the extraordinary performances of a new generation of actors. But most affecting was the film's evocation of a unique historical period and the confident innocence that existed in the New Frontier era, but which would soon be lost to drugs, the sexual revolution, political assassinations, and the expanding war in Vietnam. One of the countless kids who saw the film in 1973 and wrote to Lucas said, "I'm sixteen and stoned all the time, and I didn't realize that you could have so much fun being a kid." As sad as the comment is, it says a great deal about the achievement of the film. Exactly twenty-five years ago, you were writing the screenplay for* American Graffiti *with great pleasure yet with very little confidence that it would ever be anything more than a little, low-budget film—hardly an American classic. What's your opinion of it now, after all these years?*

KATZ: After all these years, it's amazing to me how tremendously fresh the movie is, and it's all to George's credit—it's a truly inventive and innovative film. Nowadays, when you see nothing but bullshit coming out of the film industry, it's important to remind ourselves that films like that really can be made—films that are truly unique.

Well, the dialogue's a major part of that lasting "freshness." It still holds up, and, strangely enough, it doesn't seem dated. So often, people write contemporary films, and the dialogue quickly dates. But you had to write a film about something that happened ten years earlier—in a different era with a different terminology—and it still doesn't feel dated. It captures the period, but still seems alive.

KATZ: I think that's a product—which no longer exists—of not being forced through the studio machine. If we submitted that script today, we'd have to sit around in endless story conferences with dozens of executives, and, believe me, the dialogue would be the first thing to go. So would the Goat Killer—and everything else unusual about the script. Everything that was original would be taken out.

HUYCK: Yes, all the eccentricities. You can't sit in a room with a group of people and reach a unanimous decision about anything that's eccentric because somebody's bound to say, "Well, that doesn't work for me." And you can't go forward until everyone agrees, and, eventually, you have to give up. And when they do finally agree, it's always something extremely mild—something mundane.

Like a lowest common denominator?

KATZ: That's right.

HUYCK: It has to be that way because the studio people really aren't very creative, so the action of the script always has to be something they've seen before. Which, in the end, is invariably uninteresting.

So on this score, Francis Coppola would have to get a lot of credit because he allowed you and Lucas to do your own film?

HUYCK: Absolutely.

KATZ: Francis was wonderful! Things were very different back then.

HUYCK: Even with *Star Wars*, once Alan Ladd decided that George should make the film, there weren't development people sitting around in story conferences messing things up. *Never.* Once the decision was made, the filmmaker went out and made the movie. For better or worse.

Well, with American Graffiti, *the result was a true American classic, and you were both a crucial part of the film's great success.*

KATZ: Thank you.

HUYCK: Thanks.

CHAPTER 10

The Sting (1973)

A CONVERSATION WITH DAVID S. WARD

Born in Rhode Island and raised in Cleveland, Ohio, David S. Ward attended Pomona College in California where his major shifted several times, beginning with premed and ending up with cinema. After a year of graduate school at USC, he attended UCLA where he completed an MFA in Film in 1970. A year later, his screenplay, *Steelyard Blues*, was made into a feature film starring Jane Fonda and Donald Sutherland. His next script, *The Sting* (1973), was directed by George Roy Hill and featured Paul Newman and Robert Redford. The film received seven Academy Awards, including Oscars for Best Picture and Best Screenwriting. In 1982, Ward adapted and directed John Steinbeck's *Cannery Row*, starring Nick Nolte and Debra Winger. He subsequently directed a number of feature films including *Major League* (1989) with Charlie Sheen, *The Program* (1993) with James Caan and Halle Berry, *Major League II* (1994), and *Down Periscope* (1996) with Kelsey Grammer. He also continued to write screenplays for other directors, most notably *The Milagro Beanfield War* (1988) for Robert Redford; *Sleepless in Seattle* (cowriter, 1993), starring Tom Hanks and Meg Ryan, for which he received a second Oscar nomination for screenwriting; and *Flyboys* (2006), directed by Tony Bill and starring James Franco.

Looking back at the films of the early seventies in Hollywood, The Sting *seems a radical departure from the many self-conscious, heavily dramatized, contemporary films being produced at the time. What inspired you to write such an intricately plotted, humorous, entertaining period-piece about con men in the thirties?*

WARD: The idea for the film first hit me when I was researching a pick-pocketing sequence for my first movie, *Steelyard Blues*. Not knowing any-thing about the subject, I started reading about grifters, and I soon learned that pickpockets were at the bottom end of the grifters' scale and confi-dence men were at the top. I found the con men particularly fascinating, especially their contention that they didn't really "steal" their victim's money, since their marks willingly gave it to them, out of greed, knowing full well they were involved in something illegal. Another reason that con men sat at the top of the grifters' chain is that they were never physically violent and their final success was always the result of elaborately staged productions that required both intelligence and nerve. They also needed the subtle ability to pick out an appropriate mark—a person who possessed such a powerful streak of greed that it bordered on larceny. So I thought they were an extremely interesting American subculture, and, back in the early seventies, there was a serious interest in exploring the more unusual and curious aspects of Americana—which, unfortunately, you don't see much in today's contemporary films. So I became fascinated with con men and the bizarre world they lived in, and since I'd never actually seen a movie specifically focused on confidence men, I decided to give it a shot and see if I could do the subject justice.

   Did you know any con men?

WARD: I talked to a number of older con artists, and one or two of them had played the big time. The heyday of the big con was the thirties and early forties. After that, the world changed in various ways that made it almost impossible to pull off the big con—for example, it became extremely difficult to set up the elaborate con "stores" like they did in the old days. So I learned a lot from those old-timers, and I read everything that was ever written about con men. I also researched the time period in terms of its music, its culture, and its current events. Since all this happened long before I was born, I had to rely on interviews and source materials to tell the story, and I tried to be very accurate, even structuring the script to carefully follow the actual stages of the traditional big con.

   After Alan Myerson's successful direction of Steelyard Blues, *how did you get your next script,* The Sting, *in the hands of director George Roy Hill?*

WARD: *Steelyard Blues* was produced by Tony Bill and Michael Phillips, and while we were making the film, they asked me if I had any other ideas, and I said, "Yes, I've been thinking a lot about confidence men." So I told them the story, and they were really taken with the idea. Now, at the time, Tony had a very close relationship with Robert Redford, and they were talking about doing a movie about barnstorming that eventually became

The Great Waldo Pepper, so Tony said, "Why don't you make up an audio-tape of your con man idea, and I'll send it to Bob, and we'll see if he's interested." So I spoke my story into a cassette player—which really shows how much the business has changed—and Tony sent it to Redford, and he liked it. So the next time Redford came to Los Angeles, we had a meeting about it, and he said, "Well, I really like the idea, but I can't commit to it right now. I need to see the script first, so get it to me as soon as it's done." So I wrote the script, we sent it to Redford, and he loved it. Then he sent it to George Hill, and George sent it to Paul Newman.

I read that you were originally hoping to direct the film. How did you feel when Robert Redford brought in George Roy Hill?

WARD: I did want to start a career as a director, and I'd been hoping to direct my new script, but when it started to attract people like Robert Redford, I knew no one would let me direct it. It was clear that the film, which I'd first envisioned as a little independent, now had big picture potential, and I was more than willing to let a distinguished director like George Hill take over. So I was actually very grateful. I thought it would be better for the movie—and better for me in the long run.

Although your original draft of The Sting *didn't change very much in production, there were a few important adjustments, especially the character of Henry Gondorff. Originally, you described him as a large "imposing" man who looked like a "lumberjack." Is it true that you wrote the part with Peter Boyle in mind?*

WARD: Well, I loved Peter, and I thought he was great in *Steelyard,* but I didn't write the role with him in mind. Before Redford got involved, my initial vision of the two main characters was that Hooker was very young—maybe a nineteen-year-old kid—and Henry Gondorff was a steely, tough Lee Van Cleef-type. So I originally saw them as a young "hotshot"—quite full of himself—and an older, somewhat austere Lee Van Cleef-type. So their relationship would develop as a mentor/student—even a father/son—relationship. Obviously, when the roles went to Redford and Newman, it would no longer work as a father/son relationship, even though Newman still calls him "kid" in the picture, but the mentor/student relationship was never changed. As far as Gondorff being described as a stocky lumberjack type in one of the earlier versions of the script, I have to admit, I don't even remember that. But I do remember one important result of the casting of Paul Newman was that George and I felt that more humor was appropriate to the role, so I added that to the script.

According to several biographies, Newman vacillated back and forth about accepting the role of Henry Gondorff. Eventually, Hill and Redford and Newman met at Newman's apartment in New York City to discuss the script. Where you there?

WARD: No, I wasn't at that meeting, and I didn't know about the vacil-lation. You have to remember that I was just a young buck in the industry at the time, and I wasn't privy to all the things that were happening behind the scenes. I was only told after something like that was decided—or not decided—and I never knew all the details of how it got to that point.

Supposedly, Newman vacillated throughout the meeting—even suggesting to Hill and Redford other actors whom he felt could play the role of Gondorff. Finally, when the meeting ended unresolved, Newman walked his guests out to the elevator, and while they were waiting there in the silence, George Roy Hill supposedly said, "What are we worried about? The Sting is a pop piece, we enjoy working together, and we'll have fun, so let's do it"? And Newman agreed and said yes.

WARD: Well, I'm sure glad he said yes! After *Butch Cassidy and the Sun-dance Kid*, those three men had a very special relationship that, of course, preexisted my involvement, so I'm very grateful that George and Bob con-vinced Paul to take the part. It was crucial to the success of the film.

George Roy Hill was reputed to be meticulous about everything. Is that correct?

WARD: Yes, it is. In preproduction, George went over every scene in the script with a fine-tooth comb. He went over every single line of dialogue—always examining how everything revealed character and tied into the plot. He wanted to be absolutely sure that we were never "cheating" the audi-ence by giving them information that was unfairly false. So once George started shooting the picture, he was completely satisfied with the script, and he stuck to it very closely. There were only a few changes in script on the set, and all of them were minor. That was George's style: meticulously tech the script in preproduction and then stick to it in production. He's one of the most prepared and thorough people I've ever met.

I'd like to ask you about a few of the important changes that you'd made in the gradual metamorphosis of the script before the shooting began. One of the most important additions to your original script is Luther's wife and family. This dramatically humanizes the con artists, engages the audience more, and increases Hooker's motivation for revenge. How did that come about?

WARD: When I wrote the first draft of *The Sting*, it took me about six months to write, and I wasn't happy with it. I felt that it didn't do justice to the subject. It was a good recitation of how the big con really works, but I wanted to do more than just "involve" the audience in a con game. I wanted the film itself to become an *actual* confidence game that takes in the audience. I definitely didn't want anyone walking out of the theater saying, "Well, I'd never fall for anything like that." So it wasn't until I got the idea about the fake FBI agents that I felt confident I could "take in" the audience.

So then you worked backwards?

WARD: Yes. I realized that the fake FBI guys needed something very strong to make Hooker turn against Gondorff—it would have to be something extremely powerful to make him sell out Gondorff. Originally, I had him threatened with "twenty years, without parole" in the penitentiary, but I didn't feel that was enough, so I conjured up the idea that the Feds would threaten to put Alva, Luther's wife, in jail. I hoped that Hooker's fears for Alva would be creditable enough to make the audience believe that Hooker would give in to the Feds. Then, once I made that decision, I had to go back and make Alva and Luther's family more significant in the film and in Hooker's life, and that also helped to create more empathy for Luther.

One omission from your original script is the clever sequence where Hooker pulls a counterfeit con in the train station when he first arrives in Chicago. Apparently, Redford liked the scene very much, but Hill felt that the film needed to get to Gondorff quicker. Was that scene actually shot?

WARD: I'm not sure if they shot that scene because during the production of *The Sting*, there was a writer's strike going on, and I was prohibited from crossing the picket line. So I only saw about the first three weeks of shooting, and then I was off the set. But I do understand why the scene was cut: George wanted to keep the pace moving along and get right into the heart of the story, which is Gondorff and Hooker taking on Lonnegan.

How did you conceive of some of the script's ingenious plot twists? Like the clever FBI/Salino/black-gloved man subplot, or the fake shootings at the end of the film.

WARD: I originally got the idea about the faked deaths when I was reading an article about squibs—those little exploding packs of fake blood that they rig up on performers to make the "blood" squirt through their clothes. As I was reading the article, I started thinking, "Maybe they could kill each other, and *not* kill each other at the same time!"—which would be a perfect way to wrap up the con. First, it would frighten the audience; second, it would allow for another plot reversal; and third, it would be a clever way to terminate the con and convince the Charles Durning character that Hooker and Gondorff were really dead. Even Lonnegan would have no one to seek revenge against. So it neatly tied everything up. Did you notice that it was recently ripped off in the film *Bandits*?

No, I haven't seen it.

WARD: At the end of the film, Billy Bob Thornton and Bruce Willis shoot each other in a faked death scene.

Which is a tribute to The Sting. *And how about that other clever plot turn, when the mysterious man with the black glove comes down the alley and shoots Salino in the forehead. Do you remember the genesis of that?*

WARD: I can't remember it specifically, but I do remember thinking that the script was short on women, so I decided to create some kind of relationship for Hooker. Then I thought it would be good idea to turn the relationship upside down and make it potentially lethal for Hooker, even though he and the audience would be unaware of it. So I made Salino a hit man, something I'd never seen in a film before, and which I thought the audience would find quite surprising. Of course, since then, the idea's been reused quite a bit in other movies.

Another extremely ingenious aspect of the plot is the clever use of the word "place" in the final Western Union telephone call to the gangster Lonnegan concerning which specific horse he should bet his money on. The phone message is, "Place it on Lucky Dan, third race, at Riverside Park," which makes it completely believable, later in the film, when Lonnegan learns that he was supposed to bet the horse to "place"—not to "win." This is very significant because Lonnegan's definitely not stupid, and the confusion over the meaning of the word "place" doesn't arouse his suspicions.

WARD: Well, I can't take credit for that, because that's how that specific con game—the Wire—was actually played. It was a very subtle element in the con, just like the earlier "shutout" where the mark *almost* gets the bet down, and then sees that he would have won if he'd placed it in time. In the old days, there were two kinds of wire cons: one was horse racing, and the other was a stock market swindle—which I didn't think was as interesting. It would have been harder to explain to the audience, and it wasn't as visual as having an announcer actually call the horse race. So, the cleverness of the word "place" was part of the old racing con.

When the audience is actually watching the film, given its increasing pace at that point, they might not actually get the "place" idea, but later, thinking about it, they can certainly appreciate its ingenuousness.

WARD: Yes, those con guys were awfully smart. Of course, for them, the idea wasn't just to con the mark, but to do it in such a way that the mark would never even realize that he'd been taken—and thus never seek revenge. In real life, sometimes the marks did figure it out later, but they were usually reluctant to pursue the con men because it was admission that they'd been duped and that they'd been involved in something illegal. So the con men tried to cover themselves in a number of ways.

One line from your script that was unfortunately cut from the film occurs at the end of the actual sting when the phony FBI agents raid the betting parlor. As instructed, the Joliet policeman Snyder, who isn't aware of the con, quickly hustles Lonnegan out of the raided parlor to prevent the mobster's involvement in a "scandal." In the script, Lonnegan, despite the potential scandal, is naturally hesitant to leave his money behind, and he says, questioningly, "But my money?" and Snyder says "We'll worry about that later." But those lines were cut from the film, even though for the con to really work—and for the audience to believe it—it's much better to have Lonnegan believe that he'll eventually get his money back. Do you know why the lines were cut?

WARD: The decision to do that was probably made on the set, and, of course, I wasn't there at the time. Another slight change at the end is the way Hooker says, "It's not enough." When he says it in the movie, he says it in a kind of upbeat way, but in the script, he really means it. He reflects on the fact that even the successful con could never make up for what happened to his good friend Luther. But for the kind of movie *The Sting* turned out to be, I actually think that George had Bob read it the right way. As you know, the original script was much grittier, but given the overall tone of George's version, I think he did the right thing. At that point in the film, the audience doesn't want some deep and somber introspection from Hooker. They want him to celebrate this victory with everyone else, and that's appropriate. As a writer, you always have to deal with directors or actors changing your lines somewhat, and, as I mentioned earlier, I was very grateful that there was very little of that on *The Sting*—and sometimes it was for the best. So I certainly can't complain.

Is it true that George Hill suggested the Saturday Evening Post *designs for the title cards?*

WARD: Yes, it was George and Henry Bumstead, who was the art director—we didn't call them production designers in those days. I'd written those chapter headings right into the script, and George's idea of using the old-fashioned title cards as well as the outdated visual effects—like the wipes, and the iris-ins, and the iris-outs—definitely helped to create the feel of the period.

I've read that Walker Evans's Depression photographs were studied for the look of the film, especially its grittier beginning? Were you aware of that?

WARD: I didn't know about that, but I wouldn't be surprised. George was extremely meticulous.

One anachronism in the film is the wonderful Scott Joplin music, which wasn't added until after the initial rough cut. Where did the music come from?

WARD: That happened in a rather odd way. George is actually an accomplished musician, a pianist. And I would often hear him playing Bach or something like that on the piano. At that time, I'd been listening to Scott Joplin played by Joshua Rifkin on his Nonesuch album. Rifkin played the tunes rather slowly, and I thought the music was just wonderful. So I brought it to George thinking that it might be something he'd enjoy playing on the piano, never thinking that it might end up in the movie. As you know, in the script, the music I suggested was all blues from the Depression period—Robert Johnson, Bessie Smith, Ida Cox, and others—because

I wanted the film to have a gritty, earthy feel. But when George heard the Joplin music, he thought it would be perfect for the movie. And I said, "But George, that's not the right period, it's turn of the century music, not thirties music." And he said, "David, you and I will be the only ones in the whole world who'll know that. And even if some other people know it, no one will care, because the music represents the *tone* of the movie. It's exactly the mood I want to create in the film, and if the tone of the film is consistent with the music, no one will question it." And George was right. The music works perfectly for the movie, and I'm glad he made the decision, despite my concerns.

A blues sound track would have created a much different movie.

WARD: Yes. One of the first things that appealed to me about the old-time confidence men was that I envisioned them as social outlaws. These were men who weren't privileged with an affluent upbringing, and they were generally uneducated, but they could definitely hold their own with the more privileged elements of society. So I had a certain empathy for them and for their uncanny ability to transcend their humble beginnings. When I was writing the script, it was a time in our country's history when revolutionary thinking was very popular among people of my age group. So I tended to idealize—actually over-idealize—outlaws to a certain degree. And this group of outlaws was easier to idealize since they never killed people, and they didn't even "steal" in the traditional sense of the word. Basically, they were exposing and exploiting the greed of the well-to-do, and I found a certain nobility in that, and I wanted to create an honest and realistic context for the lives they led—and where they came from. Thus, the blues. But once Redford and Newman got involved, *The Sting* became much more than a little grifter film, and rightfully so, and George made all the right choices to make the film more universally appealing, and the Scott Joplin music was an integral part of that.

I'd like to ask a few questions about casting and the subsequent performances. I've read that George Roy Hill originally wanted Richard Boone for the mobster Lonnegan. Is that correct?

WARD: There was definitely talk about Richard Boone for Lonnegan, but it fell through. I think Boone would have made a very good Lonnegan, but then we ended up with Robert Shaw, and it's hard to top that.

After the film's release, Pauline Kael criticized Paul Newman's performance in The Sting, *claiming that he seemed disinterested. But almost everyone else thought that Newman stole the film with his natural charm and magnetism. How did you feel about that?*

WARD: Well, to be honest, I thought everyone was terrific in the film, and I thought that Newman played the character of Gondorff to perfection—tough, but with a strong sense of compassion and humor. He was hard on Hooker when he needed to be, and he was compassionate when that was appropriate. Paul also managed to project just the right sense of world-weariness in the character, and then he proceeded to show how Gondorff's initial negativism was gradually overcome by his innate sense of justice. This was crucial since the audience needed to believe that Gondorff had a higher motivation than just the money. I've always believed that what really bothered some of critics about *The Sting* was simply the reteaming of Newman and Redford after the huge box office success of *Butch Cassidy.* Some of them seemed to think the re-pairing was a cynical, Hollywood attempt to cash in on their recent success, which, of course, isn't how the film came to be made—or cast. It's very interesting that Charles Champlin, the film critic for *The L.A. Times,* didn't include *The Sting* in his list of the top 25 movies for the whole year—and that wasn't an especially strong year! I later heard that he had some kind of problem with the producers, Zanuck and Brown, and maybe that influenced him. Clearly, all film critics, like everyone else, have their own agendas, and that's their prerogative. And they often take an over-jaundiced view of anything they feel might be a cynical, Hollywood fabrication. But, as you know, Redford and Newman were *not* planning to do another film together, and I suspect that part of Newman's reservations about doing *The Sting* had to do with the prospect of their working together again so soon after *Butch Cassidy.* Paul Newman's an incredibly modest person who always assumes that there are many other performers who can do his roles just as well as he can, but he's wrong about that. He was an extraordinary Henry Gondorff—subtle, powerful, and humorous when he had to be. Pauline Kael was often an excellent critic, but she always tried to be a bit iconoclastic, and I was definitely chagrined by her review. But that's the business. You have to learn to live with that.

Is it true that Newman watched fifteen William Powell movies to study his Thin Man *elegance and sophistication?*

WARD: Well, I wouldn't be surprised because Paul's so thorough and meticulous. On the other hand, I'm not sure that Paul Newman needs to learn about elegance or sophistication from anybody—even William Powell. But that's Paul's modesty again. Personally, I think Paul can play any role he sets his mind to do.

When he dresses up in The Sting, *he's certainly dressed to kill.*

WARD: That's true, and he's definitely got that William Powell mustache, so maybe he was watching all the *Thin Man* films! This might be a little off the topic, but I think it says a lot about Paul's obsessive professionalism. When I was watching the rehearsals for *The Sting,* it didn't seem to me like Paul was doing very much, especially in the scenes with Robert Shaw, who seemed to be dominating. Shaw, of course, was a distinguished stage actor, and he was used to projecting, but I was still worried. So I went to George

Hill, rather surreptitiously, and I said, "George, is that the way Paul's going to do it?" And George said, "Don't worry, David, Paul always knows exactly where the camera is, and there's no camera here right now. But as soon as there's a camera in the room, you'll see Paul come to life. Don't worry, he'll 'show up.'" And he certainly did, and Pauline Kael's absolutely wrong. Sure, it wasn't a heavy dramatic part in the sense of Tennessee Williams or something like *Cool Hand Luke*, but that didn't mean that it was an easier role to perform. In some ways, it was harder.

    A perfect example is the poker scene.

WARD: Exactly, everything's done perfectly and subtly: Paul's facial expressions, the way he looks at his cards, the way he turns and looks at Lonnegan's thug, the way he explodes, and the way he fakes his drunkenness. That's great acting, pure and simple. You can't write that into your script!

    Some critics have speculated about the lack of typically beautiful female performers in The Sting, *and they've even suggested that this was done intentionally to focus on the good looks and charisma of Redford and Newman.*

WARD: Yes, I've always felt that idea was pretty ridiculous. In casting the film, George chose Dimitra Arliss to play Salino because he wanted someone with "exotic" good looks, and definitely not the typical Hollywood beauty. If she was too conventionally beautiful, the audience might not have believed that she was a murderer-for-hire. In today's world, that idea would seem much more acceptable to a contemporary audience, but back then, it was the first time that audiences saw a female hit man, and I think George was definitely right to cast someone who wasn't typically beautiful.

    After the film was shot, were you at the wrap party where Paul Newman, a notorious practical joker, had George Roy Hill's new sports car literally blowtorched in half?

WARD: No, I missed that party, but I do know that Paul is a huge practical joker, so I'm not at all surprised. He and George had a very interesting relationship. One time, before shooting actually began, George came up to me and said, "Look, David, Paul loves to talk about his character. He likes to work psychologically, and he's going to come up to you, and want to discuss his character. But everything you say, he'll later bring up with me, and he'll drive me crazy. So I don't want you talking to Paul on the set." So there I was, this young kid, suddenly on the set with the legendary Paul Newman, and every time he walked in my direction, I'd turn around and go in the other direction. It was very awkward, and it seemed that I was spending all my time on the set trying to avoid Paul Newman. Finally, one day, when I was standing alone, two arms suddenly wrapped around me from behind, and Paul turned me around, and said, "You've been avoiding me, haven't you?" So I didn't know what to say, so I admitted that I was. But Paul knew exactly what was going on, and he asked, "So George told you not to talk to me, right?" And I said yes, and Paul just laughed about it, and we kidded with George about it later, and I was very relieved.

One of the most interesting aspects of The Sting *is the relationship of the creation of the "big" con to the actual making of a film. Both are carefully plotted and elaborate deceptions, and Edward Shores, in his book on George Roy Hill, discusses the analogy at length. He points out that the "big con" involves "preproduction" meetings, "script" discussions, the building of sets, the hiring of performers and extras (con artists), costumes, makeup, "rewriting to meet contingencies," and even special effects. Was this extended analogy on your mind when you were writing the script?*

WARD: It was. All theater and drama is a manipulation. The dramatist wants us to *feel* a certain thing, so he sets us up in such a way that we'll respond accordingly. But that doesn't necessarily mean it's false, because it's constructive. But it's still manipulative—subtly manipulative. Now, of course, there's an obvious difference between honest effective drama and a heavy-handed manipulation of the baser emotions. So the writer has to be very careful. As for mystery and caper films, they're all, in a sense, a "con," since the audience is kept in the dark about certain things. The fun of such films is trying to discover what's *really* going on, and learning that what you previously believed to be true is actually false. In constructing such a film, it's crucial to avoid doing things that would "unfairly" lead the audience to a wrong conclusion, because, in a sense, you have a contract with the audience that, if they're clever enough, they can actually figure it out. Now, hopefully, you craft it in such a way that they'll never do that, even though, when it's over, you want them to say to themselves, "Yes, *now* I see how everything works out. Why didn't I see that coming?" And they feel perfectly comfortable with that—as long as you haven't broken the contract and unfairly manipulated them. In film, it's a case of the victim actually enjoying the con.

Relating to this question of "fairness," a number of commentators on The Sting *have made offhanded remarks about plot inconsistencies in the film. For example, Elena Oumano in her book about Paul Newman, refers to the "obvious loopholes" in the film without giving any specific examples. Surely, there are a number of coincidences in the plot—like the fact that Lonnegan, who knows where Hooker is living, never connects him with the man Salino is hunting down. But that's carefully covered in the script by Salino's well-known independence and secrecy. I've never found any plot holes in the script, and I wonder if you've ever discovered any after the fact?*

WARD: No, I'm delighted to say. No one has ever cited a specific or actual loophole in the plot—which is very gratifying. George and I went over that script a million times, and it paid off. George is a real blood-hound for "slips" in the story line, and together, we managed to cover all the turns in the plot.

Was there anything in the story that you worried about? Something, for example, that you felt might unnecessarily confuse your audience?

WARD: Not really, for the same reason. We'd gone over the script so carefully in preproduction that I knew exactly what George was going to do on the set. So I felt that the story line was clean and honest, and I had no concerns about George "losing" or confusing the audience.

Edward Shores in his book on George Roy Hill claims that Henry Gondorff, although a good friend of Luther's, is far less concerned about "justice" than Hooker. He makes much of Gondorff's warning to Hooker that "Revenge is for suckers," and he claims that the older con man is much more interested in the self-gratification that comes from a successful sting, than with any notions of avenging Luther's death. How do you feel about that?

WARD: I feel it's a definite misreading of the film. It's true that at the beginning of the film Gondorff is cynical—a bit like Bogart in *Casablanca*—and that he looks at the world in a slightly jaundiced way. In his past, he's done a lot of cons for a lot of different reasons, and he doesn't want to guarantee Hooker any kind of personal satisfaction. But as the movie progresses, it's clear that Gondorff gets personally involved and that he detests Lonnegan not just as a greedy mark, but as the man who had Luther Coleman killed. So, he eventually comes to share Hooker's sense that their big con has more to do with a deeper kind of justice than it does with the simple satisfactions of the con.

I couldn't agree more. After the first editing go through, I wonder if you attended the initial rough cut screening in New York? There were apparently some concerns at that point.

WARD: No, I wasn't at the rough cut screening in New York, but I attended several of the previews here in Los Angeles.

Had the opticals and music been added by then?

WARD: Yes, and the previews were a huge success. I can still remember a preview in Long Beach where I was sitting behind a middle-aged woman. At the end of the film when Gondorff and Hooker shoot each other, she was so distraught that she said out loud, "Oh, I hate it when they do this in movies!" And I remember feeling such a great satisfaction that I actually leaned over, and touched the woman gently on her shoulder, and whispered, "Don't worry, it'll be ok." Then, of course, the reversal happened, and she turned around, very pleased, and she said, "How did you know that?"

Well, I hope you told her!

WARD: I never did. I'm not sure why. But I was so delighted that she'd enjoyed the film so much. I'll never forget it.

All the previews were fantastic.

WARD: The previews were great, but of course they were much different in those days.

Did you realize that the film was a potential blockbuster?

WARD: Not really. I thought to myself, "This is a really terrific movie, and if people don't like this film, maybe I'm in the wrong business." But things were done quite a bit differently back then; they weren't so quantitative. Also, I was still a young kid, only two or three years out of film school, and I didn't know much about the business side of things. I didn't know anything about "preview scores." All I did was watch the audience respond, and they obviously loved it, but I never attempted to quantify it in my mind, and I didn't even keep up with the grosses after the picture opened. So I had no idea how much money *The Sting* was making until it was out for about six or seven weeks. I remember talking to Mike, and Julia, and Tony, and asking, "How's the film doing?" and they all said, "Fine, great," but it really didn't register just how well it was doing. Another reason was that, at the time, everyone was talking about *The Exorcist*. That was the "watercooler movie" back then, and everyone was talking about Linda Blair's head turning around, and the pea soup, and the endless lines around the block at all the theaters. So *The Sting* was rather quietly doing great business, but the real media event was *The Exorcist*. Then people started to realize, myself included, that *The Sting* had been maintaining extraordinary box office for over ten weeks, with no discernible drop off. It just played and played and played.

How much did it total? I've read several figures?

WARD: I always thought it was $129 million, but when I went to the Austin Film Festival, I was told that it was $169 million, but maybe that was the worldwide figure, I'm not sure. But to keep it in proper perspective, I think it's important to remember that movie tickets were only $3 back then, so we're talking about "nonadjusted" figures.

The critical reviews, as we touched on earlier, were mixed, although the most critical of all critics, John Simon, recognized the film for exactly what it was—a marvelously crafted entertainment—and he praised it accordingly. Were you surprised by any of the critical reactions?

WARD: Well, I read Pauline Kael, and I thought she was dead wrong, even though I always respected her as a critic. But, to be honest, I didn't read most of the reviews, and I still don't. Unless there's a unanimous chorus out there about something I *really* need to hear, I'd rather not wrestle around in my mind with every little quibble that every single movie reviewer can come up with. So, in general, I don't find reviews very helpful, and I avoid them. I do remember thumbing through *Time* magazine back then and seeing Richard Schickel's review, which I believe he titled "Con Job," and I didn't even bother to read it. I knew in my heart that we'd made the very best movie we could make, and I knew that many people had enjoyed it, and that was enough for me. The truth is, reviewers very seldom tell you anything you don't already know, so even now, as a director, I don't find them very useful—whether they're good or bad or somewhere in the middle.

The Sting was nominated for ten Oscars and won seven. Were you surprised, as many people were, that Redford was nominated but Paul Newman was not?

WARD: Yes, I was very surprised that Paul wasn't nominated. Maybe the reason was that Gondorff doesn't appear in the film until twenty minutes have passed—and the entire film clearly revolves around the Hooker character. So maybe the Academy didn't know whether the role was a "supporting" or "leading" role, and Paul got caught in between. I also think it's very hard for movies with as much comedy as *The Sting* to be taken seriously by the Academy, especially in the acting categories. That's unfortunate, but that's the way it is.

Did you attend the Oscars that year, where your film won the Best Picture of 1973 and you won a Screenwriting Oscar?

WARD: I did attend, and it was very exciting. I remember riding in our limos to the Oscars with Michael, Julia, and Tony, and they all felt we had a very good chance to win, but I honestly believed that *The Exorcist* would win everything. Certainly, *The Exorcist* had all the early publicity and buzz, but *The Sting* did come on strong at the end. Nevertheless, I was quite surprised, and I really hadn't prepared much of a speech, so when I won the writing award, I got up on the stage, and there were all these bright lights flashing in my face, and I couldn't see a thing. I didn't even know where to look. I wasn't used to being on stage, and I was extremely nervous, so I just stared straight ahead into the lights and said something—I'm not sure what. It was all rather amazing and very exciting.

The Sting is a truly original script, especially given its carefully plotted complication, and the fact that it wasn't an adaptation of some kind.

WARD: Well, I worked very hard on the intricacies of that script, but I still had six people sue me! Everybody who'd ever written a book about confidence men tried, unsuccessfully, to cash in. *The Sting* took me about a year to write, and it was one of the most difficult scripts I've ever written because of all the various, intersecting plot lines. There were times when I got very confused and frustrated, and there were times when I couldn't write a single word for a over week—even ten days sometimes—because I couldn't unscramble everything. Sometimes, I couldn't even get my mind properly oriented—thinking, OK, I've done this, and I've done that, now where do I have the room to weave this in? It was like a huge puzzle, and the writing of the script was often like trying to create the puzzle without all the pieces. On those days when I didn't have the pieces, I was often in real despair. But, ultimately, everything came to me. You always want the pieces to come to you exactly when you need them, but they seldom do, so you have to be patient. Very patient.

After the extraordinary success of The Sting, *you've gone on to write and direct a wide variety of pictures over the past three decades, but I wonder if you were ever stereotyped as a writer after the huge success of* The Sting?

WARD: Not so much as a *type* of writer, but I did feel a certain pressure to produce another "big" picture. So, for my next script, I wrote a huge epic Western, called *San Joaquin.* I spent two years on the script, and I loved it, and then *Heaven's Gate* came out and pretty much killed the Western, and the script was never made. Generally, in this industry, when you're young and still developing as a writer, people are willing to give you a certain amount of slack. They expect that you'll continue to develop, so they're not quite as hard on you as they might be on an established writer of forty-five or so. The problem for me was that once you win the Academy Award, everyone assumes that you've *already* arrived. But *The Sting* was only my second script. Since that time, I've done some better writing in terms of dialogue and character development, but a story as great as *The Sting* is hard to come by. So after the demise of *San Joaquin,* I decided to go back to my original directorial ambitions, and I adapted and then directed John Steinbeck's *Cannery Row,* which was a smaller, literary piece, although still a comedy like *The Sting.* So I convinced myself not to be at the mercy of all the expectations I'd created about myself, and to stay with the kind of movies I was always interested in—and like to see. I never set out to write *The Sting* as an extravaganza; it just metamorphized into a huge movie. So I eventually learned to write what I like, and direct what I like, and not worry about anything else.

When you look back now, having written a classic American film that will continue to entertain movie audiences as long as people continue to watch films, do you have any favorite memories or recollections?

WARD: Well, as far as moviemaking experiences go, *The Sting* was one of the best—if not the very best—I've ever had. Everyone involved liked each other, and there was always a great sense of fun and excitement about making the picture. That, of course, says a great deal about the personalities and professionalism of Robert Redford, Paul Newman, George Hill, Bob Shaw, and everyone else. So it was an extraordinary experience. But looking back, my most gratifying experience regarding *The Sting* happened, oddly enough, just three years ago, when I watched the film with my two daughters who'd never seen it before.

They'd never seen it before?
WARD: No.

That's amazing. How old were they at the time?
WARD: Eighteen and seventeen. They'd, of course, grown up seeing the movies of their own generation, and, personally, I'm never very interested in going back to watch my old films. As a matter of fact, once they're in the theaters, I never look at them again. I'm just too critical. I get frustrated and say, "Oh, I could have written a much better line than that," or "Oh, I should have gone deeper with the character right there," and so on. I always feel that I've already *had* my opportunity to do things just right, and I've missed it in various ways, so it's very difficult for me to sit there and watch my own work. In truth, it's very hard for me to imagine that *anyone* will still be watching *The Sting* in years to come, let alone a hundred years or something like that.

But it's already been thirty years, and people are still watching the film and enjoying it.
WARD: I know, and I greatly appreciate that. But generally, I put it out of my mind. Nevertheless, about three years ago, I watched *The Sting* with my daughters, and I was very worried about what their reactions might be. Let's face it, the pace of the film is very deliberate, and it's certainly not the kind of hyper-paced movie that young kids are used to. So I thought the kids would find it a bit slow, maybe even ponderous. But, of course, the pace of *The Sting*, as George directed it, is part of its charm. It's like a pact that the film and the audience make, and they grow accustomed to it—and more appreciative of it—as the movie goes along. Anyway, when it was over, my kids came up to me and said, "Dad, I can't believe you wrote that movie!" The loved it, and they even called it "cool," and that was one of the best moments I've ever had. Not only because it pleased my kids—which was the most important thing—but because it made me wonder if the film might actually, in some way, stand the test of time.

That's a great place to end. Thanks, David.
WARD: Thank you, Bill.

CHAPTER 11

The Exorcist (1973)

A CONVERSATION WITH WILLIAM PETER BLATTY

William Peter Blatty was born in New York City, the youngest child of Leb-
anese immigrants. After attending Georgetown University on a scholarship,
he received a master's degree in English from George Washington University. In 1955, he entered the foreign service, working at the U.S. Information Agency in Beirut, Lebanon, where he edited the weekly magazine,
News Review. Later he moved to Los Angeles where he was the publicity
director at USC, and then the public relations director at Loyola University. In 1960, his first novel, *Which Way to Mecca, Jack?* was published, and
three years later his first produced screenplay, *The Man from the Diner's
Club* (1963), starring Danny Kaye, was released. By the time he wrote *The
Exorcist* in 1970, he'd written four previous novels and seven produced
screenplays, including the Inspector Clouseau film, *A Shot in the Dark*
(1966), featuring Peter Sellers, which Blatty cowrote with the film's director, Blake Edwards. He also wrote the screenplay for Edwards's *Darling
Lili* (1970), which starred Julie Andrews and Rock Hudson. After the
phenomenal success of his novel of possession, Blatty wrote the screenplay
and served as producer for the film version of *The Exorcist* (1973), starring
Ellen Burstyn, Linda Blair, and Jason Miller. The film was directed by
William Friedkin, and Blatty received the Best Screenwriting Award at the
1973 Oscars. Since that time, he's written several other novels, including
Legion (1983), and several other screenplays including two that he directed
himself: *The Ninth Configuration* (1980), starring Stacy Keach and Scott

Wilson, and The *Exorcist III* (1990), starring George C. Scott and Jason Miller. More recently, Blatty wrote a prequel to *The Exorcist* which has been released in two variants, Renny Harlin's *Exorcist: The Beginning* (2004) and Paul Schrader's *Dominion: Prequel to the Exorcist* (2005), both starring Stellan Skarsgård.

The genesis of The Exorcist *began long before you were a professional writer when you were still a junior at Georgetown University.*

BLATTY: It all started when I was taking a class in the New Testament with Fr. Gallagher, a Jesuit teacher. One day, Fr. Gallagher told us about a case of alleged possession and exorcism that was currently taking place somewhere in the environs of Georgetown, which I later discovered was Cottage City, Maryland, near Mt. Rainier. It seemed that one of the priests involved in the exorcism was being billeted at the Georgetown campus, which was how Fr. Gallagher knew some of the details. It was all quite fascinating, and we discussed some of the paranormal phenomena in class. As it turned out, a few of the things we heard about in class turned out to be inaccurate. One was that a book—the text of the Latin rituals which one of the priests was reciting during the exorcism—suddenly exploded into hundreds of thousands of tiny pieces of paper. Later, when I learned the details about the case, I learned that it never really happened, but I used it later in *The Exorcist III*.

So you'd heard about the case even before the account appeared in The Washington Post?

BLATTY: Yes, but the article in the *Post* was equally riveting and full of interesting details. I was intrigued to learn that the victim, a young boy, was not Roman Catholic. He was from a family of Evangelical Lutherans, and when the phenomena first started—the various poltergeist activities— his family sent him to their minister who suggested that the boy spend a night at his home so he could observe the boy throughout the night and see if anything unusual was really happening. Well, a lot happened! The boy's bed slid all over the place and chairs started flying around the room. Feeling helpless, the minister suggested to the family that the Roman Catholic Church might be able to help, since the Catholic clergy had a tradition of dealing with that kind of inexplicable phenomena. Anyway, that's what got the ball rolling, and both the *Post* article and our discussions in Fr. Gallagher's class made a powerful and lasting impression on me.

Your interest in the story was apparently motivated by the fact that it was a period of wavering faith in your own life.

BLATTY: I hadn't actually lost my faith, and I'd certainly had a lot of rational support for my beliefs from my studies in philosophical psychology at Georgetown, which attempted to show evidence, if not proof, of the existence of the human soul. But at the same time, I knew it wouldn't have hurt my faith to witness some kind of supernatural phenomenon, some manifestation of transcendence. Miracles can definitely strengthen faith, and if my bed in the dormitory wasn't going to levitate a foot or two some night, at least this case of possession might serve the same function if some of the events I'd learned about proved to be true.

After graduating from Georgetown and receiving a master's degree from George Washington University, you entered the foreign service, working in Beirut, Lebanon. Later you moved to Los Angeles where you were the publicity director at USC and then the public relations director at Loyola University. In 1960, your first novel, Which Way to Mecca, Jack? *was published, and three years later your first produced screenplay,* The Man from the Diner's Club, *was released by Columbia Pictures. By the time you wrote* The Exorcist *in 1970, you'd written four novels and seven produced screenplays, including the best of Peter Sellers's Inspector Clouseau films,* A Shot in the Dark *(1966), which you cowrote with the film's director, Blake Edwards. Yet, despite all these successes, it seems that you'd unintentionally stereotyped yourself in Hollywood as a "comic" writer.*

BLATTY: In a sense, I had, but I'd never really focused on the matter until the film industry hit a period where comedies were no longer "hot" items. Suddenly, the studios were no longer interested in making comedies because they'd fallen off as moneymakers. At the time, although novel writing was my first love, I still made my living from writing screenplays, and when my agent told me that my opportunities were dwindling, it seemed that I had nothing else to do except queue up at the unemployment line. So, I finally decided to try my hand at that "novel about possession" that I'd been planning to write for twenty years. But I began the book with great trepidation and a total lack of confidence.

Is it true that everyone tried to discourage you from writing the novel? Including your agent and your publisher?

BLATTY: That's right. When I told my agent the premise of the book, he dismissed it immediately, and even derided it. I couldn't get anyone interested in the idea, but then I had a very lucky break. I was invited to a New Year's party by the writer Burton Wohl. I love his book *A Cold Wind in August,* and even though I never go to New Year's Eve parties, I decided to go because I liked Burton so much and also because I was feeling rather lonely and had nothing else to do. That night at the party, I ran into Marc Jaffe, the editor in chief at Bantam Books. We'd met before in passing, and he remembered me, and he came over and asked me what I was doing. So I told him that I was looking for screen work, and then added, "Well, I've also had this novel idea for a long time." Then I told him the premise of the book about demonic possession, and in less than two minutes, he said, "I'll publish that." It was amazing, the kind of thing that doesn't happen very often in life. But then Marc started to have his doubts, he thought about my former comic novels like *Which Way to Mecca, Jack?*, and my screenplays like *A Shot in the Dark*, and he starting thinking, "Come on, Blatty's going to write a serious novel?" Finally, after about four months of soul-searching, he sent me a contract and a minimal advance, and I had to get going.

Is that when you went to the cabin in Lake Tahoe?

BLATTY: Yes, I rented a very cheap cabin in Incline Village, and I spent six weeks, completely alone, writing the first paragraph over and over again. Do you remember the scene in *The Shining* when Nicholson keeps writing, "All work and no play makes Jack a dull boy"? Well, that was me, only I was writing, "The mysterious rappings began on the night of April 11th." Then I'd think, "No, the rhythm's not right," so I'd change it to April 2 or April 1, or change it back to April 11. That's pretty much all I did for six weeks when the phone rang one day, and I was offered another job. It was the screenplay for a Paul Newman film that never got made, but, thank God, it got me away from Tahoe. When the screenplay was done, I went back to writing the novel, and I finally realized what had hung me up so much on the first paragraph. I was starting the book in the wrong place. So I set the opening in Iraq, and everything went pretty smoothly after that.

In your continuing researches into the original Maryland case, you eventually made contact with the exorcist, Fr. William Bowdern, and asked for more information.

BLATTY: Fr. Bowdern wanted to help me because he felt that a book about the reality of possession would be beneficial to the public, whether it was a nonfiction account as I'd once suggested or a novelized version. So he went to both the cardinal of his diocese and the boy's family to try and get permission, but the answer was no. That's when I decided to novelize the general idea, and make the victim a girl, so the book wouldn't be associated with the original case. But maybe the family was right because after the novel came out, they were quite disturbed by a number of connections that people started making between the case described in the old *Washington Post* article and *The Exorcist*.

Even though Fr. Bowdern was unable to help, you've often described his letter as "electrifying."

BLATTY: That was because he said, rather emphatically, "I can assure you of one thing: the case in which I was involved was the real thing. I had no doubt about it then, and I have no doubts about it now." I believed him, and I was highly motivated by his conviction and honesty.

You've admitted that even while you were writing the novel, you felt certain that it would be a huge success.

BLATTY: I always felt that it had that potential, but there were still some problems in the writing process. The truth is when I started the novel, I really didn't know what was going to happen at the end. All I knew was there was going to be a young boy—now a girl—who was going to appear possessed and that an exorcist was going to be called in to deal with it. That's all I started with. So I wrote the book, chapter by chapter, building each new scene on everything that had preceded it, and praying to God that I wouldn't paint myself into a corner. In the past, I'd always worked this way. I'd never use an outline. But, of course, with the comic novels, if you can just keep your readers laughing—maybe eight little laughs a page and a gut-wrenching belly laugh every seven pages—then everything'll be fine. The plot doesn't really matter that much. When Martin Levin reviewed *Twinkle, Twinkle, "Killer" Kane* in *The New York Times*, he started his piece by saying, "Nobody can write funnier lines than William Peter Blatty. Even so, it's a virtue which often requires some modicum of mucilage to gum his lines together." But now I was trying to write a highly dramatic novel, and I was worried. At the three-quarters mark, I looked things over, and I thought it was a very good book so far, one that would hold the reader's interest. I certainly felt that it had a commercial future. So I took a break and showed what I'd done so far to my first screenwriting mentor, Bill Bloom from Columbia Pictures. At the time, I was living in a little cottage in Staten Island, so Bill came by and read over the first three-quarters of the book. When he was done, he put the manuscript down, but he seemed exhausted. When I said, "Do you want to hear what happens next?" he said, "What, the book goes on?" and I said, "Yeah, I'm planning on another hundred pages or so." Then Bill almost screamed at me, "You can't do that to your reader! It's too emotionally draining." Of course, this unexpected advice was very appealing, since I really didn't want to write another hundred pages. I'd already reached the point in the story where Fr. Merrin dies, so I thought over Bill's advice for a few days, and I decided he was right. I also knew how to end the novel, and I wrapped it up quickly—in a week. It was another lucky break.

Apparently, the screen rights for the novel, which eventually sold over thirteen million copies, were turned down by every studio in Hollywood, even Warner Bros., which eventually financed the film.

BLATTY: In fairness to them, that all happened before the novel was published. But it's true, before the novel's success, nobody in Hollywood wanted to touch it. Every studio in town rejected it—even a number of fly-by-night production companies. Generally, all I got for my efforts was a form rejection letter. Everyone turned it down, even a number of movie stars who were approached about the project, like Barbra Streisand. As for the book itself, it also had the same problem. For the first five weeks or six weeks after *The Exorcist* was published in hardback by Harper's, nobody was buying it. I'd been set up with a twenty-to-thirty cities promotion tour, and, almost invariably, I'd be greeted at the ramp as I was coming off the plane by a representative from Harper & Row telling me that the bookstores had returned the books and the promotion was off. I remember at B. Altman's in New York, I was supposed to pre-sign some books, and the clerk said, "Just a minute," and she rushed back to talk to the manager. When she came back out, she told me that I couldn't sign the books because then the manager couldn't return them if they didn't sell. But then, I had another stroke of luck. Before heading back to Los Angeles, I pre-auditioned for *The Dick Cavett Show*. In those days, if you wanted to sell a book, that was the TV talk show you needed to get booked on. At the pre-audition, I was told, "This is fascinating stuff," but I was also told, "Don't hold your breath"—meaning that I probably wouldn't get on the show. Then one afternoon, I was having lunch at the Four Seasons with some people from Harper & Row, and we got a call from the home office that someone had canceled out of the *Cavett* tapings that day and they were desperate for another guest. So I rushed over to the studio, got through makeup, and waited patiently for my six minutes at the end of the show. But the first guest was rather boring, so they gave him the hook quickly and moved on to the second guest, who was not only boring, but drunk as well. So they gave him the hook too, and then, too late, they realized that there was nobody left but me. I was going to have forty-five minutes of airtime on the *Dick Cavett Show*! When it was time, I went on, and Cavett looked at me and said, "I'm sorry, Mr. Blatty, but I haven't read your book." So I said, "Would you like me to tell you about it?" and he said, "Oh, please do." So I did. Not long after that I was at Kennedy Airport ready to fly back to Los Angeles, and I picked up a copy of *Time* magazine, and when I looked at the book section, *The Exorcist* was already listed at number four in the country. That single appearance on *The Cavett Show* had made all the difference.

Eventually, Warner Bros., at the insistence of John Calley, the studio's head of production, bought the screen rights for $400,000. Is that correct?

BLATTY: Originally, Paul Monash, the producer of *Butch Cassidy and the Sundance Kid*, represented himself as the buyer at an auction, and that was the $400,000 figure, with a six-month pay-or-play option. But behind the scenes, it was really Warner Bros., and the deal came through at the oddball figure of $641,000. Johnny Carson once asked me on *The Tonight Show*, "Why $641,000?" and I didn't know the answer then, and I still don't.

Eventually, you ended up the sole producer on the picture.

BLATTY: Yes, as part of the final deal, I took over Monash's position as producer, and I was given a $4,200,000 budget. The final cost of the picture was $12 million.

For various reasons, the film was turned down by such well-known directors as Stanley Kubrick, Arthur Penn, and Mike Nichols. But all along, you'd really wanted to hire William Friedkin, but the studio wouldn't agree. Why not?

BLATTY: At the beginning, I'd submitted a list to Warner Bros. of seven "preapproved" directors which included Billy Friedkin, but after the more established directors had turned the picture down, they kept scratching Billy's name off the list, saying, "You need to find somebody else." In the meantime, they were negotiating behind my back with a young director named Mark Rydell. Now Mark was a terrific director for certain kinds of material, especially films that could tolerate his slow, deliberate pacing and his long pregnant pauses between the lines of dialogue. In his version of D. H. Lawrence's *The Fox*, that interminable pace worked pretty well some of the time, but it seemed pretentious at other times. Regardless, it was perfectly clear to me that *The Exorcist* needed a driving, intense, narrative pace. So I had my lawyers look over my contract, and they informed me that the studio did have the legal right to overrule me. So, I bluffed. I called up Frank Wells at Warner Bros., and I said, "Frank, I've just consulted with my lawyers, and there's no way in hell that you can get away with this! It's a monumental breach of contract." Then I slammed down the phone, and, for some reason, their lawyers believed me. In the meantime, *The French Connection* had come out, and I told the executives to screen it, and they did, and Billy was finally approved for the picture.

Somewhere between the writing of the novel and the writing of the screenplay, you came into possession of the diary written by Fr. Raymond Bishop who'd assisted Fr. Bowdern in the Maryland exorcism. Did this lead to anything new that was used in the script?

BLATTY: Not really, it was very interesting, but it didn't lead to anything new in the screenplay.

Your original script was about 225 pages, with a potential running time of over three hours, so it obviously had to be cut down. Among other things, you reduced the role of Detective Kinderman and eliminated some of the medical scenes. Most of these cuts worked very well to tighten and strengthen the film, but I'd like to ask you about one that led to some subsequent confusions: removing the sub-plot regarding Karl, the family's housekeeper, and his surreptitious aid to his drug-addicted daughter. In the novel and the first screenplay, Karl's activities make him a prime suspect in the demon's murder of Burke Dennings. Yet, despite the removal of the subplot, the film still carries various suspicions about Karl. Was he an accessory of the demon? Did he put the Ouija board—which led to Regan's first involvement with the demon—in the closet? Did he perpetrate the church desecrations? Did he give the demon the crucifix for the purpose of sacrilege? The novel, of course, makes it perfectly clear that Karl is innocent, but the film never resolves the Ouija board, the desecrations, or the crucifix.

BLATTY: Yes, cutting out the Karl subplot created a number of confusions. A few years ago, when we put together our revised and extended version of the film, I went searching for an unused shot that had been made for the original film and which I'd always felt was sorely missed. It was supposed to appear sometime during the exorcism, and it showed, for the first time, a shot of Karl and his wife, Lilly, in their bedroom. Since the room was filled with religious icons, it made it perfectly clear that it was Karl who'd put the crucifix in the room with Regan, in the hope that it would protect her. It was an act of piety. Unfortunately, we could never find the shot in the vault. It could have resolved a lot of problems.

So who did the desecrations? The film seems to point to the possessed Regan?

BLATTY: Yes, the film rightly gives the impression that Regan committed the desecrations herself, but it's definitely not as clear as it could have been. One indication, of course, is when Detective Kinderman is prowling around near the bottom of the steps where Dennings's body had been discovered, and he finds a piece of one of Regan's clay sculptures—which we've already seen in the MacNeil household.

One of the crucial changes from the first script was Friedkin's insistence that the film open in Iraq just like the novel. Why didn't you include it in the original screenplay?

BLATTY: There were two reasons. One, and certainly the lesser reason, was that time was obviously a factor. I wanted to make sure that the film wouldn't run over two hours. Also, there was a residue of nagging doubt in my mind about that scene because back before the novel was published, the one thing that the publisher's entire editorial board had fought for, and pleaded with me to omit from the novel, was the opening scene in Iraq. Back then, I refused to do it, but when it came to writing the screenplay, I started thinking that maybe the film should start in a more "normal" environment like Georgetown. But Billy Friedkin insisted otherwise, saying, "What are you doing? You can't do that!" He always wanted to stay as close to the novel as he could, and he was right.

The casting of The Exorcist *was impeccable, and the performance of young Linda Blair was particularly remarkable. But I know that you'd always wanted Shirley MacLaine to play the mother. MacLaine, your former neighbor, had been the original model for Chris when you first wrote the novel. So how do you feel about it now?*

BLATTY: Ellen Burstyn gave a sensational performance in *The Exorcist*, but I'd always felt that the ideal person for the role would be someone who'd been a musical entertainer. Someone the audience would *never* think could have had a possessed child. That's why both the novel and film were set in Washington, D.C., and not someplace like Salem. The point is that this could happen anywhere, and in any family. So I always imagined Chris MacNeil as someone rather bouncy and saucy and funny and cute. So it would really shock the audience when things started to go wrong. But the film took another direction, and Ellen's performance was astonishing.

I've heard that a number of other actresses, including Jane Fonda, were considered for the role of Chris MacNeil?

BLATTY: Fonda was one of the first ones we went to, and, although she later denied it to me in person, we were told that she'd sent an angry telegram to her agent saying, "Who'd ever want to make this capitalist, rip-off bullshit?" Whatever that means! Then, I went to Barbra Streisand, but apparently I shook her hand too hard. The meeting was arranged in Las Vegas, where she was performing at the time, and I was a bit nervous about meeting her, and when I shook her hand, I must have squeezed too hard, and I ruined everything. I learned later that she'd been a bit terrified and told her staff, "Keep him away from me!" Although she seemed a bit unlikely for the role, I still think she could have gotten away with it. And Cher could have gotten away with it too, but Shirley MacLaine would have been sensational.

Maybe the most inspired piece of casting in a flawless cast is the great Swedish actor Max von Sydow who portrayed the old exorcist priest, Fr. Merrin. How did that come about?

BLATTY: At that point in his career, Max hadn't appeared in very many American films, so I'd already written to Paul Scofield and sent him a copy of the novel. Eventually, Scofield wrote back and said, "Yes, I'd be interested in playing Fr. Merrin." But by then, Max was already involved, and he was so vehement about wanting the role, that we gave it to him. He knew exactly what he wanted, and he was great in the role.

Apparently, you weren't on the set very much. Why not?

BLATTY: I was there in the beginning, for consultation, and trying not to get in the way of Billy and the actors. I wanted to support Billy since he was my somewhat controversial choice for director, but I didn't want to create any more tensions on the set than there already were. So when the company packed up to leave Georgetown and head back to New York, I said, "Billy, I'm writing a little book about my mother, and I think I'll stay behind and finish it up." So I kept out of things for a while, but when I finally returned to New York, I was very welcome. Billy's often told me, "You kept me straight many times."

Where did the daring idea of refrigerating the set of the MacNeil home—which was shot at the Ceco Studios in New York City—come about?

BLATTY: That was the special effects department, and it was quite a challenge for everyone. I remember one day when I stood in for Jason Miller for some off camera stuff in the refrigerated bedroom. The shot was on Max and Linda, but my voice was needed in the room. Initially, all kinds of things froze up in the cold—like eyeglasses—but when the big lights came on, they heated up the room so quickly that the cast and crew only had about two minutes to shoot before they'd have to stop and refreeze the room. It was very difficult in production, but it was very visually effective in the film.

Where did Mike Oldfield's "Tubular Bells" come from?

BLATTY: Billy was dissatisfied with the score, so he and the music director started creating a new score from recordings. Among the many recordings we considered was a beautiful little theme that we all liked for Regan. It seemed light and sweet and lovely. Just what we wanted. But, of course, in time, the film changed the "meaning" of the music, and we were all quite surprised to learn that our lovely musical theme for an innocent little girl was conjuring up a frightful and sinister ambiance.

One of William Friedkin's most interesting additions to the movie is the St. Joseph medal that first pops up in the archeological dig at Nineveh, then appears in Fr. Karras's nightmare about his mother, is later ripped from the priest's neck by the demon, and is finally rediscovered at the end of the movie in Regan's bedroom. A number of commentators on the film have claimed that Fr. Karras's mother is also wearing the medal in her scenes with her son, but I've never seen it. Nevertheless, there's still the problem of how a medal found by Fr. Merrin in Iraq ends up in the possession of Fr. Karras. Since the medal itself is a rather common, English-language sacramental, is it reasonable to assume that there were two medals? Or did Friedkin back himself into a corner?

BLATTY: I didn't go to Iraq for the filming of those opening scenes, and when I saw the rushes for the first time, I said to Billy, "What's that St. Joseph's medal doing in that four-thousand-year-old archeological site?" And he just looked at me, and he said, "Resonance." Then he turned around and walked away. So that's all I can tell you about it. Maybe it's best left as "resonance."

What do you make of all the press accounts that the picture was "cursed," and William Friedkin's subsequent exorcism of the set?

BLATTY: It was preposterous. Ridiculous! I was there the day it all started. Billy was being interviewed by *Newsweek* and the reporter raised the subject, "You know, I've been doing a little research and a lot of things have gone wrong during the production of this film, including illnesses and a death. Do you think there's a curse on this picture?" Well, Billy couldn't believe his incredible luck. He was being offered some amazing—and free—publicity and promotion for the movie, and he instantly responded, "Yes, I do. Exactly." Now of course, we did have a number of unfortunate things happen on the set, and it's true that Jack McGowran died back in England after his role in the film was completed. But there was nothing supernatural or paranormal about any of it, with one minor exception. Anyone who works on a film project for over a year understands that mishaps and tragedies will happen. Just as they do in real life. But Billy milked it for all it was worth, and he even had the set officially exorcised.

What was the minor exception?

BLATTY: I'd once read a book called *Breakthrough* written by a Latvian scientist who claimed that inexplicable human voices can sometimes appear on tape recordings without any apparent source. Then one day when I was with Chris Newman, our soundman, and we were listening to some recordings from the set, we heard what seemed to be a faint human voice and a series of rapping sounds. As a result, we had to redo the sound for the scene. Now, everyone knows how movies work. The soundman listens to everything with his earphones on, and if he hears a pin drop, or if he hears an airplane fifty miles away, or if he hears someone's stomach rumble, he'll stop the taping and they'll do the scene over. But Chris Newman, our Academy Award winner for sound, had heard nothing on the set, and he'd let the scene play through. It wasn't until later that we heard the inexplicable sounds, and it was very eerie.

Didn't you also have some unsettling occurrences at a Ouija board?

BLATTY: That was back when I was researching the novel. I bought a Ouija board, put it on my desk, and put my fingers on it very lightly. Even though I'd never used a Ouija board before, my fingers soon started gliding across the board to specific letters. But when I wrote the letters down, they made no sense. Then I realized that the letter "u" means "you," and the letter "r" means "are," and so on. I also realized that the vowels, unless they're absolutely necessary, were generally dropped. So "Peter," for example, would become "p-t-r." I was alone, and it went on for three days, and it was very eerie. Eventually, I started asking questions and getting answers, and, at one point, I was contacted by a girl who claimed that her name was "Vats." She said she was Hungarian and sixteen years old, and she would say things like, "You can be my friend." We had numerous conversations, and it was all very creepy, so I used it in *The Exorcist*.

Much has been made of the so-called subliminals in the film, especially the flashes of the demon's face and the "demonized" face of Fr. Karras. In his book Media Sexploitation, *Wilson Bryan Key dedicated a whole chapter to the various technical and psychological "manipulations" of* The Exorcist, *especially the "subliminals," which he describes as dangerous psychological reconditionings of the audience that supposedly led to illnesses, "possessions," and even criminal acts. Friedkin and the studio never denied using what they referred to as "subliminals" in the film, and you've admitted that some "demon face" flashes were eliminated from the trailer for fear of heart attacks and potential lawsuits. So I'd like to hear your opinion about all of this, and I'd also like to know why these visual flashes are constantly referred to as "subliminals" when they can be clearly seen in the film?*

BLATTY: Well, on the last point, you're absolutely right. By definition, a subliminal is a visual that's flashed so fast that it can't be apprehended by our conscious minds—only the unconscious is aware of it because it's so fleeting and rapid. Well, then there are no such subliminals in *The Exorcist*. Billy used a few brief flashes of certain shots, but since you can clearly see them, they're not subliminal. On the other hand, it's true that one of the early trailers did use some real subliminal flashes of the faces of the demon. I never saw that trailer, and it was used only once because the studio decided that was too dangerous. They were worried about possible heart attacks and subsequent lawsuits, so the trailer was pulled.

You first saw the completed film in a 140-minute cut on a Moviola at William Friedkin's office in New York City, which was eerily located at 666 6th Avenue. What was your reaction?

BLATTY: I was absolutely electrified. I have to admit that I thought it was a masterpiece. So over and over, I insisted to the studio executives that they give the film a wide release—the *Godfather* treatment—but, instead, we got twenty-six theaters. For some reason, the Warner's executives were worried that *The Exorcist* was going to bomb, and they had absolutely no confidence in the film.

Then John Calley and others in the studio started pressuring Friedkin to trim down the film against your advice. These prerelease edits cut approximately eleven minutes from the film, and they included: the first doctor scene, the spider walk, the conversation between the priests during the break in the exorcism, the transfer of the St. Joseph medal back to Chris, and the coda with Fr. Dyer and Detective Kinderman. Friedkin's admitted that the cuts were done to "play down the metaphysics and play up the horror." Is it true that you were banned from the Warner's lot while all this was going on?

BLATTY: Yes. I got the word from my agent that I was barred from the lot, even though I was the film's producer! But there was nothing I could do about it.

Despite the vulgar language of the demon, The Exorcist *got an R rating. Were you surprised?*

BLATTY: I was very surprised. Not only because of the language, but also because of the crucifix scene. When I wrote that scene, I'd always expected that the director would make the point without showing very much, but Billy shot it very graphically. In time, I learned that the head of the ratings board was a psychologist, and maybe that had something to do with the film's R rating.

Regarding those obscenities, I've read that it was a priest who pointed out that in real-life possessions, a demon's language would be much more obscene than the dialogue you'd originally written.

BLATTY: Yes, one of the priests mentioned it to Billy during the shooting, and Billy immediately insisted that I come up with some really awful stuff for the next day's shoot. So I sat down and wrote the ugliest stuff I could possibly think of. Of course, the priest was absolutely right, and I'd known that before I'd written either the book or the screenplay, but I never knew how far I should take it. Years later, when we redid the sound track for the restoration, Billy did the whole track in digital, and when I heard it I was shocked. In the past, the dialogue was always muddled and muddy, but now every word was crisp and right in your face, and I wanted to slink down in my seat. The fact that my son was sitting next to me made it much worse.

The Exorcist *was truly a blockbuster, setting box office records, and eventually making $165 million—which adjusted for inflation is an astounding $415 million. The critical reaction to the film was mixed, but interestingly enough most Catholic publications, including the very orthodox journal* Triumph, *actually praised the film.*

BLATTY: Earlier, the Vatican itself had praised the novel in its official literary journal, *Civiltà Cattolica*, and when the film was released, the Catholic press, with a few reservations, praised it as well. As a matter of fact, over the past ten years or so, Cardinal John J. O'Connor has referred to the book a number of times in his Sunday homilies. He's even read excerpts from the novel in St. Patrick's Cathedral, and, of course, Cardinal O'Connor was a very conservative cleric.

The Exorcist *was nominated for ten Oscars that year, winning two—best screenplay for you and best sound for Robert Knudson and Chris Newman—while losing out to* The Sting *for best picture. Were you there that night? And how did you feel about everything?*

BLATTY: I was there that night, and I was fully prepared for the backlash against *The Exorcist*. The studio had spent a tremendous amount of money promoting the film, and we'd learned that there were a number of "elders" in the Academy who were banding together against it. When the Oscar voting for best special effects came in, *The Exorcist* won, so George Cukor announced that no film was really worthy of the award that year and the category was canceled. Cukor, along with Robert Aldrich, led the crusade against *The Exorcist*, and I only recently found out about Aldrich's role. Naturally, I was quite shocked because Aldrich had actually come to my home before we started production trying to convince me that he should be the director of the film! Cukor's attitude, I could better understand. Apparently, at one of the Academy's meetings, he said of *The Exorcist*, "What? Is this what it's come to? This is entertainment?" Now, I'm sure he was thinking about the obscenity and how he didn't want it to be considered along with some of the great films he'd done—like the ones with Tracy and Hepburn. So at least I can understand his motives.

Despite the phenomenal success of The Exorcist, *you felt that the prerelease edits had undermined the overall meaning of the film, and you were also astonished to discover that many people in the audience were misinterpreting the crucial death scene of Fr. Karras thinking that he was killed by the demon—meaning that evil had "triumphed" and the film was a "downer." This is very interesting because there'd been similar reactions to the book, and both you and William Friedkin were determined to make the final confrontation between Fr. Karras and the demon perfectly clear in the film, spending a great deal of time on the crucial climactic scene, meticulously going over it shot by shot. What went wrong?*

BLATTY: At first, I thought the point of the film was only being missed by the more obtuse members of the audience, but I had to abandon that idea when my wife and I went to a dinner party at the home of Frank Wells, the president of Warner Bros. At one point, Frank and I were sitting in his den, and I started complaining about the all the "dumb" members of the audience who'd misread the ending, "They actually think the demon takes Karras out of the window at the end—and not the other way around!" Then there was a long silence in the room. Finally, Frank, bless his soul for his honesty, said, "Well, that's what I thought, too." So I realized that it obviously wasn't a simple matter of IQ. Eventually, I came to the conclusion that the audience, at that crucial moment in the picture, was in a state of shock. They've been stunned by everything that's happened, and, as a result, they can't see things clearly. Even though Billy and I choreographed that scene over and over to make absolutely sure that no one could possibly misunderstand it, we were still thinking of it shot by shot, rather than seeing it within the context of the furious flurry of activity that numbed and confused many people in the audience.

When I saw the film back in 1973, I had no doubts about what Fr. Karras had done, but his reasoning seemed unclear. The most important shot— Karras's hands approaching Regan's neck—lasts for only about a second, and it doesn't really register on the audience in the flurry of the scene's activity. Did you ever consider showing the priest's hands clearly around the child's neck?

BLATTY: We didn't think it was needed. The approach of Karras's hands actually lasts a little more than a second—a second and a half, or maybe two. But you're right, if the audience doesn't fully comprehend that the demon is using Karras to try and kill the girl, they'll be completely lost. They won't understand that his death is actually a sacrificial act of heroism, a final act of love to protect the young girl.

And if we don't understand that Fr. Karras kills himself to prevent the death of the child, then his death seems like an unsatisfying suicide. That's how I reacted when I first saw it, and I wonder if you've heard that reaction from other people?

BLATTY: Yes, I have, and it was still a point of disagreement between Billy and myself when we did the extended version in 2000. Billy added a quasi-subliminal flash, a near-subliminal, into that scene. When the bedroom curtains billow out, there's a face flashed, and it's Karras's mother. I was very worried that the audience would think that Fr. Karras then commits suicide over his guilt about his mother, but Billy insisted, and it's still in the revised version.

One more question about the climatic scene. In the Gospels of St. Mark and St. Luke, Jesus casts a multitude of demons from a possessed man into a herd of swine, but I've never heard about the idea of a possessing demon actually "jumping" of its own volition from one human victim to another. Is there any precedent for such a thing?

BLATTY: There might have been in the much-discussed Loudun possessions of the late sixteenth century, which are often dismissed as an outbreak of group hysteria. While it may be true that most of the Loudun phenomena were the result of hysteria, it's also quite possible that it was a true case of possession that set the hysteria in motion. In the aftermath of the outbreak, three of the four exorcist priests were successively possessed, beginning with Tranquille, passing to Lactance, and then finally passing to Lucas. Each priest, in his turn, died soon after the hysteria from cardiac exhaustion resulting from exactly the kinds of psychomotor fits that are so common in cases of genuine possession. None of the three priests was over the age of forty-three at the time of their deaths, and the fourth exorcist, Fr. Surin—who was thirty-three and one of the most renowned intellects in France—went completely insane and never recovered. So, if one believes the evidence of the times, there's definitely a precedent for the concept of "leaping" possession. Of course, even if it isn't true, it's still a chilling possibility for a fictional story.

Given the various misinterpretations by many in the audiences and your concerns about the prerelease edits, you apparently wanted to make some changes in the film despite its extraordinary success. So a number of additional endings were proposed to give the movie more "uplift" at the end. Friedkin suggested a final shot where Fr. Dyer would actually see the dead Fr. Karras ascending the stairs, and you suggested an epilogue twenty-five years later where Fr. Dyer would encounter a jogger and realize that it was the "spirit" of Fr. Karras. Finally, after twenty-seven years of effort, you managed to convince William Friedkin and the studio to release the film in 2000 with the 1973 edits restored. Let's start with the famous "spider walk." This amazing scene is the creepiest moment in a film crammed with unsettling moments. Out of nowhere, Regan suddenly scurries down the stairs facing upwards using her arms and legs like a spider. Why was it cut back in 1973?

BLATTY: You could see the cables. It was unusable. But in 2000, we could take them out with a computer. I was very disappointed back in 1973 when we had to cut that scene, but we had no choice.

Also restored is the brief, mid-exorcism conversation between Fr. Merrin and Fr. Karras. Friedkin felt it was a "showstopper" and that it was similar to the much maligned coda in Hitchcock's Psycho, *but you felt that the scene contained the "moral center of the film."*

BLATTY: Well, it *was* the moral center of the film. In the book, of course, it runs on for two pages, and I can still remember the day on the set when Billy refused to shoot it. So I tried cutting it down from my original script, and I finally got it down to three or four sentences. I was adamant that it be in the film, but Billy refused, saying, "I'm not making a commercial for the Catholic Church," and he even added, "And if you shoot it without me, I'll cut it later." But the scene was hardly a commercial; it's the moment in the film when you realize that everything's really about Karras. It's not about the little girl. It's about the struggle for Karras's soul. *He's* the "exorcist" of the title, not Fr. Merrin. In my view, many of the people who saw the film felt guilty about it. After all, there's a little girl masturbating with a crucifix, and lots of vomit, and head spinning and all the rest of it. And that scene where the priests talk for a moment explains why it's appropriate to see all these terrible things—because there's a war going on, and something very important is at stake. *The Exorcist* isn't a pointless, rambling demonic visitation; it's about the struggle for a man's soul.

Also included in the revised version is the final transfer of the St. Joseph medal back to Chris MacNeil, an avowed atheist. Her acceptance of the medal from Fr. Dyer implies a new spiritual openness in her life. Why was this effective moment cut in 1973?

BLATTY: The truth is Billy never fully understood it. He shot it back then, but he cut out the final transfer of the medal. I was always disappointed about that, so when we did the 2000 version, we went back to the vault and discovered that Billy never got full coverage on the scene. But we did have a close-up of Dyer's hands passing the medal to Chris's, so we added a voice-over, and it works.

Also restored in the 2000 version is the final scene between Detective Kinderman and Fr. Dyer indicating that they'll eventually develop a friendship like the one that was forming between Kinderman and Fr. Karras. But I must admit, I still think it's a bit anticlimactic.

BLATTY: Well, it's not a very powerful scene, but I like it because I think it prevents the film from ending as a "downer." It lets the audience know that despite everything that's happened, everything's all right now. If it wasn't for the fact that so many in the audience misinterpreted the ending of the film—thinking that the demon won—I wouldn't have pushed so hard for that scene to be added in the 2000 expanded version.

One of the most ludicrous "interpretations" of The Exorcist *is that it's, as Mark Kermode puts it, "a pedophobic tract" expressing a male disgust with female maturation—or what Peter Biskind in* Easy Riders, Raging Bulls *calls "menstrual panic." Yet, ironically, you'd originally planned to write the story about a boy, only later changing it to a girl in order to deflect similarities with the Maryland case.*

BLATTY: It's so preposterous that I never know what to say about it. It's really not worth discussing—or encouraging the ridiculous people who come up with these things.

Speaking of the Maryland exorcism, for many years you've known the whereabouts of the principal in that case, who was a ten-year-old boy back in 1949, and who's now, apparently, a practicing Catholic. I also know that, although you've always wanted to meet with him, you've carefully respected his privacy. Have you ever heard about his response to the film?

BLATTY: I've never heard how he reacted to the film—or if he even saw it. I do remember that one time on *The Tonight Show*, Billy mentioned that the film was related to a real-life case of possession, and he received a passionate letter from the family saying that they were very disturbed by what he'd said.

Do you have any idea if the victim in the Maryland case knows that you'd like to meet with him?

BLATTY: I don't know about that either. I'd like to think that he'd be curious about meeting with me since I was so inspired by his case.

The result of that inspiration was a best-selling novel, a masterful script, and a classic film. What memory would you like to end with today?

BLATTY: On the night of the first screening of *The Exorcist*, my agent was nervously pacing up and down in the lobby of the Academy Theater. When the picture ended, one of the Warner Bros. executives came out to the lobby, and my agent asked rather anxiously, "So what do you think?" And the executive answered, "We've got our *Cleopatra*." But he was wrong, dead wrong, just as the studio had been wrong when they'd refused to hire Billy Friedkin until I finally threatened to sue them. They always felt that *any* director could make this film, but it's my conviction that in the hands of almost any other director in Hollywood, *The Exorcist* could have easily descended into an unintentionally hilarious comedy. So I'm very grateful to Billy, and to everyone else who dedicated themselves to the film.

Especially you. Thanks.

BLATTY: And thank you, Bill.

CHAPTER 12

Jaws (1975)

A CONVERSATION WITH CARL GOTTLIEB

A graduate of Syracuse University, Carl Gottlieb joined the popular San Francisco improv troupe known as The Committee in the mid-sixties. He later began writing for the *Smothers Brothers Comedy Hour*, for which he won an Emmy Award in 1969. He subsequently wrote for other television shows including *The Odd Couple*, *The Bob Newhart Show*, *Flip Wilson*, and *All in the Family*. In 1974, he was hired to rewrite Steven Spielberg's *Jaws*, sharing the credit with the author of the best-selling novel, Peter Benchley, and receiving a nomination for a Golden Globe Award. His other screenwriting credits include *Jaws II*, *Jaws 3D*, *The Jerk* featuring Steve Martin, *Doctor Detroit* starring Dan Aykroyd, and *Which Way is Up?* starring Richard Pryor. In 1977, he directed *The Absent Minded Waiter*, a comedy short featuring Steve Martin that was nominated for an Academy Award. He also directed *Caveman* and *Paul Reiser: Out on a Whim*, and various television shows including *Laverne and Shirley*, the *George Burns Comedy Week*, and *Honey, I Shrunk the Kids*. As an actor, he's appeared in a wide variety of films including *M*A*S*H*, *Up the Sandbox*, *Jaws*, *The Jerk*, and *Clueless*. His various books include *Long Time Gone: The Autobiography of David Crosby*, *The Jerk*, and his best-selling account of the making of *Jaws* entitled *The Jaws Log* (1975), which has been reissued numerous times, most recently in 2005.

In 1974, when you were first brought on the Jaws *project, you were Script Editor at ABC's* The Odd Couple, *as well as an old friend of Steven Spielberg. Did you meet during your college days at Long Beach?*

GOTTLIEB: No, I first met Steven at Universal when he was still doing *Night Gallery.* I forget who introduced us, but it was probably our mutual agent, Mike Medavoy, who, in 1968, had signed up an amazing group of Hollywood newcomers to their first agency contract: Steven, Terrence Malick, John Milius, myself, and even Michelangelo Antonioni and others. From the very beginning, Medavoy believed in the synergy of putting his various clients together on different projects, and he kept combining me with Steven. Soon we became good friends, and we spent a lot of time together. That was probably 1969. So by 1974, we'd known each other for five years, and I'd appeared in two of his television movies, doing "day player" parts and improvisation. I had a background in improvisation, and I was part of a comedy troupe known as The Committee, which played in Los Angeles in '68, '69, and '72. So, I was pretty well known for that kind of work, and I was generally considered, at the time, a comedy writer.

I read somewhere that you were "astonished" when Spielberg asked you to rewrite Jaws.

GOTTLIEB: I was surprised, but I wasn't astonished. We'd collaborated before, having written about a half dozen treatments together.

Wasn't one a dogfight script?

GOTTLIEB: Yes, we wrote one about World War I flyers, and we had a bunch of other ideas that we'd go out and pitch together—for me to write and for Steven to direct. At the time, our agent insisted that Steven had to be guaranteed direction on any of the ideas he pitched, and nobody was quite ready to do that yet. Eventually, Zanuck and Brown hired him for *The Sugarland Express,* and when he was finishing up the film, he sent me a copy of the script for *Jaws* with a note on the cover saying: "Eviscerate it." So I read it carefully, and I sent him a memo describing what I would do to improve the script. Oddly enough, that memo was later discovered by a very thorough archivist who was preparing the *Jaws* DVD for Pioneer, and it was very interesting to read it again because when I wrote that memo, dated January 1974, I told Steven that if the film was made, and if it was done right, audiences would "feel about the ocean, the same way they felt about showers after *Psycho.*" And for the past twenty-five years, that's always the first comment that Steven or I hear about the film, "After I saw *Jaws,* I couldn't go into the water!"

The film actually decreased beach attendance the summer it was released.

GOTTLIEB: That's right, so we must have done something right! Anyway, back in 1974, I sent my memo off to Steven, and that's the last I thought about it. He was finishing up *Sugarland* and preparing *Jaws*—and having casting problems—and I was working on *The Odd Couple.* Then early one Sunday morning, I get a telephone call from Steven, and he says, "Listen, I'm over at the Bel Air Hotel with Zanuck and Brown, and I've

shown them your memo. Can you come over here and discuss it with us?"
So I drove over to the Bel Air Hotel, had lox and bagels, and we discussed
the script, and its strengths and weaknesses, and what I would do to rewrite
it, and so on. And we talked until 7:00 that evening, until the sun went
down, talking for eight straight hours about the film. When we finally left,
Steven said, "Can you quit your day job and come East and do the
movie?" and I said, "I think so." The very next day, Monday, they made
me an offer for a very minimal deal, and Tuesday I was on the plane to
Boston with Steven. That was May 2nd, only nine days before the com-
mencement of principal photography.

*Had you already been hired to play the role of Meadows, the local newspaper
editor?*

GOTTLIEB: Yes, in the weeks preceding that meeting, Steven had said,
"Maybe you should come out as an actor, and we can work on improvisation together, especially in the crowd scenes." So I looked at the script
again and suggested "Meadows," and Steven said, "Well, I was thinking of
using a woman for that role." But I pointed out that it was a perfect part
for me because Meadows is in most of the crowd scenes. So Steven said,
"OK, but you have to pass casting with Universal," which I did. So I was
already on the picture as an actor when I got hired to do what was being
called, on paper, "a one-week dialogue polish" at the Writers Guild minimum. As things turned out, Steven and I lived together in a house on the
Vineyard for the next nine weeks, and I rewrote the whole script while he
directed the film. When the script was done, Steven had finished almost all
of the dialogue scenes and was focusing on the action scenes in the ocean.
So in midsummer, I left behind the completed script, and Steven still had
about two more months of shooting at sea.

How much did you make?

GOTTLIEB: I was *very* happy to make $15,000—$8,000 for the writing
and another $7,000 for the acting. I bought a brand new BMW for
$5,900, and my wife and I drove down to Nashville where some of our
friends were making a movie called *Nashville*. So we hung out in Tennessee
for a while, traded war stories, watched the filming, and then drove back to
Los Angeles and waited for Steven to get back from New England.

*Before you came on the scene, there were two earlier screenwriters. The first
was Peter Benchley, the author of the hugely popular novel that had sold over
ten million copies in the United States alone. He wrote three drafts, but
admitted that he wasn't "a competent screenwriter," and finally said, "I give
up." Then Howard Sackler, the Pulitzer Prize winning author of* The Great
White Hope, *did a five-week rewrite at the Bel Air Hotel. By the time you
saw the Sackler script, had the two subplots from the novel—the mayor's mob*

connections and the adulterous affair between Hooper and the Police Chief's wife—been completely eliminated?

GOTTLIEB: I'm not positive, but I think both elements survived in the Sackler draft.

Both were crucial aspects of the novel.

GOTTLIEB: They were, and I remember that we were still arguing about them even while Steven was shooting the film. The mob aspect was definitely the first to go since it was truly extraneous to the focus of the movie. But the affair between Ellen Brody and Hooper was much more complicated since it would greatly affect the film, and we were still debating its ramifications right up to principal photography. Since the first things Steven shot on location were the party on the beach, the discovery of the body, and the first day in the Brody's new house, we were able to postpone dealing with the issue for another week or two, but then we finally had to make a decision. Earlier, the problem was further complicated by the fact that Jan Michael Vincent was being considered for the role of Hooper, which would have added a natural sexual energy to the relationship, but, eventually, we agreed that he wasn't right for the part.

Eliminating the adultery not only helped the relationship between the husband and the wife, but it also created the strong bond at the end between Brody and Hooper. The book doesn't have that bond.

GOTTLIEB: Right, which is why Hooper gets killed at the end in the novel. But we didn't want to do that to our young hero, whom the audience is rooting for and wants to succeed. Besides, it's quite a formulaic construction to have the adulterous male punished—in this case eaten by a shark—in spite of his good deeds, so, in the end, we were happy to see it go.

Did you ever discuss the screenplay with either Peter Benchley or Howard Sackler while you were rewriting the script?

GOTTLIEB: No, I never met Sackler, and I never talked to Peter Benchley until after the film was completed.

Steven Spielberg called the filming of Jaws *on Martha's Vineyard "the worst experience of my life," and Bill Gilmore, the executive producer, claims that it was "the most difficult film ever made." Things were so bad that the film was being called* Flaws, *and the reasons were countless: problems with the mechanical sharks, strong ocean currents, varying water color, unmatchable cloud patterns, rainstorms, other boats sailing into the frame, union problems, intrusive press, mutinous crew, disgruntled actors, and various mishaps. Is it true that you actually took a dangerous plunge into the ocean?*

GOTTLIEB: I did, and it resulted in a wonderful film clip that we showed on *The Tonight Show*. At one point early in the metamorphosis of the script, the body of Ben Garner was discovered by Hooper, Brody, and

Meadows in the daytime. On the day we tried to shoot it, the ocean was very rough, but we had a schedule to meet, and we went out in our little boats to film the scene. The original staging required me to lean over the edge of our search boat and discover the mutilated remains, but while we were doing the shot, the center of gravity shifted, and the boat tipped, and I fell headfirst into the water between the two boats. I went down and popped up very quickly. There was lots of shouting, but I wasn't that uncomfortable, and they got me out of the water within thirty seconds. But I was very close to the propeller, and there were also sharks in the area.

Then later you must have written yourself out of the scene.

GOTTLIEB: That's right, and it was very painful! Right after I'd fallen in the water, a huge wave came up and crashed down on the sound man, and the recorders were soaked with a ton of salt water. The sound guy called out, "That's a wrap for sound," and the whole day was a washout, and we moved on to other things. Eventually, as the script continued to evolve, we moved the scene after the dinner at Brody's house, so Hooper and Brody could find Ben Gardner at night. Part of that was a practical consideration because, by that time, we were back in Los Angeles, and we didn't have the luxury of shooting at the Vineyard. So we shot it at night on the back lot at the lake with some ground fog. So various events conspired to make that scene much better than it would have been if we'd done it the way it was originally written.

You must have written yourself out of other scenes as well, given that the part of Meadows is much larger in the novel?

GOTTLIEB: Yes, and much larger in the billing too, but it definitely made more sense to have most of Meadows's dialogue said by the mayor. So, I cut myself out of a number of scenes and cut my dialogue down in others. Murray Hamilton was a wonderful actor, and he perfectly embodied the character of the mayor, so it was best to let him absorb most of what Meadows had to say.

How was the writing actually done on the set?

GOTTLIEB: Steven and I shared the house with his personal assistant, Rick Fields. Before shooting began, we spent all our time talking, discussing, making notes, and writing outlines—mostly working out the final plot outline, and making sure that the story elements lined up properly. Once we started shooting, Steven would go off to the set in the morning, and I would stay behind and work at my typewriter, an IBM Selectric. I had an outline of the script, on four pieces of yellow paper taped together, pinned to the wall along with all the shark research. I worked in a separate area of the house, which became my writing studio, and I typed most of the day. When Steven came back from shooting all day, we'd go to dailies and discuss the shots with the producers, and then we'd head back to the house and have dinner with Verna Fields, the editor. Zanuck and Brown, if they were in town, would come by sometimes, and frequently the actors would show up, especially Roy and Richard. During dinner, we'd discuss the changes I'd made in the script and all the ramifications of those changes.

It was a fabulous process because the actors would naturally look at the movie from the point-of-view of their characters, while Verna Fields looked at everything from a storytelling POV: "How can I cut the footage together?" and "What images do I need?" I was always looking at the film from an over-all construction point of view, and Steven had to keep everything in mind, especially how to shoot it and how to get strong performances from his actors. By the end of dinner, there would generally be some consensus, and I would clean up the pages, and do final revisions. Then a typist from the production office would type up the pages, usually around 10–11 P.M., and have them Xeroxed and ready for everyone by 4–5 A.M. the next morning. In general, my first assignment was to write what was next on the schedule, and then to try and write ahead as fast as I possibly could so that there wouldn't be so much pressure to finish the pages. But there were still quite a few scenes that came out of the typewriter the night before they were shot.

Let me ask you about the improvisation. Spielberg once said that "all the dialogue from Jaws *came from improvisation." How do you feel about that?*

GOTTLIEB: There was definitely some excellent improvisation at dinner that helped me write the scenes, but all the speeches spoken by the professional actors were very well scripted. Naturally, there were various asides and expressions that were ad-libbed on the set, but no one ad-libbed substantial dialogue. Personally, I'm never offended when an actor improvises "in character"—when he or she is so present in the role that whatever the performer says is appropriate to the moment. The only reason that an actor can do such is thing is because the writer has fashioned an appropriate character and milieu, and any good writer should appreciate it. But on the set of *Jaws*, the speeches were never significantly altered from the script, with a few exceptions. One of those exceptions provided the biggest laugh in the movie when Roy Scheider, having finally seen the shark, backs away from the edge of the boat into the cabin and says to Quint, "You're gonna need a bigger boat." Roy made that up, I didn't write it, and it's exactly true to the character, and I'm glad he came up with it. On the other hand, there's a number of other scenes that might seem like they were improvised, but they weren't. Like the scene where Hooper comes to dinner and eats Brody's meal, or when Quint and Hooper compare scars, or when Hooper and the mayor argue in front of the billboard sign.

Is it true that Sid Sheinberg, the head of Universal, visited the island, saw the way you were rewriting the script, and said in disbelief, "My God! This is the way this is being done?"

GOTTLIEB: I wouldn't be surprised. I don't remember hearing those exact words, but I wouldn't be surprised that he felt that way. You have to remember that Sid came out of the television side of the studio before he became the head of production. *Jaws* was very early in his tenure as production head, and I don't know how many feature films he'd actually seen being made. He was certainly familiar with the process, but he was an attorney. He wasn't a guy who'd come up like Dick Zanuck, working as a laborer, a grip, and a props guy before ascending through the ranks because his father was the head of the studio.

I've read that the rushes were sent to Los Angeles for processing and that they weren't seen on the set until forty-eight hours after they were shot. Did this affect your constant state of revision?

GOTTLIEB: Not as much as you might think, and not all the rushes were delayed that long. On the set, they'd generally "break the film" in the early afternoon to get it on the night flight to Los Angeles. Anything that got to Los Angeles by midnight would be processed by the lab and be ready to come back the next day. So in the dailies, we'd see some work from the previous day and some from a day earlier. But we'd planned for everything over our long shooting schedule, and it caused very few revision problems.

Bruce, the mechanical shark, apparently named for Spielberg's lawyer Bruce Ramen, was actually three twenty-four-foot-long mechanical sharks designed by Bob Mattey. In the Atlantic Ocean, they malfunctioned in every kind of conceivable way—sinking, exploding, corroding, etc.—but some people feel that Spielberg's inability to shoot the shark actually enhanced the film because it forced him to keep the predator hidden from the audience even longer than he'd intended. How do you feel about that?

GOTTLIEB: When it became obvious, early on, that the shark was going to be a problem, Steven and I agreed that one of our favorite suspense movies was an old sci-fi film called *It Came from Outer Space* which takes place in a rocket research station where an extraterrestrial being is inhabiting the subterranean tunnels. It was the precursor to a great many films, including *Alien*, and Steven and I loved how the suspense was built up in that film because the creature was always just off camera. You could see the results of its carnage, and they used the clever device of the Geiger counter, which accelerated its clicking every time the radioactive creature was nearby. Sometimes the Geiger counter would click up to a great roar, and you'd expect the creature to burst into view, and instead there'd be a red herring of some kind. So we decided to concentrate on showing the "effects" of the shark rather than the shark itself, and that's evident from the very first shot of the movie, which is made from the shark's point of view, cruising beneath the water, and then, a little later, underneath the young girl's legs. One of things that's so chilling about the opening death of Chrissie is the colossal force of the unseen creature sweeping her back and forth in the ocean. This continues later in the film when the unseen shark pulls the dock apart, and when it pulls the barrels beneath the water. All these scenes were dictated in part by the failure of the shark to function, combined with a very calculated plot decision to hold off revealing the shark as long as possible.

While Spielberg was shooting at Martha's Vineyard, the famous shark photographers, Ron and Valerie Taylor, were off the Australian coast trying to get footage of a great white attacking an undersized shark cage containing Carl Rizzo, a midget stunt man filling in for the Hooper (Dreyfuss) character. When they actually came upon a huge great white, Rizzo refused to get in the cage, but the Taylors managed to get some great footage of the shark attacking the empty cage. Is it true that, in an effort to use the footage, the script was rewritten so that Hooper—who was killed in his cage in the novel— now, escapes, hides at the bottom of the ocean, and survives?

GOTTLIEB: We wanted to use whatever spectacular footage we had. So we had this empty cage being battered around by a vicious shark, and that led logically to an eerie shot of the twisted wreckage of the cage being hauled out of the sea, leaving the fate of Hooper uncertain. So all we needed was a tank shot of Hooper swimming away from the cage to create confusion as to whether he survived or not, and to allow the audience to accept the fact that he's all right when he surfaces after the confrontation.

Was the Hooper character plotted to be killed up to that point?

GOTTLIEB: No, we'd already decided that Hooper would survive, unlike the novel.

John Baxter, author of Steven Spielberg, *claims that Hal Barwood and Matthew Robbins made unattributed contributions to the script. Is that correct?*

GOTTLIEB: They're very good writers, actually a writer/director team, and they were peers of Steven and George Lucas who did some very successful films like *I Wanna Hold Your Hand*, which Steven produced. Back in those days, there was a much more collegial sense of community among filmmakers in general. First of all, there were fewer people involved in the business, and you tended to know everyone—especially the ones your own age.

Didn't that group hang out at the beach?

GOTTLIEB: Yes, at the beach, at parties, everywhere. Margot Kidder had a great beach house in Malibu that was very popular. So there was a real sense of community, and if you had a film problem, there wasn't such a big "ego investment" back in 1974 as there is today. It was common to ask others for help, and to lend out your script to others. I read *Jaws* when

I had no hope of being a writer on the picture; I felt lucky to be an actor on the film—and get a five-week acting job. As I mentioned earlier, I did a fairly lengthy dissection of the script for my friend Steven. Well, Steven also showed the script to others as well, including Barwood and Robbins, and I don't doubt that they made some useful suggestions, and I don't doubt that some of those suggestions ended up in the film—as did some by John Milius and others—but I have no idea what they might have been.

One of Howard Sackler's most interesting contributions to the screenplay was Quint's powerful story about being on the USS Indianapolis *at the end of World War II. The ship, which had delivered the atom bomb for Hiroshima, was sunk by a Japanese submarine, and hundreds of the helpless crew were killed by subsequent shark attacks. Supposedly, John Milius expanded Quint's memorable speech, and then Robert Shaw, drinking whiskey, improvised the lines on the set. Is that accurate?*

GOTTLIEB: That's not quite correct, and, of course, a great deal of mythology had been written about Milius's role in the creation of the *Indianapolis* speech. The truth of the matter is that the scene was *always* planned as a very big moment in the film—it's the last dialogue scene in the movie and it's followed by forty-five minutes of hard action. Steven and I always referred to that scene in our outlines as the "just before the battle mother" speech. The speech was clearly an analogue of the countless war movies where soldiers are sitting in their foxholes before going over the top in WWI, and they talk about their past and about the coming battle, when, suddenly, they're interrupted by a barrage and the final confrontation starts. Now John Milius was a surfer and a self-styled macho man, and he may have come up with the *idea* of the men comparing their scars, but I wrote that dialogue word for word as it appears in the script and in the film. As for the long monologue about the *Indianapolis*, that speech in Sackler's version was quite long, running a couple of pages. But Steven wasn't satisfied with it, and he appealed to everybody to help him, and many people contributed drafts and suggestions including John Milius. I was present during at least one conference call with Milius, and I took notes from what he said, and the only complete line of dialogue from John Milius that appears in the film is, "I'll find him for three, but I'll catch him, and kill him, for ten."

But that's from Quint's first scene at the town meeting.

GOTTLIEB: That's right. I liked the line, and I put it in the script. As for the *Indianapolis* speech, I'd collected quite a mélange of materials: Sackler's version, two or three drafts that I'd written, notes from various people, and Milius's suggestions over the phone. The upshot was that I gave all these materials to Robert Shaw so he could look them over. Then one night when we were eating dinner—very close to when the scene was going to be shot—Shaw stopped by, which he rarely did, and after dinner he said, "I think I've got that speech licked." Then he took out a piece of paper and proceeded to read the speech almost exactly as it appears in the movie. Shaw, you have to remember, was a distinguished playwright. He'd written *The Man in the Glass Booth*, and he also had several novels to his credit. He was very literate, and very stage-wise, and he basically created that speech out of text I'd written, along with the Sackler version, and the notes from Milius and others. So it was Robert Shaw who put that speech together, organized it, and performed it for us after dinner. Then he performed it exactly the same way on the set, two days running: one day with the other actors, when he was sober, and the next day with the same actors, when he was drunk.

Which was used in the film, the drunk or the sober version?

GOTTLIEB: They were cut together.

Were you excited when you first heard Shaw's version of the speech?

GOTTLIEB: Incredibly, you have to imagine the setting. We're at dinner, it's 8 or 9 in the evening, we're all exhausted from a long day of shooting, and we have to be up at 6:00 A.M. the next morning. Then, unexpectedly, Shaw comes in and joins us for dessert. Then the housekeeper dims the lights and leaves, creating this marvelous ambiance, this magical moment, and then Shaw started his monologue. Everything suited him theatrically, and ever the performer, he gave an unforgettable and powerful reading. Afterwards, there was total silence in the room. Finally, Steven said, "That's it. That's what we're going to shoot." And that was that.

You felt that way too?

GOTTLIEB: Absolutely. So I believe that Robert Shaw wrote that speech. He organized the materials, improvised a bit, and decided exactly what words he was going to say. So I think he deserves the credit, and certainly not John Milius. In the end, your readers will have to decide whether they believe the guy who was there and says he didn't write it, or the guy who *wasn't* there and says he did.

It's good to set the record straight. Now I'd like to run down the casting of the three main characters, starting with Chief Brody. Originally, Charlton Heston wanted the part, but Spielberg preferred someone less well known. When he couldn't convince Universal to approve Joseph Bologna, Robert Duvall was offered the part. But Duvall wanted the role of Quint, and finally the lead went to Roy Scheider.

GOTTLIEB: That sounds correct, although most of it happened before I came on board. But I do remember when I was reading the Sackler draft that Steven once rolled his eyes and told me that the studio wanted him to use Charlton Heston and Jan Michael Vincent.

OK, then let's talk about the role of Matt Hooper, the young ichthyologist. It was first turned down by Jon Voight, and then a number of other actors were considered—Timothy Bottoms, Jeff Bridges, Joel Grey, and, as you've told me today, Jan Michael Vincent. Then the part was offered to Richard Dreyfuss who initially refused it as "meaningless," but then, claiming he was "prostituting" himself, he finally agreed to do it. Does that sound right?

GOTTLIEB: Yes, right up until Richard and how he got the part. It's true that, initially, he turned it down, and, as a matter of fact, when I first went to Boston with Steven, nine days before the start of principal photography, neither Hooper nor Quint had been cast. Neither appeared in the first two weeks of the schedule, but time was obviously running out. You certainly don't want to start rolling a multimillion dollar picture without the lead characters cast. Back in those days, I had a very strong relationship with Richard Dreyfuss—I still do—we'd done improvisational theater together, and I knew him before Steven did. At the time, I was very happy for Richard because he'd just made *The Apprenticeship of Duddy Kravitz*. So Steven and I were sitting together in Boston, and he told me that Richard had turned it down. So I said, "Let's let him know that I'm rewriting the film, and see if we can get him to change his mind." So I called my wife and said, "Where's Dreyfuss?" and she called me right back and said, "You're lucky, he's in New York on a press tour for *Kravitz*." So I called Richard in New York, and I convinced him to come up to Boston, even though he was totally exhausted from his three-week promotion tour. I told him I was rewriting the script, that it was going to be very different, with a lot more humor, and I made some promises that Steven had agreed to. When he finally showed up at the hotel, the Holiday Inn in Boston, he was wearing his Hooper outfit. He had the little glasses on, and the hat, and the beard, and we said, "Don't change a thing. Don't even get a haircut."

He did it intentionally?

GOTTLIEB: No, it was just how he was dressed. So he asked what we were up to, and we began discussing the film, and somewhere in the course of our discussions, somebody crushed a Styrofoam cup, and we all said, "We have to put that in the movie." Quint would crush a beer can, and Hooper would crush a Styrofoam cup. So we had a great discussion, especially about the character of Hooper, and how we would reinvent the character for Richard. Then Steven offered him the money he wanted, and Richard accepted the role.

Had the reviews from Duddy Kravitz *come out yet?*

GOTTLIEB: I think the first reviews were in, but I don't think the full impact—the huge ego stroke—of all those reviews had hit yet.

There's a line of thinking about all this that Dreyfuss felt his performance in Kravitz *was terrible and that his career had been destroyed. So he took* Jaws *because he was afraid he wouldn't be offered anything else.*

GOTTLIEB: There may be some truth to that, but I think the main reason that Richard took the film was that Steven and I were willing to recreate the Hooper character to suit his talents.

How about Quint, the sea-hardened captain on a personal mission? Apparently, Lee Marvin was the first choice, but he turned it down. Then Sterling Hayden was considered, but his tax problems eventually eliminated him. Finally, Robert Shaw, who felt the project was "a piece of shit," took his wife's advice and accepted the role.

GOTTLIEB: That's right, and I pushed very hard for Sterling Hayden. I'd met Sterling a few times, and I'd read his book, and I was convinced that he was Quint. Robert Shaw, of course, did a great job, and Robert Shaw's a great actor, but I think that Sterling Hayden would have given a performance that would still be remembered as the equivalent of what he'd done in *Dr. Strangelove*. But he had those huge tax problems at the time. Basically, all of his income as an actor went directly to the IRS, but he was somehow able to keep his income as a writer. He'd been living in Paris, and he'd just returned, and we met at my house in Los Angeles and at his private railroad car near Sausalito, but he just couldn't take the part.

One final question about the casting. The role of Ellen Brody, the wife of the police chief, was given to Lorraine Gary, the wife of the studio head, Sid Sheinberg. Although a major character in the novel, her role was constantly shrinking on the set, and I understand she wasn't happy about it. Was this difficult for you?

GOTTLIEB: Cynics would say, and have said, that casting Lorraine was the best insurance policy Steven ever had—and that it was a very calculated movement on his part. In Steven's defense, he'd known Lorraine from television where she'd distinguished herself in a number of roles, including Telly Savalas's girlfriend in a *Kojak* movie of the week. She was a very good actress.

She was terrific in Jaws.

GOTTLIEB: She was, and she'd been terrific in a number of things before *Jaws*, so it wasn't a purely political move on Steven's part, although, obviously, it didn't hurt. But, Sid Sheinberg, like Lew Wasserman before him, had only one master and that was MCA. If he felt his wife was wrong for the film and that she might hurt the picture, he would have fired her in a minute. I'm sure of that. Also, in Sid's defense, I can tell you that we never heard a word from him promoting Lorraine in the dailies. He never pushed for more screen time, or questioned our story decisions about her role in the film. It was all completely professional.

Now, I'd like to ask you about a number of excellent ideas and added scenes that were not in the original novel. For example, when the shark attacks the young boy on the raft, Brody, off duty, is sitting on the beach amid the Amity sunbathers, and this allowed Spielberg to do his very effective Vertigo *"zoom-dolly back" shot.*

GOTTLIEB: Yes, that's one of the places where Steven said, "I want to do a trick shot." Usually, he doesn't like to do them, but it seemed right in that scene, and it worked perfectly. But I'm not sure who first moved that scene to the beach—maybe Sackler.

Then there's the town meeting and the first appearance of Quint—and his scratching his fingernails on the blackboard.

GOTTLIEB: That's probably Steven staging the scene to get the audience's attention. It still makes me cringe when I hear it, and it has that same effect on the audience.

There's also that humorous, though potentially deadly, new scene about the two guys who decide to capture the shark with the family roast.

GOTTLIEB: I added that scene for a little comic relief, and Steven cast two local guys who were perfectly and appropriately silly.

The misidentification of the captured tiger shark and its dissection were excellent additions to the film.

GOTTLIEB: Steven and I always referred to *Jaws* as "*Moby Dick* meets *Enemy of the People*," so we created those scenes to establish the credentials of Hooper, the young oceanographer—and to make Brody his reluctant ally. For the dissection scene, I had lots of information about the different things that people have found inside the guts of sharks. So it was very natural to have Hooper pull out all kinds of funny stuff. On the other hand, the scene also had the suspense of the darkened warehouse, and the overriding tension of the ongoing conflict between the mayor and Brody regarding the safety of the town.

The scene with the two young kids and the fake fin causing a panic on the beach is especially effective.

GOTTLIEB: In earlier drafts, Steven had wanted a little group of local hooligans roaming the town. That concept didn't survive, except when Brody's secretary reports on some of the kids' mischief, and, more effectively, in the fake fin scene at the beach. Steven had also wanted a false alarm in the film, and we felt that it should be perpetrated by the kids. If it was adults, it would have seemed very malicious and ugly, but with the kids, it seemed more prankish and mischievous. So I wrote that scene to satisfy two of Steven's objectives.

How about the scene when Ellen Brody looks at the book while her kid is sitting in his boat at the dock?

GOTTLIEB: That was an added scene that came out of the set's physical location and the constant effort to compress exposition. I'm very proud of the exposition in *Jaws*. There's very little talking at blackboards, or characters telling other characters what they want them to know. Yet there's quite a bit of exposition in *Jaws*, and that scene was designed to reinforce the looming specter of the shark. When Ellen Brody looks at the book and sees the picture of the shark attack, she immediately gets frightened, looks down at her kid playing by the dock, and calls the boy out of the boat. I think Lorraine performed that moment perfectly.

Apparently, Peter Benchley was very opposed to the idea of killing the shark with one of Hooper's air tanks, but when he saw the film, he felt that Spielberg had "absolutely pulled it off."

GOTTLIEB: I can't remember how the shark was killed in the earlier drafts, but once the decision was made to use one of the air tanks, all I had to do was establish how lethal they could be in an earlier scene.

With the mob and adultery subplots eliminated from the movie, and the town's opposition to Brody eventually overcome by the ferociousness of the shark's attacks, the last act becomes a straight adventure story. I've read that Spielberg had Spencer Tracy's Captains Courageous *in mind. Did you ever discuss it?*

GOTTLIEB: I don't remember that. I always thought *Jaws* was much more like Hemingway's *Old Man and the Sea* than Kipling. Kipling's story is more of a morality tale than an extended struggle—when Spencer Tracy dies, he's saving the kid. *Jaws* is more of a titanic struggle, like Melville or Hemingway.

Peter Benchley originally decided to write the novel after he read about a fisherman named Frank Mundus who killed a 4,550-pound shark off Long Island in 1964. I've also read that Quint was modeled on an old Martha's Vineyard sea captain. Did you ever meet either of these men?

GOTTLIEB: I never met Frank Mundus, but I read his book, *Sportfishing for Sharks*, as part of my research. He was a guy who ran a fishing boat off Montauk, and he realized, somewhere along the line, that everybody hates sharks—that people like to catch them and shoot them and kill them—so he developed sportfishing for sharks. As it turns out, there are some very huge sharks off Long Island, and he did, in fact, catch a monster shark in 1964. So, in the abstract, Mundus was the model for the Quint character, and I think he sued the studio because Steven had interviewed him before the shooting began, and he felt that his life story was being expropriated—which people tend to do. But behaviorally, the real model for Quint was a guy named Craig Kingsbury who lived on the island and who played Ben Gardner in the film. Kingsbury was an old sea dog and a super colorful island character who'd experienced pretty much everything that could possibly happen to a sea fisherman. Quite a lot of Quint's dialogue was lifted from the verbal mannerisms of Craig Kingsbury. He was a very self-possessed "man's man," very confident, and he didn't get camera shy at all. Steven would tell him what to do, and he'd just do it. He tended to improvise his lines a bit, and, for a while, I followed him around with a tape recorder and a notepad taking down all the colorful things he said, and then I gave them to Robert Shaw in the form of Quint's dialogue.

Jaws is full of many memorable lines, and we've already discussed a few, including "You're going to need a bigger boat." I'd like to ask you about the last two lines in the film, which are perfectly ironic, as Brody says to Hooper while they're kicking to shore: "I used to hate the water," and Hooper responds, "I can't imagine why." It was a great way to end the film.

GOTTLIEB: Those lines came very late, after the picture was finished in fact. During final production, I was brought back on payroll for another week to do the incidental and background dialogue during the looping or ADR [Automated Dialogue Replacement] process. In the script, there were a few places that were actually marked "dialogue to be added during looping," and it was at that time, when we were looking for a way to finally end the movie, that I wrote those two lines.

I've read that Spielberg was considering a final shot in the film where the audience would see a number of shark fins heading towards the coast. Do you know anything about that?

GOTTLIEB: Yes, the idea was that the tank explosion of the huge shark, with all the blood and commotion in the water, would draw the other sharks, who would then, rather ominously and ambiguously, head for shore. It was like the hand coming out of the grave at the end of *Carrie*, a creepy postscript.

Who talked him out of it?

GOTTLIEB: I think we all did. Besides, it would have been a huge process shot, and we were already $3 million over budget.

Jaws was the first picture to go one-hundred days over schedule (nearly tripling from a scheduled fifty-five days to one-hundred fifty-five), and it more than doubled its original budget. Were there any concerns on the set that the picture would be scrapped or that Spielberg would be replaced? Especially considering the fact that Zanuck had once fired Kurosawa from the set of Tora! Tora! Tora!

GOTTLIEB: But Zanuck and Brown were great fans and champions of Steven. They'd done *Sugarland Express* together, and even though the film tanked, they remained perfectly loyal. I don't think they ever would have replaced him, despite all the problems.

Well, all the concerns about the film were quickly forgotten after the extraordinary success of its two preview screenings in Dallas and Long Beach, but Spielberg still felt that he could turn a "four scream" picture into a "five scream" picture by improving the underwater "head" scene, which he reshot in Verna Fields' backyard swimming pool with Richard Dreyfuss. How did that work?

GOTTLIEB: Actually, I thought the "head in the boat" shot was redone before the previews. I was at that exciting Long Beach screening, but I'm not positive. Regardless, whatever the timing, Steven was definitely not satisfied with the original shot, but since there was no money left and very little time, he decided to do it quickly and pay for it himself. All the props were still on the lot, so he threw a crew together and, instead of going to a tank, he went to the swimming pool. He got a dummy head, threw a half gallon of milk into the water to make it look murky, and Rexford Metz did the underwater photography. They set it up in the afternoon, made the shot that evening, and it became one of the most unforgettable moments in the film.

Jaws opened in 463 theaters in the United States and Canada on June 20, 1975, and sixty-four days later it passed The Godfather as the highest grossing film of all time. It eventually made $458 million in worldwide box office returns.

GOTTLIEB: Yes, and *Jaws* was a revolutionary picture in the history of film distribution. Back in those days, a picture had a platform release in some big cities and then filtered down to the public, eventually playing for a year or two. The concept of saturating a movie in many theaters over the summer and making a lot of money very fast didn't exist until *Jaws*, although it's now the standard release pattern for summer films. Ironically, when *Jaws* first opened, it wasn't particularly well received. *Time* and *Newsweek* and *The New York Times* pretty much dismissed it as a "potboiler" movie based on a "potboiler" best seller. In the very beginning, we didn't even have the good theaters in Los Angeles. We had one in Westwood and one on Hollywood Boulevard, and both were insignificant. There was no Grauman's Chinese, or the Egyptian, or the Pacific, so nobody knew much about the film.

But after the second preview in Long Beach, with the audience going nuts and coming out of the theater buzzing, Lou Wasserman, Sid Sheinberg, and Charlie Powell, who was head of publicity, huddled together in the men's room at the movie theater—since it was the only place they could get some privacy—and they basically scrapped the original release plans for *Jaws*. They decided to call all their salesmen, and call all their field reps, and put the film in as many theaters as they could get on short notice—and they got quite a lot of them. Four-hundred sixty screens in 1975 compares to two thousand today. And that decision, and its amazing success, changed how movies have been released ever since. It's also very interesting that, previously, one of those big mainframe computers had been fed all kinds of information about *Jaws*, and it predicted that the film was going to gross $65 million domestic, and no one believed it. They felt it needed to be reprogrammed because it just wasn't logical. In the end, of course, the film grossed over $100 million domestic. At one point that summer, *Time* magazine reported that the film was grossing a million dollars a day—in 1975 dollars!—which was unbelievable. No picture had ever grossed that kind of money.

The following February, a very confident Spielberg invited a Los Angeles TV crew to his office to record his reactions to the Oscar nominations. But he was visibly shaken when the film only received four nominations, and he was overlooked for Best Director. The common explanation is that the film's popular success created a critical reaction. How do you feel about that?

GOTTLIEB: Nowadays, when a big film like *Titanic* wins everything, nobody has a problem with it. But in those days, there was almost always a backlash against the most popular picture of the year. Big films like *Airport* and *Towering Inferno* might get some special effects nominations but not much more. Nevertheless, *Jaws* was nominated for Best Picture because they simply couldn't ignore it, and, generally, when a picture got a Best Picture nomination, its director would get a Best Director nomination. But Steven didn't, and it came as kind of a shock. It was, of course, a bit hubristic of Steven to have a TV crew standing by for the nominations, but you have to remember that everything was new to him back then. He was the "boy wonder," even subtracting a year from his age in order to be "the youngest director ever." And he'd been nominated for the Golden Globes—we were all nominated for the Golden Globes—and the British Academy had nominated us for Best Picture, Best Director, and Best Screenplay. So it was a disappointment when we were ignored by the Academy, except for John Williams winning Best Score and Verna Fields winning Best Editing. Yet, at the very same time, Steven was quickly becoming the center of an enormous cult of personality, which he definitely encouraged. And why wouldn't he? He was only twenty-eight years old and ready to rewrite film history.

Many people gave Oscar-winner Verna Fields, the film's editor, a great deal of credit for the finished film, and Spielberg was naturally quite angry over claims that she'd "saved" the picture. Even though that's obviously an exaggeration, how would you assess her role?

GOTTLIEB: Nobody could ever suggest that Verna Fields didn't deserve an Oscar for her work on *Jaws*, but no editor ever cut a film that hadn't been framed and shot by the director. Editors don't shoot the film, they work with what they're given. So it's definitely unfair for people to say that she "saved" the movie. She did, however, make the most of what she was given. It's important to also remember that Steven didn't just walk away from the film when the shooting was over; he was present for the editing and had very strong ideas about how things should be cut.

You talked earlier about the effect Jaws *had on distribution strategies, and many people similarly feel that the film initiated the "blockbuster mentality" in Hollywood which encouraged the studios to allocate tremendous resources to a limited number of commercially potential films—while eliminating many other more varied and "serious" projects. What's your reaction to that?*

GOTTLIEB: It's not the first time that artists have suffered for commerce. I think it's true that *Jaws* initiated "blockbuster" thinking, but it was really solidified by *Star Wars* and *Raiders of the Lost Ark*. Eventually, there was a brief period when Lucas and Spielberg, between them, had eight of the top-ten grossing films of all time. So you can't blame the corporations for committing to those kinds of projects. Unfortunately, the same mentality has also crept into the record business, book publishing, and Broadway. Another problem is that the transnational global corporations eventually acquired most of the studios. Movies used to be a much cozier family business, but now it's much more corporate. We all know that the budget of one picture like *Armageddon* could have financed fifteen smaller films, but those films won't keep the studio open. It's the same thing in New York; publishers don't want thirty novels selling thirty thousand copies, they want one novel selling nine-hundred thousand copies. I guess I feel that it was all inevitable—if *Jaws* hadn't kicked it off, something else would have.

Spielberg once admitted that he was very good at making "shock-value films," and he referred to Jaws *as a "primal scream movie." But like all the best horror and adventure films,* Jaws *was profoundly successful because it explored fundamental fears, phobias, and anxieties. How much did you think about these universal themes when you were actually working on the script?*

GOTTLIEB: During the day-to-day writing of a movie, you're less concerned with grand themes than you are with practical matters like: "How do I plant the fact that the air tanks are volatile?" But as a storyteller, I never really lost sight of the fact that I was dealing with a primal creature and all the primordial fears it inspires. All of the story elements and all of the crucial personal relationships in the film were predicated on that fundamental fact.

At least one critic had raised the possibility that Quint, being "guilty" for delivering the A-bomb and having survived the sinking of the USS Indianap-olis *and its aftermath, is destined to die. Did that ever occur to you during the rewritings?*

GOTTLIEB: No, but it's a marvelous coincidence that gives texture to the film. The basic story fact regarding *Jaws* is that we had to let the shark kill at least one of the three men at the end of the film, and we felt very strongly that it shouldn't be either Brody or Hooper.

Fairly recently, Steven Spielberg has actually apologized for the film as being "violent, nasty, and crude," and Peter Benchley feels that both his book and the film unjustly malign sharks, feeling that they're "more victim than vil-lain." How do you react to that?

GOTTLIEB: I think they're both belittling their own contributions to the project and carrying political correctness a bit too far. On the other hand, it's true that the maligning of sharks was an unfortunate by-product of the film. They're not as bad as we made them out to be, and they're just doing what's necessary for their survival. In reality, there are relatively few shark attacks on humans—whom they really don't like to eat, which is why there are so many survivors of shark attacks.

But, on the other hand, Moby Dick *isn't a typical sperm whale, he's a very special one with a malign intelligence.*

GOTTLIEB: That's right, and Benchley's genius in the book—following after Melville—was his creation of a shark, usually a rather brainless creature, with a malevolent personality combined with an aggressive fixation and a kind of omnipotent ability. And all of that plays very nicely into our natural fear of sharks. As Mundus pointed out in his book, sharks are like spiders and rats and snakes. Let's face it, nobody really likes them, and the film benefited from those almost inexplicable primordial feelings by playing off the mythos of the shark, and I certainly don't feel guilty about it.

Well, you shouldn't! Thanks, Carl.

GOTTLIEB: Thank you. It was fun.

CHAPTER 13

Rocky (1976)

A CONVERSATION WITH SYLVESTER STALLONE

Born in New York City but raised mostly in Philadelphia, Sylvester Stallone attended the American College in Switzerland and the University of Miami before returning to New York City as an actor and an aspiring screenwriter. After various small roles on television and some bit parts in feature films, Stallone costarred in *The Lords of Flatbush* (1974) with Perry King, Henry Winkler, and Paul Mace. Moving to Los Angeles the same year, he sold his first feature-length script, *Hell's Kitchen*, in 1975. Later the same year, he wrote and sold his screenplay, *Rocky,* to producers David Chartoff and Irving Winkler, and the film, starring Stallone and directed by John Avildsen, was released in 1976. The film received the Best Picture of the Year award at the Academy Awards, and it also received five other Oscar nominations, including two for Stallone: Best Actor and Best Screenplay. He subsequently wrote and starred in five *Rocky* sequels (1979, 1982, 1985, 1990, and 2006), directing *Rocky II*, *III*, *IV*, and *Rocky Balboa*. He also wrote and starred in the popular *Rambo* sequence of feature films (1982, 1985, and 1988). An international movie star, Stallone has appeared in many other films since *Rocky*, including Renny Harlin's *Cliffhanger* (1993) with John Lithgow, from a script by Stallone; Rob Cohen's *Daylight* (1996) with Amy Brenneman; James Mangold's *Cop Land* (1997) with Harvey Keitel and Robert De Niro; and Stephen Kay's *Get Carter* (2000) with Miranda Richardson.

On March 19, 1975, as a struggling young actor and screenwriter, you took the night off and went to see Muhammad Ali defeat Chuck Wepner, the so-called "Bayonne Bleeder," and retain his heavyweight title. What affected you so much about that fight?

STALLONE: Chuck Wepner was basically a guy who everybody considered a joke. He was known as the "Bayonne Bleeder," and it was clear that his only notable contribution to the history of pugilism would be *just* how badly Ali would destroy him. No one considered whether he could win the fight, that was out of the question, but everyone was wondering just how much of a beating he'd take—and how long it would last—and how much pain he'd absorb before he crashed to the canvas. The odds on Wepner were basically a zillion-to-one, and they couldn't even take bets on the fight. So I'm sitting there watching the fight, with an especially bloodthirsty crowd, and it was terrible. The guy didn't even look like a fighter. He was terribly awkward and unskilled, and he looked like a heavy bag with eyeballs. It was really sad. Then, all of a sudden, something incredible happened. From nowhere, Wepner knocked down the immortal Ali. It was like a bolt of lightning from some Greek god in the sky, and, almost instantly, Wepner became the crowed favorite—in a matter of seconds. Suddenly, he went from being a complete joke to being somebody whom everybody watching could identify with—because everybody's thinking, "Yes, I'd like to do that! I'd like to do the impossible, even if only for a moment, and be recognized for it—and have the crowd cheer." So it made everyone think to himself, "If this totally inept guy can put down Muhammad Ali, who knows what *I* can do." So I'm sitting there watching all this, and at some point I realize that the whole thing's a metaphor, and I realized that it wasn't really about boxing. Actually, *Rocky* was never really about boxing, it was about personal triumph.

One biographer claimed that, "Rocky was born that night." Did you immediately think of the Wepner fight as a screenwriting possibility?

STALLONE: Not immediately. At the time, I'd already written a script called *Hell's Kitchen* about three brothers struggling to rise up out of the mean streets of New York, and one of the brothers was a club fighter. Eventually I sold the rights to *Hell's Kitchen* to Ron Suppa and John Roach, who were two young guys, backed with a little Texas oil money, who'd just created a production company called Force 10. I was completely broke at the time, they gave me a little money, and, in my heart, I never really believed that they'd actually make the film—but, of course, I was hopeful that they would. Then one day, I had an acting audition for the well-known producers, David Chartoff and Irving Winkler, and when it was over, I had the feeling that nothing was going to come of it, so as I was walking out, I said, "Oh, by the way, I write a little bit"—which I knew they heard all the time, but they said, "OK, bring us what you've got." So I gave them *Hell's Kitchen*, and they liked it, and they had a meeting with Suppa and Roach. But afterwards, Chartoff and Winkler said to me, "Sorry, Sly, but it's just impossible; we can't work with these neophytes. They don't really understand the business, so we'll have to pass." So there I was watching all my dreams go right down the drain, but when I got home that night, I said to myself, "But the window of opportunity is still open." So I decided to do another script just for them. Since I was obsessed with the idea of personal redemption, I kept saying to myself, "Redemption, redemption, redemption ... but whose redemption?" So I considered a gangster, then a cowboy, then an actor, all kinds of people, until I finally came back to the Wepner fight. Why not a loser, an over-the-hill boxer? I loved the visuals, and the warrior aspect, and the grand symbolism, so, bang!, it all crystallized. I said, "That's it," and I went to work immediately. A door had opened, and my youthful ambition was cresting.

Then you wrote Rocky *in three-and-a-half furious days, in a continuous "heat," with your wife typing the manuscript. Is the legend true?*
STALLONE: Yes, it is. I had this opportunity with Chartoff and Winkler, and I wasn't going to let it slip by. I was young, and I had an incredible amount of energy, and I wrote it in a fury. I was very excited about the whole thing. I had a feel for the streets, and I loved films like *Mean Streets*, and *Marty*, and *On the Waterfront*, and I felt inspired.

Now when you first gave the new script to Chartoff and Winkler, they apparently suggested a few changes?
STALLONE: That's right. The original draft was only about eighty-nine pages long, and it was rather hastily thrown together. At that point, Rocky wasn't really Rocky yet. He was much harder, more caustic, and his face was heavily damaged from all the blows he'd taken. As for Adrian, she was Jewish in the first draft, with a brother and a mother, and the mother couldn't stand Rocky for all kinds of reasons: he was Italian, he was poor, he was semi-punchy, and he was a low-level gangster. Also, the mother really didn't want her daughter to get married and leave her. She wanted to keep her right where she was, as a kind of permanent indentured servant. So, at that point, with the suggestions of the producers, the two main characters started to change. Rocky became a much nicer guy, rather naïve, even sweet in a way, and he was much less of a thug, and more on the fringes of the mob. Eventually, Adrian also became Italian, and her mother was cut out, and the brother took over the role of the needy relative who didn't want to lose her—and who only suggests that Rocky take his sister out on a date because he wants a job.

I've read that Mickey was a blatant racist in the first draft?
STALLONE: He was, and it was very overdone, so I changed it.

Also, in the original script, Rocky actually "threw" the fight. What was that all about?

STALLONE: Well, this was the original story line: Rocky was, quite willingly, being used as a promotional gimmick by the champion, and, at the beginning, Mickey says, "Look, kid, the champ's getting along in years, and if you train right, you can give him a good fight." But, of course, in real life, people only truly reveal themselves when they're under great pressure—where they're so desperate they can't hide their true character anymore. So, during the title fight, as Rocky starts to hurt Apollo, Mickey's bloodlust rises up. He's suddenly on the cusp of being the manager of the heavyweight champion of the world, and he starts salivating at the idea that he's finally about to get some respect and recognition, and his true character comes out. Suddenly, he can't contain himself, and he starts yelling at Rocky, "Kill that black bastard!" But Rocky is put off—he starts to realize what's *really* going on. He senses it in Mickey and in the whole crowd, "Kill him! Kill him!" and he's turned off by all the bloodlust, and the underlying racism, and he realizes that it's not really what he wants. He actually starts feeling sorry for the older champion who's given him his break, even while he continues to pound the guy. It's like that Damon Runyon story "Bred for Battle." Or it's like the time that Marciano beat the aging Joe Louis. So Rocky says to himself, "I've already proved myself, but I don't want to be part of this, and if I beat this man, I *am* part of it. So he takes a dive. He goes down intentionally, and when he hits the canvas he cuts himself, and the fight is stopped—or he loses by decision, I can't remember—but he's content. He's got his self-respect, and he takes his money, and he and Adrian buy the pet shop at the end of the script.

That's an interesting motivation.

STALLONE: I liked it at first, but as other things started to transform in the script, I eventually went back to the original "Wepner idea" of a guy who really doesn't have the ability to pull it off, but still conducts himself in such a way that he earns self-respect. Also, I liked the idea of a vigorous young Apollo rather than a fading old champ. I think it gave more life to the film.

Now, I'd like to back up a little bit here, because one of the great misconceptions that resulted from the success of the film is that you were an "overnight" success, but you'd actually been writing scripts for years, ever since you first saw Easy Rider *and felt that you could write a low-budget screenplay. Before writing* Rocky, *you'd written at least eight screenplays, including* Hell's Kitchen, *and I wonder if you saw screenwriting as a way to create a leading role for yourself, since you were being type-cast in your acting roles?*

STALLONE: Definitely. No doubt.

You had that nice co-lead in The Lords of Flatbush, *but almost everything else was a thug or a mugger.*

STALLONE: Yes, I was always the mugger, the intimidator, which actually seemed quite strange to me since I'd never perceived myself in that way. I was a bit tough as a teenager, but I'm not really that big, and I never felt that I had an intimidating presence, but every time I was called in for an audition, it was never for the good guy, or the pleasant guy, or the bright guy, it was always the bad guy. So I thought that I should try and write something that would still have a somewhat intimidating character—Rocky's an enforcer, after all—but one who'd be much more complex and interesting. So I wrote a whole pile of scripts—*The Bogus Kingdom, The Bully, Cheerful Charlie, Promises Written on Water*—trying, in every case, to create possibilities for myself as an actor.

You even wrote an episode for the anthology show Touch of Evil *hosted by Anthony Quail.*

STALLONE: That's right, my friend and I heard that they were looking for ideas, so we had a kind of writing contest one night over the phone, and I eventually sold five of my ideas to the show. Five treatments in one night! Mostly, it was derivative stuff—a lot of stealing from Poe and others—but they all worked, and they actually made the one called "The Monster of Manchester" which they retitled "Heart-to-Heart." So my wife and I had some food to eat for awhile.

Somewhere in the midst of all the bit acting parts and the screenwriting, you made a vow to push even harder for success, and you went back and recon-sidered all the scripts you'd written, and you decided that they were too nega-tive. You felt that they were too much like a lot of the other antihero stuff that was current at the time.

STALLONE: Absolutely, and that led to *Hell's Kitchen*, which was much more uplifting. Previously, for example, I'd written a script based on the life of Charles Becker who had the dubious distinction of being the only police lieutenant in New York City history to go to the electric chair—back in 1915. He'd set up this big murder in the Tenderloin area, and the trial was so sensational that the D.A. who got him convicted was later elected gover-nor. It was a pretty good screenplay—dramatic and interesting—but it was *very* negative. I did another one about the life of Edgar Allan Poe, which is an idea that I'm still struggling with to this day. It's quite a challenge, and, of course, it also has to be very negative. How can you have an upbeat end-ing with *that* man's life? So I thought, "Why not try to do something dif-ferent, something more up-beat?" and since I'd always loved Damon Runyon's stuff, I thought I'd try to set it on the streets. That's something I knew about and could relate to, and I felt that I had a feel for the vernac-ular, so I wrote *Hell's Kitchen* about three brothers in the late forties trying to rise up out of the New York City slums. One of the brothers, as I mentioned earlier, was a club fighter, and later, after *Rocky*, when the script was finally made as *Paradise Alley*, the boxer became a wrestler.

OK, let's get back to Rocky *and the great "gamble." At the time, you had $106 in the bank, your wife was pregnant, and Chartoff and Winkler offered you $75,000 for the script. They had a number of major stars—like Ryan O'Neal, James Caan, and Burt Reynolds—all interested in the role, but you turned them down, insisting that you play the lead. Over time, the producers kept increasing their offer until it was up to $265,000, and you finally told them that "Even if the price goes up to a million, I still won't sell it."*

STALLONE: Yes, at the time, they had John Boorman committed to direct the picture, but he said, "What? I can't work with Sylvester Stallone. Who's that?" So he backed out.

So why'd you do it? You were broke.

STALLONE: I was completely broke. I had to sell my dog, Butkus, and my $40 car, which wasn't working anyway. Things were pretty bad. It was so hot in the place we were living that my wife would get nosebleeds when she tried to cook. It was very rough. All I can say, looking back, is that it was youthful naïveté. I was at an age where I was still full of raging optimism. If it had been ten years later, I would have been a lot more jaded, and I probably would have given in. But at that point in my life, I still felt that the sky was the limit, "Let's just go for it, and take the chance." After all, the worst case scenario was that we end up right back where we were. So, let's face it, it wasn't a matter of life and death. Things were tough, but no one was going to end up dead. On the other hand, I really believed that I was at a dead end with the acting, so the dye was cast. I'd become, at best, a guest shot on some of the TV shows like Chuck Connors's *Police Story*, and *Kojak*, and some others. But that was it, and I was convinced that I'd never be offered anything more. So I told my wife, Sasha, how I felt about it, and she said, "I think you're crazy, but I'll back you up. Let's go for it." So we did. We were just two naïve kids in the valley taking a ridiculous risk, and it worked.

Finally, Chartoff and Winkler agreed, but the film's budget was very low for that time period. I've read about $1,100,000?

STALLONE: Actually, I think even that figure's inflated. Sometimes studios, after the fact, get embarrassed to tell the real story and give the actual facts. But when the producers cut the deal with the studio, it was a $900,000 budget, and Chartoff and Winkler had to put a bond on their homes to secure the deal. Then they still had to get the blessing of United Artists about the casting of the main role, but the executives naturally said, "Well, who's Sylvester Stallone?" So they screened *The Lords of Flatbush*, and while they were watching it, one of them asked, "How come he's

Italian if he's got blond hair and blue eyes?" And either Chartoff or Winkler said, "There's lots of Italians up in northern Italy that have blonde hair and blue eyes." So the executive nodded, and he said, "OK, he looks pretty good," and they all agreed.

That's amazing! They approved Perry King!

STALLONE: That's right! And no one told them otherwise. As a matter of fact, early in the screening, one of the UA people said, "You're not talking about that goon next to him?"—meaning me, of course—but when no one answered him, they all continued focusing on my costar, Perry King, thinking that he was Sylvester Stallone. Looking back, it's truly amazing that *Rocky* ever got made, given all the obstacles, and it certainly must have been quite a shock for those studio executives when they finally saw the completed film.

Then John Avildsen, the talented and budget-conscious director of Joe *and* Save the Tiger, *was brought in to direct the film. Avildsen was so committed to the picture that he actually took a cut in salary for a higher percentage. That must have boosted your confidence?*

STALLONE: It sure did. John's an incredibly focused person—and director—adamant and stubborn to the point that it's almost legendary. And those traits worked perfectly on *Rocky*, because the picture needed exactly that kind of commitment. I know I sure did. John was relentless and audacious. Even the opening titles of the film were indicative of his boldness as those gigantic letters appear across the screen spelling out *R-O-C-K-Y.* It was just amazing. After all, this was a little film about a nobody character, but John opens up the movie with huge titles, and with trumpets and fanfare—it was gladiatorial. I remember when I first saw it, and I said, "Damn, that's amazing!" There was a kind of reckless abandon and bravado about the opening, and John approached the entire picture that way, right down to the final scene where you see this losing fighter calling out, "I love you. I love you," and the music is blaring into an ever-increasing crescendo. There was no little, ditty theme song; it was classical, and it was fully orchestrated. It was truly amazing, and, believe it or not, Bill Conti recorded the whole *Rocky* score in one day. That's how tight the budget was! But John got it done. He was absolutely relentless.

I have a few questions about the casting. Originally, Carrie Snodgrass was offered the role of Adrian, but when her agent held out for a better deal, Talia Shire, who'd been nominated for The Godfather, *was given the role. Is it true that you requested that she test for Adrian?*

STALLONE: Definitely, but there were several other actresses in between, like Bette Midler and Cher.

And they turned it down?

STALLONE: Yes, they did. Both of them. Then we went to Susan Saran-don, but she seemed too beautiful for the role, so I suggested that we ask Talia to read, and she did, and she was extraordinary.

I've read that Kenny Norton, the famous heavyweight boxer who'd starred in Mandingo, *was the first choice for Apollo Creed. Is that right?*
STALLONE: Actually, the first candidate was Roger Mosley, the guy who starred on *Magnum, P.I.* with Tom Selleck, but he started asking, "How come every time *you* throw a punch, it's a 'thunderous' punch, but when *I* throw a punch, it's just flicking jabs?" So we knew immediately that this guy wouldn't work out if he was worrying about the adjectives in the script! Then we tried a couple of other guys before Kenny Norton came in. Ken's a massive guy, but he had a certain feel for it, and then one day, right before we're ready go, he says, "I just got a better offer. I'm going to be in the ABC Superstars competition, and it's got a $25,000 grand prize." And I said, "But Ken, that's only *if* you win the competition, but this picture's something your kids'll love and be proud of forever." And I stood there waiting anxiously, but he shook his head and left, and it turned out to be the best thing that could have happened—because, from nowhere, in walked the *real* Apollo Creed—Carl Withers.

Who was naturally cocky.
STALLONE: Carl's ego arrived ten minutes before he did. He was per-fect for the part. He had the arrogance. He had the voice. He could act. And he was very athletic. Also, he was much better proportioned to me.

Height-wise?
STALLONE: Yes. We matched up very well.

Burgess Meredith was an obviously inspired choice for the role of Mickey, but I understand that many well-known actors in Hollywood wanted that role?
STALLONE: Yes, it was a terribly painful process. John was great with the film, but that was the one aspect of the process that I found very unset-tling. He'd make all these legendary actors actually read for the part. Origi-nally, I'd written the role of Mickey with Lee J. Cobb in mind, and when he came into to meet us, he brought along some props, and said, "I guess I should wear a mustache?" and he had all kinds of other ideas about the role. Then, after ten minutes, John says, "OK, let's turn to page sixteen," and Lee J. Cobb says, "Why?" And John says, "Because I want you to read." So Cobb gets furious, and he says, "Look, I've only read for one other bastard in this business, years ago, and I'm not about to read for another one." Then he turned around to me and said, "I'm sorry, Mr. Stallone, but I can't do that, and if I could write like you, I wouldn't have to work for people like that." Then he left. I was astonished, and I looked over at John, and I said, "I think he knows how to act." But John was adamant,

"*Everyone's* going to read. No exceptions." Then he made Lee Strasberg, who'd recently been nominated for an Oscar, read for the part. Then Lew Ayres, then Victor Jory—who'd done 230 films—then Broderick Crawford. Finally, Burgess, who'd been nominated the year before for *The Day of the Locust*, came in, and he was great, and he put an end to the whole painful process.

He was perfect.

STALLONE: He was. So I guess it all worked out in the end, but it was very painful sitting there and watching it all. Whenever they'd come into the room, I'd just sit there in dread, ducking my head, knowing what was coming. Then John would say, "Let's turn to page sixteen," and the men would go ashen.

On the first day of shooting, January 9, 1976, in the frigid early-morning darkness of Philadelphia's Fishtown, you were suddenly so overcome with fear that you had to be left alone for awhile. Were you concerned about the script or about whether you could pull off the role?

STALLONE: I was worried about me, as an actor. Sometimes our ambitions exceed our abilities, and I'd never carried a film before, and now I was in almost every scene. So there was this terrible moment of doubt; it was like a voice that was saying inside my head, "You're going to go out there and be exposed as a total fraud." I knew that for the next three weeks, I had to totally embody this character, Rocky, and I had to completely surrender my own ego. If Rocky looks bad, I have to look bad. If Rocky drinks raw eggs and there's drool running down his chin, then I have to do it. Ironically, I think it was a bit like those moments before the fighter actually steps into the ring, or before the opening bell rings. There's all kinds of doubt in your mind. You're not really sure if you can do what you have to do. But then you collect yourself and you go ahead. So John and the crew gave me a little time that first day, and I got a grip on myself, and we pressed ahead, but the nagging doubts were still there. Very often, I'd be doing a scene, and I'd feel like it was a parody of some scene from another movie. I might, for example, be doing something down on the docks, or even kissing Adrian, and I'd think to myself, "I've seen this before. I'm just imitating something else." But, regardless—and maybe like the prizefighter once again—as time went by, my confidence grew, and I started to believe in myself and what we were doing. But let's face it, I was pretty inexperienced to be carrying a feature film.

Rocky was shot very quickly in twenty days in both Philly and at the Los Angeles Sports Arena. While maintaining this blistering pace, Avildsen, as you've often pointed out, "stuck almost religiously to the script." But there were some changes and deletions that I'd like to discuss. One such addition is Mickey's crucial tirade in the gym. He calls Rocky, "a dumb Dago," and he claims that, "You had the talent to become a good fighter, and instead of that, you became a leg-breaker to some cheap second-rate loan shark." These are crucial lines on several counts: they set up Mickey's offer to be his manager, they allow the audience to believe that Rocky might be able to last fifteen rounds, and they highlight the crucial "bum" motif. But these lines were not in the master script dated January 7, two days before shooting began. Do you remember writing them on the set?

STALLONE: Yes, with Burgess's help. We felt the scene needed more than Rocky just walking into the gym and telling Mickey that he's going to be a sparring partner for the champ. It seemed a good place to give more depth to their relationship, and I remember asking Burgess what he thought Mickey might be feeling inside when he hears the news, and he said, "Maybe I'm raging with jealousy. Maybe I can't stand the idea that you're going to be associated with the champ. Maybe I can't contain myself anymore and I even call you a 'dumb Dago' or something like that." And I thought he was exactly right, so I started writing the extra dialogue, and I realized that this would be the perfect moment for Rocky to probe even deeper—to force Mickey to explain why the old man's treated him so badly over the years. So I added the part where Rocky yells across the gym, "I've been coming here for six years, and for six years you've been sticking it to me, and I want to know how come?" And when Mickey dismisses him saying, "You don't want to know," Rocky keeps insisting and finally calls out angrily, "I want to know *now*!" So Mickey tells him, and I always felt very good about those changes in that scene, and I owe a lot to Burgess.

What happened to the ice skating scene? And the 400 extras?

STALLONE: It was supposed to be a huge scene. We had a big rink all lined up in Philly, with night lights and hundreds of extras, and we'd even done 8-millimeter tests of the location, and then one day, in the midst of our hectic schedule, John comes up and he says, "We can't do the ice skating rink." It was a matter of time and money, so I said, "Okay, we'll make it a roller skating rink, and we'll do it in Los Angeles. We'll sneak in when nobody's there."

Which turned out to be perfect since, in the script, it's Thanksgiving.

STALLONE: Exactly. So all we needed was the guy who runs the rink, and, of course, Rocky tries to hustle the guy for a little skating time for Adrian, but the guy actually dupes Rocky. The rink guy, incidentally, was played perfectly by George Memmoli from *Mean Streets*.

And the isolation of the huge, empty rink gave much more impact to the scene.

STALLONE: Yes, it was cold, and cavernous, and it highlighted the loneliness and neediness of both Adrian and Rocky.

Also missing in the master script is Rocky's initial refusal to take the fight when it's offered, and the promoter's encouraging lines that began, "Do you believe America's the land of opportunity?"

STALLONE: Yes, I made that change on the spot. As an actor in that scene, I didn't feel fully satisfied. I felt we were only halfway there, so I said to myself, "What if we throw common sense out the window? What if Rocky, given the chance of a lifetime, actually refuses it?" At first, he's overwhelmed by the idea, but then he has a special moment of personal insight and evaluation. In truth, he doesn't even think that he's good enough to be the champ's sparring partner, let alone his opponent for the title. So he tries to explain himself to the promoter, admitting that he's just a bum, a ham-and-egger. He knows exactly "what he is" at that moment, and he has absolutely no ego, so the audience feels a great sympathy for him. They start rooting for him, and they want him to take the chance to better himself, to prove that he's not a bum.

The master script also indicates that the loan shark, played by Joe Spinell, is Rocky's older brother?

STALLONE: Yeah, I always loved that idea, but John didn't like it, and neither did the producers, so we cut it on the set.

It's very much like On the Waterfront.

STALLONE: Exactly, which is why I loved it! But it's also why John and the rest of them didn't want to do it.

Did you shoot it both ways?

STALLONE: Yes, we did. Joey's a great ad-libber. He can do anything you want.

Did he ad lib the inhaler?

STALLONE: Yes, he actually had an asthma attack while we were shooting the scene, so I said, "Don't stop, Joey. We'll use it, it's perfect." So he just kept going, and he used his inhaler when he needed it, and he was terrific.

Also cut were the two scenes where Rocky is watching fight films of Apollo Creed.

STALLONE: We shot some of that too, but it just wasn't exciting enough watching Rocky watch the films. Later, in *Rocky II*, we found a way to make it work better with Mickey, but in the first *Rocky*, we felt it was too slow, and we replaced it with the training montage and Rocky's visit to the empty arena before the fight.

Is it true that the script's original ending—with Apollo, Rocky, and Adrian all being hoisted up on the shoulders of the crowd—was scrapped because of the wild behavior of the crowd at the Los Angeles Sports Arena?

STALLONE: Yeah, we never had a chance to try it, and maybe that was all for the best. The crowd got pretty unruly that day. They didn't know who either actor was, since we were both unknowns at the time, and they got bored, and they started throwing stuff into the ring. So as we're trying to shoot the scenes, we were very worried that somebody might get hurt, and we had no idea what might happen next. So we decided to bag the ending. We let Apollo have his moment of triumph in the ring, then we let the crowd disperse, and then we shot Rocky walking out of the arena all alone. Adrian's waiting outside in the corridor, he grabs her hand, and they walk off together to his dressing room. But it was just too depressing, so we had to go back and change it.

Did you reshoot after the film was cut?

STALLONE: Yes, quite a bit afterwards, and we had no money left— maybe $20,000. So we set up everything in one corner of the ring, and we brought in everyone we knew—neighbors, friends, and relatives—and we had them all walking in circles around Rocky, and I'm calling out for "Adrian!" and I felt like the biggest fool in the world. I'm in full makeup, in this giant arena, with about twenty extras, and we're cheating the scene something terrible, and I felt like an idiot.

But you're an actor!

STALLONE: I know, but this was ridiculous. It was cold, and I'm freezing, and everyone's hungry, and the set was absurd. We didn't even have ring posts. The ropes were draped over a couple chairs. And there I am in the midst of it all, yelling over and over, "Adrian! Adrian!" and I was doing my best, but it seemed hopeless. That night, when I went home, I kept thinking to myself, "Well, that's that, we blew it. The movie's finished. It's over. It's down the tubes." It seemed to me that we'd shot the worst afternoon of filming in cinema history. All I could think was, "This stinks."

But the shots cut in perfectly.

STALLONE: They did, and it was a complete miracle! But the next time you see the film, watch that ending closely and you'll notice that it's always shot from exactly the same angle—because the place was empty!

Two of the best lines in the film were not in the script. One is Mickey's boxing rule: "Women weaken legs."

STALLONE: Yeah, I remember adding that one on the set. One of my very favorite pictures from the shooting of the film is a shot of me writing on the set. I'm sitting there in costume, both of my hands are charred, my nails are broken, I've got a cigar in my mouth, and I'm writing away. I was a mess, but whenever a good idea came up—from me or someone else—I sat right down and made the changes. It was exhausting, but also exciting. You're always hoping to make it just a little bit better.

The other new line is in the scene where Paulie goes nuts with the baseball bat, and Adrian looks over at Rocky and says, "Do you want a roommate?"

STALLONE: Yes, I think originally Adrian tried to change the mood in the room by saying something like, "Do you want to hear a joke?" But the roommate line pushed the story further along, and it was kind of an emancipation for Adrian. That was a great thing about John Avildsen. Unlike a lot of directors, he was always flexible enough to consider new ideas even though he was so careful about staying on schedule. Another example of that is the scene in Rocky's room after he's thrown out Mickey. Originally, it was a very simple scene, but we decided to let Rocky vent his anger for the first time—maybe even for the first time in his whole life. So he yells at the door, and he rants at Mickey who's left the room but can still hear what he's saying. So, once again, John was willing to try new variations within the scene, and I think it worked. I think a lot of people identified with Rocky's frustrations and his anger—especially his disappointment with people who should have treated him better over the years. Then, of course, once he's got it all out of his system, he chases after Mickey and tells the old man that he can be his manager.

One of the most famous scenes in film history is Rocky triumphant at the top of the stairs in front of the Philadelphia Museum of Art. Obviously, it's the culmination of the training sequences, but when you wrote the scene, did you have any idea that it would become one of the key moments in the film?

STALLONE: Not at all. The truth is, we were just running all around Philadelphia, my old hometown, and we were stealing scenes wherever we could get them. We'd jump out of our van, and shoot on the spot, without any sound, and with Garrett Brown still experimenting with his new camera—which was literally held together with ropes, and bolts, and washers.

The Steadicam?

STALLONE: Yes, and Garrett Brown was absolutely amazing. He's 6'7", but he could run up those steps sideways just as fast as I could run up them forwards.

In the script, you had Rocky carrying his huge dog, Butkus, up those stairs!

STALLONE: I know, I know, it sounded better on paper, but it was crazy. So when we got to the steps, I picked up the dog, who weighed about a hundred and twenty-five pounds, and I couldn't even make it half-way up the steps. It nearly killed me! So we scrapped the idea, and it came out much better in the end. I think the way that Garrett Brown swung around his steadicam at the end of the scene so the audience can see the city from behind was truly extraordinary—and even more so when you consider that we did it on the fly.

And the music's blaring away in the background . . .

STALLONE: I know. When it was cut together, it sure didn't look like a little, low-budget picture. It was pretty amazing.

You once said that you always felt that the "most important scene" in the movie is the one where Rocky talks to Adrian before the fight and admits that he can't win. Could you discuss that a little?

STALLONE: Well, I felt it was a pivotal scene because it does something that I'd never seen before in a sports film. It allowed the main character to admit that he was going to lose, and to face the fact, but then establish another goal for himself—to go the distance against the champ. So, like in the Wepner fight, Rocky finds a way to validate himself. Maybe he can't win, but he can try to last until the final bell against the best boxer in the world. So there's a potential victory even in losing because it's *how* you lose that matters. Rocky's definitely got the physical courage, but he lacks the skills to beat the champ, so he prepares himself to take a beating and salvage triumph from defeat. But when we were doing this scene, which I felt was so important, we ran out of money, and they pulled the plug. Literally! I always knew there was an expression in Hollywood about "pulling the plug," but I had no idea that when the money ran out, they literally pulled the plug in the middle of whatever was going on, and then went home. So we're doing the scene, and these guys pull out the plug and the lights go out. And I said, "Wait a minute! We have to finish this scene! Otherwise, we have to forget the whole film. It just won't work. This is the heart of the whole picture!" And they said, "Sorry, we can't do it," so I begged them, "Please, just give me a few more minutes. Just one take." So they finally relented, "OK, but just one more take." So we did the first take, and the sound was off, and I begged them again. I was so agitated, I drank down nearly a half bottle of wine, and I finally convinced them to give us one more take, and I said, "Talia, are you ready?" And she nodded, and we did it, and if you watch that scene today, you'll see it was all done in one take—all the way through. And as soon as we were finished, "Cut!" Boom! The plug was pulled out again, and the lights went out. Then the very next day, I'm leaving the lot, having missed the rushes, and one of the producers comes out of the screening room smiling, and he says, "Sly, that's the best scene in the movie." And I said, "I know it is. I've been saying that all along." So it was just another one of our many little miracles. Whenever I look back at the making of *Rocky*, it all seems so absurd to me now—the entire process. So many things that could have gone wrong, didn't, and I'm convinced that luck is a very important part of any successful film.

The key theme in Rocky, *as in* On the Waterfront, *is the notion of being a bum and trying to transcend it. In the opening scene at the Blue Door Fight Club, a woman calls out to Rocky, "You're a bum, you know that? You're a bum." And this idea is repeated in various ways throughout the film by Mickey, Gazzo's henchman, and even Rocky who refers to himself at one point as "just another bum in the neighborhood." Why was this theme so important to you?*

STALLONE: In the vernacular of boxing, a bum is either somebody who wasn't able to capitalize on a break or someone who never "had it" to begin with. He may not be a "bad" fighter, but he's still a "bum," and I've always identified with guys like that—and I think we all do to some extent. After all, how can you really call a man a "bum" if he's got the guts to walk into a boxing ring—or anywhere else in life—and take a beating. That's pretty brave. He's certainly not a "bum" in the other sense of the word: a guy who's living on the streets, who's basically given up on life, and who's living out his time on other people's handouts. But regardless, it's still pretty debilitating to be called a bum, or to feel that you might actually be one. In Rocky's case, he's heard it so long that he's come to believe it. He's fallen into the stereotype, but, inside himself, he still has unrealized potential. I've always believed that everyone, deep within their hearts, would like to have at least one opportunity to *fail* on their own terms. They might not succeed, but they'd like the chance to try, and when Rocky gets his opportunity, he makes the best of it and salvages some dignity. He may have lost to the champ, but no one will ever believe he's a "bum" again.

Also crucial to Rocky *is the love story. In her own way, Adrian, whose brother calls her a "loser," closely parallels Rocky. After the film was released, the critics consistently cited two earlier films, which they saw as relevant to* Rocky. *One was* On the Waterfront, *and the other was Paddy Chayefsky's* Marty, *the story of an ordinary butcher (Ernest Borgnine) who falls in love with a plain girl from the neighborhood (Betsy Blair). Did you have* Marty *in mind when you were writing* Rocky?

STALLONE: Sure, it's a classic coming together of two seemingly insignificant misfits. Literature's full of the theme, and *Marty* was a great expression of it for the previous generation. So *Rocky* updated the scenario for my generation, and *Marty* always reminded me not to get too eccentric with the story or the characters—keep it simple. I also think that, like *Marty* and *Waterfront*, the love story works best at the lower end of society. It's most effective down on the street, and not "up there" with the affluent, because it plays more passionate and unself-conscious that way, and it has more of a sense of authenticity and audience identification.

How about Waterfront? *That was the other film that critics often cited in the wake of* Rocky's *release, and despite the many obvious differences between the two films, there are still many similarities with Elia Kazan's* On the Waterfront— *from the brilliant script by Budd Schulberg. For example, Brando's Terry Malloy is an ex-boxer, he "could have been a contender," he's liked by a mobster, he's detested by one of the mobster's henchmen, he falls in love with a girl in the neighborhood, and he's desperately seeking for some kind of self-respect. So when you were writing* Rocky, *did you consciously have* Waterfront *in mind?*

STALLONE: I think I did. It certainly inspired me, and I'd once worked on the waterfront in Philly when I was a kid in Fishtown—right where we shot *Rocky.* I remember one time when a strike was going on, and the merchants would take the seats out of their cars, and load them up with merchandise, and I'd run them out past the mob. I was so young at the time that no one suspected that I was running big blocks of cheese and other stuff right through the strikers who were a pretty rough crowd—they were torching trucks and beating up the drivers. So I grew up knowing the docks pretty well, and even though I didn't use them like Budd did in *Waterfront*, the whole ambiance of that classic film greatly affected me. But Budd's script was much more socially relevant, even political, whereas *Rocky* was much more personal. Rocky's a guy who's almost completely unconnected. He has no parents. He has no relatives. He has no interest in politics. He has no issues, period. So unlike Terry Malloy, Rocky was even more cut off and isolated.

You once said in an interview that, "I respond very much to the theme of redemption," and Rocky *is clearly about the personal and psychological redemption of the main character. But the film is also full of religious imagery: the very first shot is a mural of Jesus, Rocky has a crucifix over his bed, he kneels down and prays on his knees before the fight, and he blesses himself before the first round. Rocky obviously becomes a better person throughout the course of the film, but did you also see it as a spiritual regeneration?*

STALLONE: I was definitely thinking about that because many athletes who constantly face danger and death—like bullfighters, and boxers, and race car drivers—have a natural inclination to rely on religious rituals and icons. Bullfighters have their little altars, for example. Now, of course, sometimes they can get too dependent on such things, but they're always looking for strength and meaning, and it's crucial to Rocky's persona. Also, in a way, *Rocky* opens like one of those old thirties or forties fantasies, with the shot of the mural of Jesus that tilts down to the fight club's ring and this rather barbaric club fighter, Rocky. Back in the thirties or forties, that would have been a clue to the audience that a miracle was probably about to happen, that maybe an angel would come down and touch this guy and help him improve his life. They would have immediately recognized him as a bad guy, or as a prodigal son, who'd eventually be brought back into the fold.

During the editing of the film, you and John Avildsen had a number of disagreements over the way the film was being cut, especially the ending. Is it true that at one point the film was left uncertain about who'd actually won the fight?

STALLONE: Yes, at first, John wanted to leave the film open-ended. But I said, "John, you can't do that!" and I eventually convinced him. But then we argued about the music because he originally cut the final fight sequence to Jimi Hendrix's "Purple Haze." And all I could say was, "No! No! No! No!" So John said, "Well, what would you like?" And I said, "Beethoven. Something grand. Something classical. Not just rock 'n' roll." So the debate went on for quite a while, but luckily Bill Conti came along and ended the problem with his brilliant and elegant score. Even though *Rocky* was just a little "street" film, there were no little pop songs or ditties on the sound track, just Bill's full-powered classical score—like Leonard Bernstein. It was great, and I was delighted.

One of the first screenings of the finished film was at USC.
STALLONE: Yes, in Arthur Knight's class. We actually showed the students the film without the ending, just to see how they'd react, and it went over pretty well—a nice applause. Then we showed them the fight scene, and the reaction was incredible.

Was that when you realized you might have a blockbuster on your hands?
STALLONE: No, that happened at the Directors Guild screening, which was very bizarre. All during the film, nobody laughed at the laughs, and there was a lot of stirring in the audience. Then, when the film ended, everybody just got up and left the theater. It was dreadful. There was nothing. No response at all. Now, by this time, we'd shown the film around town a few times, always with phenomenal results, but here, at the DGA, with an audience of our peers, there was no reaction whatsoever. So the place cleared out, and I was sitting there in that big theater, eleven hundred seats, and I was stunned. Then my mother started worrying, and we got up, left the theater, and walked over to the stairs. Then I realized that the entire lobby was jammed with the audience, and they all started applauding, and it was just tremendous. And as I was coming down to the lobby, I realized that it could *never* be any better than this—to get the recognition of all these successful filmmakers. These are the people you can't fool; they know too much. So it was a great personal moment, and one that made me realize we might have something very big on our hands.

On Oscar night, you lost the best original screenplay Oscar to Network, *written by Paddy Chayefsky, who was also, ironically, the author of* Marty.
STALLONE: Before the Oscars, Paddy Chayefsky came up to me and said, "You're not going to win."

Cockily?
STALLONE: Absolutely.

Because everyone knew him from the old days?
STALLONE: Exactly. He said, "There's no way you're going to win. I'm president of the Screen Writers Guild." So what could I say? He was a very

outspoken man; so I just shrugged my shoulders and said, "OK." And he was right, of course, so I was ready for it on Oscar night, and it really didn't bother me. But I was truly shocked and dismayed that both Bill Conti and Burgess went home empty-handed. Burgess had been in the business for thirty-five years, he'd been nominated the year before, and he was great in *Rocky*. What more did the poor guy have to do? It was terrible.

Do you think it hurt Burgess Meredith that Burt Young from Rocky *was also nominated in the same category?*

STALLONE: Maybe. Possibly. I really don't know what happened that night.

In the Best Actor category, both you and Robert De Niro, who'd been nominated for Taxi Driver, *were passed over for Peter Finch who'd played the lead in Chayefsky's* Network.

STALLONE: Yes, it was a very strong year, but we younger guys were ready for the Finch award. He'd died that year after a long career, and I was absolutely certain that he'd win posthumously. Besides, it's always hard to win in that category, but it's almost impossible to win on your first nomination.

The good news, of course, was that Rocky *won Best Picture.*

STALLONE: Yes, I was astonished. Getting nominated was incredible enough. And when you think of all the difficulties that we had making that little picture, it's truly amazing. Also, it was a boxing film, and up until that time, boxing pictures were pretty notorious for being financial failures. But I believed then, and I do now, that the key to that film was Adrian. It's the love story that makes *Rocky* work, and it's Adrian who allows Rocky to blossom into something the audience can respect.

Well, the audiences certainly showed up for Rocky. *It was extremely popular all over the world, and it grossed well over a hundred million.*

STALLONE: That film had the all-time highest ratio of dollars invested to dollars returned. The ratio was 111 to 1. It was amazing. And those were 1974 dollars!

Even more important than Rocky's *phenomenal financial success is the fact that it's become a classic American film—and a classic American screenplay. Hal Ackerman, in an article for* Creative Screenwriting *a few years ago, called the film "brilliantly written," and he suggested it as a model for other screenwriters. Since* Rocky, *you've gone on to write many other very successful screenplays, including the popular sequels and other films, but you've never, as far as I know, ever gotten back to that smaller, low-budget frame of mind.*

STALLONE: No, you're absolutely right. I haven't, but I certainly want to. Recently, I've been working on a smaller script called *Maggie's Eyes* about a girl who's going blind and gets mixed up with a thug. To be honest, that's the kind of thing I feel most comfortable with—smaller, grittier stories about so-called "little" people who achieve something.

Could you write such a film even if it had no role for you?

STALLONE: Definitely. And I think the times are right for it. There's a group of younger directors out there who prefer the little insightful stories over the bigger commercial films. So I'm hoping to get back to my roots and starting writing in the way I began.

As a result of all your success as an actor, you've been somewhat forgotten as a writer. But a big part of the Rocky *"story" when the film first came out was that you not only starred in the film, but that you also conceived the story and wrote the screenplay.*

STALLONE: That's right, and now I'm hoping to devote more time to the writing—to see if I can still create smaller and more personal screenplays.

Thanks for your time.

STALLONE: Thank you, Bill, I enjoyed it.

CHAPTER 14

Tender Mercies (1983)

A CONVERSATION WITH HORTON FOOTE

Horton Foote, the renowned playwright and screenwriter, was born in Wharton, Texas. He began his career as an actor in California and New York City, where he performed in a number of Off-Broadway productions. In 1941, his first full-length play, *Texas Town*, was produced in New York, and he subsequently managed Productions, Inc., a semi-professional theater in Washington, D.C. Eventually, he returned to New York City to work for television, writing or adapting over thirty dramas for live television anthologies like *Kraft Playhouse*, *DuPont Show of the Week*, and *Playhouse 90*. One of those teleplays, *The Trip to Bountiful* (1953), starring Lillian Gish and Eva Marie Saint, was later transformed to the stage and opened on Broadway. In 1962, he adapted the film version of Harper Lee's novel *To Kill a Mockingbird*, starring Gregory Peck, for which he won an Academy Award for screenwriting. Other film adaptations included *Baby, The Rain Must Fall* (1965), staring Steve McQueen and Lee Remick; *Hurry Sundown* (1966), featuring Michael Caine; and William Faulkner's *Tomorrow* (1972), starring Robert Duvall. In 1983, his original screenplay *Tender Mercies* was directed by Bruce Beresford, starring Robert Duvall and Tess Harper, and Foote won his second Academy Award for the script, and Robert Duvall received the Best Actor Award. In 1991, his adaptation of John Steinbeck's *Of Mice and Men* was released, starring Gary Sinise and John Malkovich. In the meantime, he has continued his successful playwriting career, with such works as his nine-part *The Orphan's Home* and *The*

Young Man from Atlanta for which he received the Pulitzer Prize in Playwriting in 1995.

In the 1970s, after very successfully writing for television and film, including an Academy Award for To Kill a Mockingbird, *you moved to New Hampshire and returned to writing plays. But in 1979, while writing your play* Night Seasons, *you decided to write another screenplay, which eventually became* Tender Mercies. *Why did you make this decision at that time, which was eight years since your last produced screenplay, an adaptation of William Faulkner's* Tomorrow?

FOOTE: I'd been a writer-for-hire—which I hated—on a couple of other film projects, but I can't even remember their names since they were never completed. I'd go out to Los Angeles, get an assignment, and write the screenplay—in order to subsidize my playwriting. But working on *Tomorrow* was a great turning point for me because it was the first independent film I'd ever worked on. We did it for only $400,000, and it was a truly collaborative effort, which I feel is necessary in both theater and film. Everyone involved with *Tomorrow* was doing it out of commitment and dedication, not just to make money, but to be part of something they really believed in. So, after that experience, my attitude toward commercial films changed dramatically. But by 1979, I was running out of money, and my agent said, "You're a very peculiar person, Horton. They're dying for you to write another film out there, and yet you refuse to pitch any ideas." And I said, "But I don't know how to pitch ideas. I don't even know what they're talking about!" But she reassured me, "Oh, don't be so nervous about it. Just think of an idea that appeals to you, and I'll set up some appointments. Then you can make some money and go back to writing plays or whatever you want to do."

So I remembered that Boatie Boatwright, whom I'd enjoyed working with on *To Kill a Mockingbird*, was now at 20th Century Fox, so I said, "Well, I always feel comfortable with Boatie, and I do have an idea that I'm interested in. My nephew, who's been passionate about the drums his whole life, went to college and met up with another young student named George Strait, and they started up a little country-western band and began playing the small clubs. He told me that sometimes, when they'd been promised a gig, they'd arrive at the club, and another band, who'd gotten there first, had already been given their job. And it reminded me of some of my own experiences as an actor, so I thought it would be an interesting subject to investigate." My agent liked the idea immediately and sent me to Boatie. So I told her my idea—almost as simply as I just told you—and, to my surprise, she thought it was very interesting. She said, "I want you to tell this to Gareth Wigan," who was an executive at Fox, "and just tell him exactly what you told me." So I told it to Gareth, and he said, "You know, I'm very interested in this idea. We just had a very successful film about young people"—which was the bicycle film ...

Breaking Away?

FOOTE: Yes, that's right. So Gareth said, "Go and see *Breaking Away*," so I went to see it, and, afterwards, he said, "Now, listen, Horton, I really like your idea, but there's one thing I'd like to suggest. I think there should be an older man in there somewhere." And I thought to myself, "Well, why not?" I must admit, at that point, I was still very skeptical of the whole thing anyway. But Gareth insisted, "Have your agent come to Los Angeles, and we'll make a deal." So my agent went out to Hollywood, and the day she arrived, she opened the trades and read that Gareth Wigan had been fired from Fox. So I said to myself, "God's trying to tell me something here, but I don't know what it is." And then, at that point, I decided to do something that I'd never done before: write a screenplay without a contract. I'd gotten very interested in the story, and I finally made up my mind to go back home, and write it, and take my chances. I must admit that the "older man" idea had really begun to hit around in my head and expand.

Whenever I write, I always "transfer" things from my own life to areas where I'm not that knowledgeable. Since I knew almost nothing about country music—except liking to listen to it—I began to think of all the people I'd know in the theater who were greatly talented but who'd destroyed themselves with drink. One line in *Tender Mercies* actually came from a very famous actress who'd been destroyed by alcohol. She once said, "I went back home, and I walked down the street, and somebody came up to me and said, 'Were you really so-and-so?'" Well, that really unlocked the door for me. So I began to think a lot about this older country singer, and I wrote the screenplay. Then, one day, my daughter, who's a friend of Duvall's—as I was—said, "Did you know he can sing?" And I said, "No, I didn't realize that." And she assured me, "Well, he can." So I called up Bob—we were very close friends—and I said, "Would you come over to my apartment?" I was living in New Hampshire at the time, but I was also renting a temporary apartment in New York City, and he said, "Sure," and I told him, "I've got a new screenplay." So I think the poor, dear man thought I was going to hand him the screenplay when he arrived at my apartment, but instead, I said, "I'm going to read it to you." I suppose I could have ruined our friendship right then and there! But he liked it a lot, and I said, "I hear you can sing, Bob." So he sang *Wings of a Dove*, and I thought to myself, "*That*'s got to be in the film." So that's the genesis of things.

You once said that "the role of lyrics in Tender Mercies ... *is very important," and the key song in* Tender Mercies *is Ferlin Husky's classic "Wings of a Dove." It's amazing that the song—which connects to so much else in the film—was added after you'd written the script.*

FOOTE: Absolutely. Life gives you these things sometimes. When I first did *The Trip to Bountiful* in the stage version, I used a hymn called "What a Friend We Have in Jesus." Then, when Richard Burton died, there was a memorial service, and Shirley Knight sang without accompaniment, "Tenderly, My Jesus Is Calling, Calling Me Home." Well, I'd been in the Methodist church all my life, but I'd never heard that song, and when I did, I thought to myself, "Whenever I do *Bountiful* again, *that's* the song I'm going to use." And that's how it ended up in the film version.

Another key song in Tender Mercies *is Lefty Frizzell's "It Hurts to Face Reality," which is not one of his most well-known songs. How did it come to your attention?*

FOOTE: Bob had a partner, a business representative, who was dating—or married to—Lefty Frizzell's daughter. So I think Bob became very interested in Frizzell's music, and he discovered the song.

Then there's the eight songs that Robert Duvall actually wrote for the film. Did you discuss them at all before he wrote them?

FOOTE: Not really. He'd go off and write the songs, and then I'd approve the ones that I felt were most useful to the script.

How much did you know about the life of George Jones, the legendary country music singer, who, like Mac Sledge, saw his career temporarily destroyed by addiction, and who'd had a tempestuous marriage to singing star Tammy Wynette?

FOOTE: Well, the film's not about him, but he thinks it is!

He does?

FOOTE: Yes, apparently he does. I *did* know about him, of course, but not in the intimate way that I knew the actors and actresses who were my real models.

Yet there's definite parallels: his drinking, his marriage to Wynette, and his rehabilitation.

FOOTE: That's true, but he wasn't a conscious model for Mac when I was writing the screenplay.

Since Tender Mercies *was the first nonadapted screenplay that you ever wrote, I wonder how the writing went? Did you have any special difficulties that you can recall?*

FOOTE: Not really. It went very well. I was very comfortable with it.

There was apparently some concern about Robert Duvall's ability to actually sing the songs for the film, and a tape was made with him singing "Wings of a Dove" and some other songs. Were you—and Robert Duvall—open to the possibility of dubbing?

FOOTE: I never knew about those concerns, and neither of us ever considered dubbing his voice. It was never an issue for us.

Is it true that he did some singing gigs in country bars in Texas?

FOOTE: He did. And to get his accent right, he traveled all over Texas, and he listened to everyone. Then he finally found this guy—I forget what the town was—in east Texas somewhere, and Bob said, "*This* is the accent I want." So he hung out with the guy and recorded him talking.

You're a Texan, how does Duvall's accent sound to you?

FOOTE: Wonderful, just perfect.

When did the Hobels get involved with the project?

FOOTE: Well, first, Bob and I tried to produce it ourselves. We got involved with Julian Schlosberg who's quite a well-known figure in New York. He's produced a number of films himself, and he had a wonderful company that promoted other films that he loved—ones which had received great critical acclaim, but were not considered very commercial. Like *Tomorrow*, for example, which he still distributes all over the place, and that wonderful film by Kazan's wife, Barbara Loden ...

Wanda?

FOOTE: That's the one. So he'd made a reputation promoting quality films, and he fell in love with the *Tender Mercies* script, but he couldn't raise the money.

Then you got involved with Philip and Mary-Ann Hobel, two people who'd produced many documentaries but no feature films.

FOOTE: That's right. And they were a perfect pleasure to work with.

As the Hobels tried to create interest in the script in Hollywood, a number of directors turned it down ...

FOOTE: It seemed like every director in Hollywood turned it down!

Could you name a few?

FOOTE: Sure. I just saw Delbert Mann the other night. I was giving a reading from my recent book, *Farewell*, and, afterwards, the lady he was with said to me, "Oh, I love *Tender Mercies* so much." And I said, "Well, Delbert turned it down." And he looked at me and said, "What?" And I said, "You turned it down, Delbert." And he looked very surprised and said, "Well, that doesn't sound like me." But it's true. Arthur Penn also turned it down, although, I must admit, quite reluctantly. And Dan Petrie turned it down, and many others. I do remember that Jonathan Demme wanted to do the picture, but things didn't work out.

You once said in an interview, that most of the directors declined because "they didn't like the material" or because you wouldn't "agree to the changes they asked for."

FOOTE: That's right.

What did they want to change?

FOOTE: Very conventional things, like more "action." Of course, what they meant by "action" wasn't my idea of action.

How about the ending?

FOOTE: Yes, they had all kinds of ideas about that, and a lot of other things, and I must say the Hobels deserve a lot of credit.

Because they hung tough?

FOOTE: Yes. And so did Barry Spikings and John Cohn from EMI. They all deserve a lot of credit.

After Spikings and Cohn agreed to finance the picture, weren't they the ones who first suggested Bruce Beresford, the highly regarded director of ten Australian films including Breaker Morant?

FOOTE: That's right. They said, "We're sending it to Bruce Beresford," and I thought they were out of their minds. So I went to see *Breaker Morant*, and I still thought they were crazy—absolutely wasting our time. But I was quite wrong, of course.

Was it because he was a foreigner, and that you didn't feel that he could apprehend the subtleties of small-town Texas life?

FOOTE: I'm really not sure what I felt. I loved *Breaker Morant*, but I thought it was just too different in too many ways. Now I realize that both pictures have a lot in common. These days, Bruce and I are very close friends—I was just with him about a month ago—and he tells me that he was very anxious when he got the screenplay. He says, "You know, I get scripts all the time, and sometimes it's two or three weeks before I can take a look. But something told me to read that script right away, and I got halfway through it, and I was so nervous that somebody else might grab it up that I cabled my agent immediately and said 'I'll do it,' even before I'd finished reading it." His only concern, as he's told me later, was that "I knew I had to meet with the author to see if we could get along." So he came to the States, and we met, and we got along very well.

I understand that you took him to Texas and traveled around a bit—to make sure he'd feel comfortable.

FOOTE: We did, and he said, "This is *just* like Australia."

One more question about EMI's involvement. All this was happening in the wake of Heaven's Gate *and its box office disaster. Were you ever concerned about the financing?*

FOOTE: I didn't know anything about the financing. If there were any problems, they didn't burden me with them.

You once mentioned that Bruce Beresford, who'd handled flashbacks so brilliantly in Breaker Morant, *convinced you to eliminate them from your own screenplay.*

FOOTE: Yes, he convinced me to cut them out—and I thought he'd love them! He just said, "We don't need these," and I agreed.

Were they flashbacks of Mac's life?

FOOTE: I can't remember exactly, but I'm sure they were.

Beresford also wanted to eliminate the narration from the early draft of the script.

FOOTE: Yes, he did, and I had no problem with that either.

Were you ever tempted to tell the story from the boy's point of view? Like To Kill a Mockingbird?

FOOTE: Not really, because it was Mac that interested me the most.

As coproducer of the film, you were involved with all aspects of the production. How was Tess Harper cast opposite Robert Duvall? She'd never had a lead before.

FOOTE: Bob was very enthusiastic about Tess.

She gave a very powerful performance.

FOOTE: She did beautifully.

Were you on the set all the time?

FOOTE: I was. And I must say, everyone was very supportive and respectful. Unlike typical Hollywood pictures, the script was never altered without my consultation and approval.

Is it true that difficulties between Beresford and Duvall nearly led to the director quitting the picture? Robert Duvall, who would win an Oscar for his extraordinary portrayal of Mac, once referred to Beresford's methods as "dictatorial."

FOOTE: Well, they're both very dear friends of mine, so I'd prefer not to discuss what happened. It's true that they both had hurt feelings, but I think it's all been finally healed. Later, I did another film with Bob called *Convicts*, which was never properly released because the company went bankrupt. But Bruce loved *Convicts* so much that he bought quite a few copies of the film when it finally came out on video, and then he gave them out as Christmas presents that year. When I told Bob about it, it pleased him a great deal. So I think the difficulties have healed and passed.

In both your plays and your films, you're justly praised for your subtle use of understatement, your ability to eliminate ordinary connecting materials, and your sense of when to end a scene. This stripping things down to essentials has,

*misleadingly, been called minimalism, since that word might imply, as it
often does in fiction, a lack of structured drama. In reading earlier versions
of the script, it seems clear that some of this effect in* Tender Mercies *comes
from a "cutting back" in your writing—a paring away—especially of more
transitional scenes.*

FOOTE: It's true that I hate overstatement and that I like to keep things
lean and, hopefully, subtle, but, as you point out, I'm certainly not a mini-
malist. So much of the paring back of things in my writing happens in my
rewritings, but on *Tender Mercies*, I was also blessed with collaborators
who had the same objectives that I did, and who were able to help me cut
back even further. I'm a very practical person, and if somebody suggests
something that makes sense, I'm glad to do it. That's the nature of effective collaboration.

*Let's discuss a few of those alterations from the screenplay. In earlier ver-
sions of the script, the character of Rosa Lee has a harder edge than the final
portrayal by Tess Harper. For example, she says to Mac of his drinking, "Well,
cut it out while you're working here," and the first time he leaves, she says to
Sonny, "That's the last we'll see of him." Later, she says of Dixie, "I never
want to lay eyes on that woman!" These lines and others are cut or modified
in the final version.*

FOOTE: Well, the editor, William Anderson, deserves a lot of the credit
for some of those cuts. Apparently, he never reads the script before editing.
He just watches the dailies and goes from there—never knowing what's
going to happen next.

That's very odd. Someone must pick his projects for him?

FOOTE: I honestly don't know how he does it, and, I must say, it made
me very nervous at first. But I trusted Bruce, who had complete faith in his
editor who'd sit there and watch the dailies and say, "Leaner, leaner" and
"Take it out, take it out." So both Anderson and Beresford had an important impact on making the script even tighter than it was.

Had he worked for Beresford before?

FOOTE: Yes, a number of times, and he did *Breaker Morant*.

Well, that would certainly give you confidence. In your Tender Mercies
*screenplay, as in the movie, Mac proposes in the garden, saying, "Would you
think about marrying me?" and Rosa Lee responds, "Yes, I will." In an early
version of the script, the next scene shows the marriage at the Preacher's house,
followed by Mac, Rosa Lee, and Sonny sitting in a motel watching TV with
their "wedding" clothes still on. But in the film, both the wedding and the
motel scene are cut out, and we learn about the marriage in a much more
interesting way when Sonny talks to some unpleasant kids at school.*

FOOTE: I remember that we shot both of those scenes, and they were cut during the editing process. Sometimes it was hard—I really liked that motel scene.

But the transition in the final cut is perfect.

FOOTE: It is.

Another scene that's cut from the earlier drafts is the trip to Sonny's grandparents' house.

FOOTE: Yes, I was very fond of that scene as well. I felt it was some of my best writing.

Did they shoot it?

FOOTE: They either shot it or they were about to shoot it, and Bruce came to me and convinced me that we should take it out.

It does seem to pull the script in a slightly different direction, and the scene at Sonny's father's grave probably says what needs to be said about his family.

FOOTE: That's true. As you can see, I was very fortunate to have great collaborators on *Tender Mercies.*

I also wanted to ask you about the cut scenes at the end of the film: Mac's presence at his daughter's funeral and gravesite, and, even more importantly, his futile visit to her bedroom to look for some kind of keepsake or memento— which is especially powerful in the script.

FOOTE: We shot that scene too, and it's still very moving to me. I can't remember exactly why we decided to cut it.

It showed that his daughter's life had been rather transient, without any rooting, and, of course, Mac was largely responsible for that.

FOOTE: That's right. It's very hard to give up the scenes you like, even if it's best for the picture as a whole.

Well, let's talk about a scene that remains in the film—one of the most powerful and thought-provoking scenes in the movie. It occurs when Mac's daughter, Sue Anne, at the end of a very moving and awkward reunion after six years, asks him about a song he used to sing to her when she was a young girl about a "snow-white dove." Mac says he can't remember, but after Sue Anne leaves, he stands at the window and sings "Wings of a Dove." The singing scene is very boldly and effectively photographed from behind in wide-shot by Beresford, without a close-up of Mac.

FOOTE: Yes. My scripts aren't like all those studio scripts where the writers put in all the shots. In my opinion, no good director will pay any attention to them anyway. But I did believe in that shot, and I put it in the script, and Bruce had the daring to let Mac sing that song with his back to the camera, just as I wanted.

Given the scene's raw emotional power, the audience naturally wonders why Mac has lied to the daughter he wants to reconcile with. Is it a fear that, despite his desire to put things right, certain significant recollections are still too hard to face? Or is it something else?

FOOTE: I'm asked that question all the time, and I've never had a very satisfying answer. It was just instinctive on my part. My own personal instincts told me that Mac would behave in that way, and I can't really articulate it any better than, I imagine, Mac could. The other thing people are always asking me about are Mac's lines in the last scene: "I don't trust happiness. I never did; I never will."

They're among the best lines in the film, but why do people ask you about them?

FOOTE: They want to know if I believe it. If Mac's speaking for me.

They think you believe what your character says?

FOOTE: Yes, which is not the case. And they're very puzzled by it.

David Sterritt once described Tender Mercies *as "a daring picture," which it is on many levels: in its spare style of writing, in its equally spare style of filmmaking, and in its willingness to confront large and difficult themes, including Christian theological themes which are so often ignored or demeaned in contemporary cinema. The title of the film is an often-repeated phrase from the Psalms that relates to the concept of God's grace, which is, as you've said elsewhere, "a very mysterious thing." Mac is struggling, just like Job, to understand why there are certain kinds of suffering in the world, and the movie gives the sense that even though it can't be fully comprehended by Mac, or by anyone else, it can be accepted and endured. Fred Chappell once described Mac's attitude as a "quizzical Christian stoicism." Is that a fair evaluation?*

FOOTE: Well, I'm delighted to hear such interpretations of the film, but, I must admit, it wasn't the impulse. When I'm actually writing, I'm not thinking about large concepts like grace. I'm thinking of very specific things relating to character and incident.

Yet you've talked about grace in relationship to Tender Mercies *on a number of occasions?*

FOOTE: Yes, because after the fact, when people have pointed out these things, I begin to think about them and say, "Yes, that's true." But at the time I was writing the screenplay, I wasn't thinking about those large concepts. It's something very unconscious. Flannery O'Connor was often extremely surprised by the symbols in her work, and that happens to me all the time. After *Tender Mercies* came out, and people pointed these things out to me, I did go to Psalms and found the passages with "tender mercies," and I felt that these thoughts really *were* in the film. So, certainly, I had some vague concept of grace, but when I was writing the script, it was still a very nebulous term for me.

Related to this complicated concept of grace is the more common theme of baptism. Mac experiences an Augustine-like "face-to-face contemplation of human degradation and regeneration," as your friend Reynolds Price has put it, and Mac's regeneration, his salvation, clearly comes from his nascent faith and baptism.

FOOTE: Well, I'm very flattered by that idea, and I just love Reynolds, but it honestly wasn't my intention during the writing.

But you do have him baptized, and his whole life changes, and he has to deal with terrible suffering?

FOOTE: But that's what people did every day of my life when I was growing up in Texas. And the little boy says, "I don't feel a whole lot different. Do you?" And Mac says, "Not yet."

But that's precisely the right answer because that's the way it's supposed to work. It's not like turning on a switch, it's a difficult and gradual process.

FOOTE: Yes, that's true. All I'm saying is that instinct took me there, not my head. There were no large thematic intentions.

How about "Wings of a Dove"? Since you've already explained that the song was added after the first draft, maybe it was just a fortuitous thing that happened?

FOOTE: Maybe it was a work of grace, I really don't know.

Well, it certainly compliments the film since it's about the baptism of Jesus by John the Baptist and the Father. You've even got a little boy in there named Sonny.

FOOTE: I know. I know. But I didn't think it out. When Bob sang the song, I felt instinctively, maybe unconsciously, that it belonged in there. Let me give you another example of this kind of thing. A number of critics in the Seattle area kept writing about my work being heavily influenced by Ozu, but I'd never heard of Ozu before. But since they were making all these comparisons, I watched his films, and I've fallen in love with them. I watch them all the time. So I'm very grateful for critical evaluation and analysis, and I'm flattered by it, and I think we can all learn from it. But if I'd tried to sit down and write a screenplay about grace, I don't think I could have done it. It's too abstract, and I work too instinctually. People always say that my plays are about people looking for "home," and I think they're right, but I never did it consciously. I'm told later that I did it, and then I look over my play again, and I say, "Well, yes, I guess I *did* do that." But I didn't realize it until someone pointed it out to me.

I know what you're saying, but it's still hard for people in our culture to see a story of regeneration like Tender Mercies *and not think of parables like the Lost Sheep and the Prodigal Son.*

FOOTE: I know that, and I appreciate it. People have actually preached sermons about the film.

When the film was first released, Vincent Canby in The New York Times *was pleased to find a film that "concerns, among other things, people who sing 'Jesus Saves,' without making fun of them."*

FOOTE: Well, I grew up with those people, and I respect them. I was raised a Methodist, not a Baptist, and we never dipped people for baptism. But I felt that Rosa Lee, being the kind of young woman she was, would be a Baptist. I actually saw my first Baptist baptism while the film was being made, so I'd never witnessed one before I wrote the script, but I knew and respected those people. And Bob and Bruce felt the same way. Bob would never tolerate any kind of condescending attitude toward American provincial life—or making fun of it in any way. He honors those people, as I do, and the film reflects it.

Yet Hollywood is always nervous about the subject.

FOOTE: Well, look at *The Apostle.* I don't know how Bob won that battle, because they wouldn't touch it. In the end, he had to put up his own money. Five million dollars and every penny of it was his.

I'm not surprised. Now I wanted to ask you when you first watched Tender Mercies *with an audience?*

FOOTE: I'd seen many of the earlier cuts, of course, but eventually we went to San Francisco for the preview.

How did it go over?

FOOTE: I was very anxious, as I always am, and, to tell you the truth, I didn't feel that it went over particularly well.

And Universal?

FOOTE: They hated the film, and they sold it to cable. They literally gave it away, and they were about to open it in Europe, so they could get the cable money, when the Hobels and Cohn and Spikings decided to screen it in New York City, and somehow they got a number of New York critics to come and see it. I don't know how they pulled it off, but they did, and they stopped Universal from opening abroad. But cable still had the rights, and two weeks before the Oscars, they were showing it for free on television.

Didn't you have similar problems with To Kill a Mockingbird?

FOOTE: Yes. The studio wanted to do the same thing—open in Europe. But what saved *Mockingbird* was that Gregory Peck had had the good sense to put in his contract that he and Bob [Mulligan] and Alan [Pakula] had the final cut. Otherwise, Universal would have ripped that picture to pieces.

So there's something to be said for star power if the star has good sense.

FOOTE: Yes, if it's somebody like Gregory, somebody with integrity.

When you finally saw Tender Mercies *with that audience in San Francisco, what was your reaction?*

FOOTE: It's hard to describe. For me, it's a very traumatic thing to see your film with a roomful of strangers. The time I most appreciated *Tender Mercies* was when my daughter came to see it with a friend. We watched it in a screening room, and I felt overwhelmingly that it was a powerful emotional experience, and I was convinced that we should all be very careful with it, because the least little change might tip it the wrong way.

You're talking about post-preview changes?

FOOTE: Yes, I was very afraid they'd take it back to Los Angeles and recut it. All the typical disastrous stuff they do when they get their preview cards back from the audience. You know, "Oh, let's change the ending," that kind of thing. Fortunately, the Hobels and Cohn and Spikings managed to prevent it, and they deserve a tremendous amount of credit.

I did want to ask you about the two kids' scenes, especially the first one where an older kid taunts Sonny in the schoolyard. It seemed to me the one weak moment in a perfectly executed film.

FOOTE: Yes, the kids were very mechanical in that scene, but everywhere else, the little boy, Sonny, was wonderful—at least, to me. And Bob deserves most of the credit. There's an old theater exercise developed by Sandy Meisner which is based on repetition. I say a word, and then you say it back to me. It creates a great rapport between actors—and concentration—and you *really* begin to talk to each other and listen. And every moment when Bob wasn't on the set, he'd get that little boy, and they'd be off somewhere doing that exercise. And the results were magical.

Yes, they were. I wonder if you attended the Academy Awards that year, when both you and Robert Duvall won Oscars?

FOOTE: Yes, I was there. You see, I didn't go for *Mockingbird*. I didn't think I was going to win, and I thought, "Oh, I'm not going to dress all up and go through all that nonsense." But this time I thought, "Well, maybe I should go."

Did you have a good time?

FOOTE: Well, it was kind of heady. You're the flavor of the month for about two seconds. At the time, I was shooting *1918*, and I had to get back to the set in Texas.

I'd like to ask you a rather general question. Could you discuss the influence of three writers on your work: Katherine Anne Porter, whom you've cited before as an influence; William Faulkner, whose work you've adapted for the screen on at least three different occasions; and Anton Chekhov, to whom you're most often compared—especially in the sense once described by Robert Duvall as a "rural Chekhov"?

FOOTE: I got into Chekhov very early when I studied acting with the Russians at the Tamara Daykarhanova School of Theatre in New York City. And, right now, I'm rereading his short stories in the Modern Library editions edited by my cousin Shelby Foote. Even though I came upon Chekhov's stories much later than his plays, I often feel they're more relevant to my work, but there's always an insatiable interest in character in all of his writings which has always greatly attracted me to his work. As a young actor, I was heavily influenced by *The Seagull*, especially the last scene. Later, when I'd begun writing, I read *The Cherry Orchard*, and I wanted to find a way, like him, to have a kind of affirmation somewhere in my work, as when the professional student talks about the future in *The Cherry Orchard*. I don't generally conceive of that affirmation in the grand cosmic ways that Chekhov did, but I always strive for it, nevertheless. In the play I've just finished, there's a Chekhovian moment which says, basically, that this thing has happened, but now you have to go on—you have to go on and on and on. Well, that's very Chekhovian. So that's one thing that I've definitely learned from his work. I'm also very fond of *The Three Sisters*. I've studied that play a great deal, and the Actors Studio production of it is very meaningful for me. I have it on tape, and I've watched it many times. Then, as I was mentioning before, there's Chekhov's short stories which I think have greatly influenced my one-act plays—there's a real affinity there. I'm often interested in the grotesque in my characters—the slightly grotesque—as he is in his short stories.

As for Katherine Anne Porter, her work, like that of Willa Cather, has a marvelous unseen music—maybe "unseen" isn't exactly right, but there's a subtle music there, a cadence, something unstated but unmistakenly felt in her work. I think I've been most influenced by her long story "Old Mortality," because it's about generations. It starts with the myth, and then it destroys the myth—which I often do myself. As for Faulkner, you simply can't escape him.

Especially not a Southerner, like yourself.

FOOTE: That's right.

Was it very useful for you to adapt his work?

FOOTE: Absolutely, although I was very nervous about it. But, apparently, he was quite pleased with what I did. Unfortunately, I never got to meet him. The first Faulkner adaptation I did was *The Old Man*, which I later did again, just two years ago.

For which you won an Emmy.
FOOTE: Yes, I did.

But Faulkner had seen the earlier version?
FOOTE: That's right, the one I did with Geraldine Page and Sterling Hayden. I was very anxious about it because I'd changed a few things, particularly Geraldine's part, but he liked it very much. Later, when I was asked to do *Tomorrow*, I didn't know how to approach it, and I almost turned it down. Back then, I was living in Nyack, New York, and, one day, I was walking by the Hudson River thinking about it, and suddenly I started concentrating on the woman in the story who's lost a child—there's only about a paragraph about her and she isn't named—but I had the feeling that she "wanted" me to do more with her. So I gave her a name, and I began to reconstruct her story. And then I thought, "What would Faulkner say about this?"—because I'm usually very strict about adaptation. But then I thought, "Oh, well, I'll just have to try it this way, and see what happens."

You've often talked about getting "obsessed" with your characters.
FOOTE: Oh, I do.

Do they take you over?
FOOTE: They do. They certainly do.

Mac, for example, wasn't even in your original idea for Tender Mercies.
FOOTE: That's right, but then he took over completely.

I have one final question. Vincent Canby, in his original New York Times *review, said that* Tender Mercies *was one of those rare films that "force one to reexamine one's relationship with the universe." This ambitious objective seems to be at the root of all your serious work, and I wonder if you've been conscious of it from the very beginning?*
FOOTE: I don't think it was conscious at the beginning, maybe subconscious. But, in time, I did realize that my work was some kind of essential search to try and make some order out of chaos. I believe that's a motivating force for me. And within that search, it's crucial for me to ask "*Why* is this happening?" and often I have to answer, "I don't know, but let's pose the question."

Thank you very much.
FOOTE: My pleasure.

Appendix: Basic Film Credits

Singin' in the Rain (1952)
Directors: Stanley Donen & Gene Kelly
Screenwriters: Betty Comden & Adolph Green
Producer: Arthur Freed
Cinematographer: Harold Rosson
Music (Songs): Arthur Freed & Nacio Herb Brown
Editor: Adrienne Fazan
Principal Cast: Gene Kelly (Don Lockwood), Debbie Reynolds (Kathy Selden),
    Donald O'Connor (Cosmo Brown), Jean Hagen (Lina Lamont), Millard
    Mitchell (R.F. Simpson)

On the Waterfront (1954)
Director: Elia Kazan
Screenwriter: Budd Schulberg
Producer: Sam Spiegel
Cinematographer: Boris Kaufman
Music: Leonard Bernstein
Editor: Gene Milford
Principal Cast: Marlon Brando (Terry Malloy), Eva Marie Saint (Edie
    Doyle), Karl Malden (Father Barry), Lee J. Cobb (Johnny Friendly),
    Rod Steiger (Charley Malloy), Pat Henning (Timothy "Kayo" Dugan)

Rebel Without a Cause (1955)
Director: Nicholas Ray
Screenwriter: Stewart Stern
Producer: David Weisbart

Cinematographer: Ernest Haller
Music: Leonard Rosenman
Editor: William Ziegler
Principal Cast: James Dean (Jim Stark), Natalie Wood (Judy), Sal Mineo (John "Plato" Crawford), Jim Backus (Frank Stark), Ann Doran (Carol Stark), Corey Allen (Buzz Gunderson)

North by Northwest (1959)
Director: Alfred Hitchcock
Screenwriter: Ernest Lehman
Producer: Alfred Hitchcock (uncredited)
Cinematographer: Robert Burks
Music: Bernard Herrmann
Editor: George Tomasini
Principal Cast: Cary Grant (Roger Thornhill), Eva Marie Saint (Eve Kendall), James Mason (Phillip Vandamn), Jessie Royce Landis (Clara Thornhill), Leo G. Carroll (The Professor), Martin Landau (Leonard)

Psycho (1960)
Director: Alfred Hitchcock
Screenwriter: Joseph Stefano
Producer: Alfred Hitchcock (uncredited)
Cinematographer: John L. Russell
Music: Bernard Herrmann
Editor: George Tomasini
Principal Cast: Anthony Perkins (Norman Bates), Janet Leigh (Marion Crane), Vera Miles (Lila Crane), John Gavin (Sam Loomis), Martin Balsam (Milton Arbogast), Simon Oakland (Dr. Fred Richmond)

Hud (1963)
Director: Martin Ritt
Screenwriters: Irving Ravetch & Harriet Frank, Jr.
Producers: Martin Ritt & Irving Ravetch
Cinematographer: James Wong Howe
Music: Elmer Bernstein
Editor: Frank Bracht
Principal Cast: Paul Newman (Hud Bannon), Patricia Neal (Alma Brown), Melvyn Douglas (Homer Bannon), Brandon de Wilde (Lonnie Bannon), Whit Bissell (Mr. Burris)

The Sound of Music (1965)
Director: Robert Wise
Screenwriter: Ernest Lehman
Producer: Robert Wise

Cinematographer: Ted D. McCord
Music: Richard Rodgers & Oscar Hammerstein II
Editor: William Reynolds
Principal Cast: Julie Andrews (Maria), Christopher Plummer (Captain Georg von Trapp), Richard Haydn (Max Detweiler), Peggy Wood (Mother Abbess), Charmian Carr (Liesl von Trapp), Doris Lloyd (Baroness Eberfeld), Ben Wright (Herr Zeller), Daniel Truhitte (Rolf)

The Wild Bunch (1969)
Director: Sam Peckinpah
Screenwriters: Walon Green & Sam Peckinpah
Producer: Phil Feldman
Cinematographer: Lucien Ballard
Music: Jerry Fielding
Editor: Lou Lombardo
Principal Cast: William Holden (Pike Bishop), Ernest Borgnine (Dutch Engstrom), Robert Ryan (Deke Thornton), Ben Johnson (Tector Gorch), Warren Oates (Lyle Gorch), Emilio Fernández (General Mapache), Strother Martin (Coffer), Bo Hopkins (Clarence Lee)

American Graffiti (1973)
Director: George Lucas
Screenwriters: Gloria Katz & Willard Huyck & George Lucas
Producer: Francis Ford Coppola
Cinematographers: Jan D'Alquen & Ron Eveslage
Editors: Verna Fields & Marcia Lucas
Principal Cast: Ronny Howard (Steve Bolander), Richard Dreyfuss (Curt Henderson), Cindy Williams (Laurie Henderson), Paul Le Mat (John Milner), Charles Martin Smith (Terry "The Toad" Fields), Candy Clark (Debbie Dunham), Mackenzie Phillips (Carol), Bo Hopkins (Joe Young), Wolfman Jack (Disc Jockey), Harrison Ford (Bob Falfa)

The Sting (1973)
Director: George Roy Hill
Screenwriter: David S. Ward
Producer: Tony Bill
Cinematographer: Robert Surtees
Music (Songs): Scott Joplin, arranged by Marvin Hamlisch
Editor: William Reynolds
Principal Cast: Paul Newman (Henry Gondorff), Robert Redford (Johnny Hooker), Robert Shaw (Doyle Lonnegan), Eileen Brennan (Billie), Charles Durning (William Snyder), Ray Walston (J.J. Singleton), Dimitra Arliss (Loretta)

The Exorcist (1973)
Director: William Friedkin
Screenwriter: William Peter Blatty
Producer: William Peter Blatty
Cinematographer: Owen Roizman
Music: Steve Boeddeker
Editors: Norman Gay & Evan Lottman & Bud Smith
Principal Cast: Ellen Burstyn (Chris MacNeil), Linda Blair (Regan MacNeil), Jason Miller (Father Damien Karras), Lee J. Cobb (William Kinderman), Max von Sydow (Father Merrin)

Jaws (1975)
Director: Steven Spielberg
Screenwriters: Carl Gottlieb & Peter Benchley
Producers: David Brown & Richard D. Zanuck
Cinematographer: Bill Butler
Music: John Williams
Editor: Verna Fields
Principal Cast: Roy Scheider (Chief Martin Brody), Richard Dreyfuss (Matt Hooper), Robert Shaw (Quint), Lorraine Gary (Ellen Brody), Murray Hamilton (Mayor Vaughn)

Rocky (1976)
Director: John G. Avildsen
Screenwriter: Sylvester Stallone
Producers: Robert Chartoff & Irving Winkler
Cinematographer: James Crabe
Music: Bill Conte
Editor: Scott Conrad
Principal Cast: Sylvester Stallone (Rocky Balboa), Talia Shire (Adrian Pennino), Burgess Meredith (Mickey Goldmill), Burt Young (Paulie), Carl Weathers (Apollo Creed), Joe Spinell (Gazzo)

Tender Mercies (1983)
Director: Bruce Beresford
Screenwriter: Horton Foote
Producer: Philip S. Hobel
Cinematographer: Russell Boyd
Editor: William Anderson
Principal Cast: Robert Duvall (Mac Sledge), Tess Harper (Rosa Lee), Betty Buckley (Dixie), Allan Hubbard (Sonny), Wilford Brimley (Harry), Ellen Barkin (Sue Anne)

Index

About the Author

WILLIAM BAER has taught film and screenwriting at the University of Evansville for the past fifteen years. He is currently the film critic at *Crisis*, and for years his work has appeared regularly in *Creative Screenwriting*. A recent Guggenheim recipient (2007), he has also received a Fulbright (Portugal) and an N.E.A. Creative Writing Grant in fiction. His published works include *Elia Kazan: Interviews*; *Luís de Camões: Selected Sonnets*; and *The Unfortunates*, for which he received the T. S. Eliot Poetry Award.